Kate Rogers

1988

Winchester Cathedral, 1795 — J.M.W. Turner

i

On Maundy Thursday, 12th April, 1979, Her Majesty the Queen attended a special service to commemorate the 900th Anniversary of Winchester Cathedral. At this she also presented the traditional Maundy Money.
To mark the occasion she was presented with a specially bound copy of "Winchester Cathedral, 1079-1979", of which Her Majesty had previously graciously and uniquely consented to write the foreword.

BUCKINGHAM PALACE

In the year in which the 900th anniversary of
the present Winchester Cathedral is to be celebrated, I
join in giving thanks for the Christian witness which
this magnificent building has exemplified, and for the
work of restoration which has been made possible in recent
years by the generosity of so many people. In doing so,
I am reminded that Winchester was, from the days of
Alfred the Great to the Norman Conquest, the capital of
the Kings of England, and that, in the new Cathedral,
begun in 1079, the Conqueror's immediate successors
frequently wore the crown at the Easter festival.

I send my good wishes to the Dean and Chapter
and to all who work with them to maintain this ancient
and living church, and I pray that through the years ahead
Winchester Cathedral may continue to be a place where all
may be refreshed and strengthened by the presence, the
power and the peace of Almighty God.

ELIZABETH R.

(Murray Davison).

The Cathedral Choir, conducted by Master of the Music Martin Neary.
Christmas, 1978.

Winchester Cathedral

1079-1979

By

FREDERICK BUSSBY
Canon Residentiary, Winchester.

Photographs by E. A. Sollars
(except where stated)

Published By
Paul Cave Publications Ltd.

Printed By
Brown and Son (Ringwood) Ltd.

UXORI MEAE
DILECTISSIMAE

First published 1979

Reprinted 1987
ISBN 0-86146-062-6

Contents

The Author

Born in Lancashire, Canon Bussby was a scholar of St. John's College, Durham and later a Senior Exhibitioner of Wadham College, Oxford. Before the Second War he served in the diocese of Liverpool and was later Vice-Principal of Clifton.

During the war, he served as a chaplain for over six years, mainly in the Middle East, and ended his military career as a Staff Chaplain to Field Marshall Viscount Montgomery.

In 1945 he returned to civilian life to be Warden at Lichfield Theological College and from 1947 onwards to serve in the diocese of Winchester.

In 1961 he was made an Honorary Canon of Winchester and in 1967 succeeded Canon Roger Lloyd as Canon Residency, becoming Vice-Dean of the Cathedral in 1970. Canon Bussby has devoted special interest to the Cathedral's library and archives and has written extensively on many of the men and women who have been associated with the Cathedral down the centuries.

Sadly he died in the Holy Land in 1981.

Tribute to Canon Bussby

This book was written to mark the nine hundredth anniversary of the foundation of Winchester Cathedral in 1079. For several years it has been out of print, and there will be many who will welcome its re-appearance.

Canon Bussby held various offices in the Cathedral. At one time he was sacrist and treasurer. And from 1970-1980 he was Vice Dean as well as Cathedral librarian and archivist. Those fortunate to work with him, or receive his ministry, remember with great affection a faithful priest, a very caring pastor, and a diligent historian and scholar.

Frederick Bussby saw the Cathedral as a whole. It was founded for the worship of Almighty God and for this purpose it has remained for over nine hundred years. The beauty of its proportions, the stonework, the woodcarving, the murals, the glass, the embroidery and the furnishings are the consecrated offerings of men and women down the centuries to this end. And they are articulated through the performance of the liturgy day by day, and the rendering of the music. This was his perception as a priest. As a pastor he loved to dwell on the lives of the people bound up with the Cathedral's story. Some of them very eminent — Jane Austen, Izaak Walton and Bishop George Morley: a special hero who re-created the library in the reign of Charles II. But he was most concerned for the lesser known men and women, the worshippers, pilgrims, monks, masons, musicians whose names are not recorded in the history books. And for him the representative figure of the smaller people was William Walker, the diver, who underpinned the wall of the Cathedral in the early years of this century.

After he died while leading a pilgrimage to the Holy Land in 1981, his family and friends presented in his memory a flagon for use at the Nave altar. This was entirely appropriate. The Nave was especially important to Frederick Bussby: the place where the people's prayers are offered. I recall him saying: "I like to imagine the many sounds of the voices that have been uttered here". Saxon and Norman, the Latin chanting of the monks, the speech of Chaucer's day, the language of Shakespeare and the Authorized version of the Bible, right through to our own time. Today English, European and North American accents mingle with those of visitors from all over the world who come to see Winchester Cathedral.

There can be fewer surer guides than Canon Bussby. His learning is worn lightly and he unfolds a fascinating story for the reader. And for those who would discover more he points to the sources, which he knew and loved as well as an historian, where a student can trace in greater detail the absorbing history of our Cathedral.

May 1987   + Colin Winton

The New Team

The Rt. Rev. Colin James, who became Bishop of Winchester in 1985.

The Very Rev. Trevor Beeson who became Dean of Winchester in 1986.

Abbreviations

A.R.	Attendance Registers	H.F.C.	Hampshire Field Club
C.A.	Chapter Books	H.M.S.O.	Her Majesty's Stationery Office
C.C.P.	Calendar of Cathedral Papers	H.R.S.	Hampshire Record Society
C.P.	Clarendon Press	L.B.	Ledger Books
C.S.P.D.	Calendar of State Papers Domestic	O.E.D.	Oxford English Dictionary
		P.R.O.	Public Record Society
C.U.P.	Cambridge University Press	R.S.	Register of Services
C & Y	Canterbury and York Society	W.C.D.	Winchester Cathedral Documents
D.N.B.	Dictionary of National Biography	W.C.C.	Winchester Cathedral Chronicle
		W.C.R.	Winchester Cathedral Record

Corrections

After the book was published Canon Bussby continued his research into the history of the Cathedral and found that (a) Adrian Batten was born in Salisbury in 1591 (not in Winchester in 1590), see p.131 and (b) Canon A. G. Robinson was Archdeacon of Surrey (not Winchester), see p.278.

List of Illustrations

The Roof of the Guardian Angels' Chapel

Henry III, who was baptised in the Cathedral in 1207, maintained his interest in the Cathedral. About 1241 he allowed one of his craftsmen, working on Westminster Abbey, to come to Winchester and paint the roof of the Guardian Angels Chapel. He was known as Master William. The painting depicts the angels peering through the windows of heaven. They were restored in 1958 by Professor and Mrs. R.W. Baker.

WINCHESTER CATHEDRAL

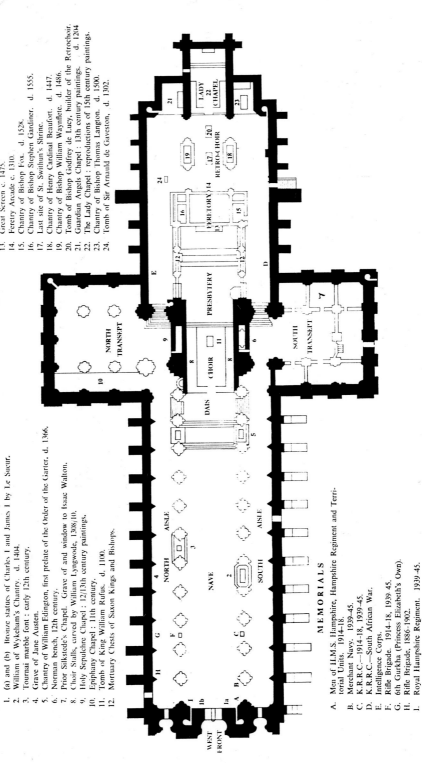

KEY TO PLAN

1. (a) and (b) Bronze statues of Charles I and James I by Le Sueur.
2. William of Wykeham's Chantry. d. 1404.
3. Tournai marble font : early 12th century.
4. Grave of Jane Austen.
5. Chantry of William Edington, first prelate of the Order of the Garter, d. 1366.
6. Norman bench, 12th century.
7. Prior Silkstede's Chapel. Grave of and window to Isaac Walton.
8. Choir Stalls, carved by William Lyngwode, 1308/10.
9. Holy Sepulchre Chapel : 12/13th century paintings.
10. Epiphany Chapel : 11th century.
11. Tomb of King William Rufus. d. 1100.
12. Mortuary Chests of Saxon Kings and Bishops.

KEY TO PLAN

13. Great Screen c. 1475.
14. Feretory Arcade c. 1310.
15. Chantry of Bishop Fox. d. 1528.
16. Chantry of Bishop Stephen Gardiner. d. 1555.
17. Last site of St. Swithun's Shrine.
18. Chantry of Henry Cardinal Beaufort. d. 1447.
19. Chantry of Bishop William Waynflete. d. 1486.
20. Tomb of Bishop Godfrey de Lucy, builder of the Retrochoir.   d. 1204
21. Guardian Angels Chapel : 13th century paintings.
22. The Lady Chapel : reproductions of 15th century paintings.
23. Chantry of Bishop Thomas Langton. d. 1500.
24. Tomb of Sir Arnauld de Gaveston. d. 1302.

MEMORIALS

A. Men of H.M.S. Hampshire, Hampshire Regiment and Territorial Units. 1914-18.
B. Merchant Navy. 1939-45.
C. K.R.R.C.—1914-18, 1939-45.
D. K.R.R.C.—South African War.
E. Intelligence Corps.
F. Rifle Brigade. 1914-18, 1939-45.
G. 6th Gurkha (Princess Elizabeth's Own).
H. Rifle Brigade, 1886-1902.
I. Royal Hampshire Regiment. 1939-45.

xiv

The South Transept with the original roof.

Ray Simpson

A southern view of the Cathedral.

Chapter I

Walkelin the builder

An important part of Norman policy, after the conquest of England in 1066, was to build great Norman churches to replace Saxon churches. In like manner Saxon churchmen were replaced by Norman churchmen. Both principles operated in Winchester where the present Cathedral was begun in 1079 in majestic Norman style which can still be envisaged by a visitor to the crypt or to the north transept of the present building.

William appointed a kinsman of his, Walkelin, who had been educated in Paris, to be the Bishop in 1070 to succeed the Saxon Stigand. He also caused Walkelin's brother, Simeon, educated at Cambrai, to be appointed Prior in the same year. Sufficient of the building was completed for it to be dedicated for worship in 1093 on April 8th of that year, probably the very day on which the building had been commenced fourteen years earlier. The stone for the building was brought by water from Quarr in the Isle of Wight. It only had to be dragged the last short distance from the river to the site. During the building operations, Simeon was made Abbot of Ely and was succeeded in 1082 by Godfrey, a scholar well known for his satirical and epigrammatic verse which still survives.

The Roof

The stonework rose quickly and seven years after the foundations had been laid the question of constructing the roof became a pressing one. Walkelin needed timber for the roof and so he asked the Conqueror for it. The Conqueror replied that he could have as much timber as he could gather in four days and nights from his wood at Hempage on the Alresford Road. Astutely, the Bishop gathered together a large number of men and denuded the royal wood entirely apart from one tree. The *Annalist* who records the occasion says: 'The King passing . . . . was struck with amazement, and cried out, Am I bewitched? or have I taken leave of my senses? Had I not once a most delectable wood in this spot? But when he understood the truth he was violently enraged. Then the bishop put on a shabby vestment, and made his way to the King's feet, humbly begging to resign the episcopate . . . . . the king was appeased only observing "I was as much too liberal in my grant as you were too greedy in availing yourself of it."'[2]

Hugh the Mason

The actual building of the Cathedral is generally attributed to Hugh *Caementarius* (the mason)[3] who lived at Chilcomb on one of the manors already in the possession of the monastery, where he held two ploughlands under Walkelin, c 1086. The general impression that the departure of the Roman legions meant the end of civilization is untrue. The traditions of builders and craftsmen were handed down, particularly in due course among the Benedictine monks who preserved books like the works of the Vitruvius who wrote *On Architecture*.[4] The builders, therefore, of the Cathedral followed the construction of the basilica rather than the pagan temple with its inappropriate associations. The basilica was an oblong shaped building usually with rows of columns to divide the nave from the aisles. At one end there was usually a semi-circular apse. This style of building recommended itself to the first church builders. It was the form followed at Winchester.

We know that the text of Vitruvius passed from the Benedictine Library of Monte Cassino via Fleury (now St. Benoît-sur-Loire) to Abingdon whither Aethelwold took both religion and learning in the tenth century. There is, therefore, nothing improbable in the availability of the text of Vitruvius to Walkelin and his advisers. A simple genealogical plan may help:-

Monte Cassino — Italy
Founded by S. Benedict
c. 529
|
(Fleury (Now St. Benoît-sur-Loire)
(Remains of St. Benedict transferred
here in 7th. century)[5]
|
Abingdon — St. Aethelwold[6]
c.954
|
Winchester — St. Aethelwold
c. 964
|
Walkelin, 1070

In 1087 the Conqueror died and was buried at Caen. Soon, the records tell of the presence of William Rufus in Winchester at Easter in the following year and regularly afterwards until his death in 1100 in the New Forest.

The Dedication

By 1093 sufficient of the building was completed to enable it to be dedicated for worship. Quoting the Winchester *Annalist* again, the ceremony "took place in the presence of nearly all the bishops and abbots of England . . . . with the utmost exultation and rejoicing".[7] What that ceremony was we can conjecture from the work on the subject by Durandus (1230-1296), who wrote about the various services of the Church in a work entitled *Rationale Divinorum Officiorum*. It is true that the work was written a good deal later than the completion of the Cathedral but nevertheless it embodies the ancient customs of the Church. In chapter six of his first book he tells how a church should be built and understood. The four walls represent the four evangelists. The foundation is faith, the roof is charity which covers a multitude of sins; altar, images, bells and churchyard all have their meaning. Coming to the dedication itself, it must be conducted by a bishop (there were many in 1093) and it must be endowed (it had received innumerable endowments since the seventh century). This was to ensure that once the worship of God had begun it should continue unbroken. In those days the notion of church collections and the voluntary support of churches had not arisen. The cathedral had to be dedicated for five main reasons:-

    1.   To drive out the devil;
    2.   To offer sanctuary;
    3.   To offer prayer;
    4.   To praise Almighty God;
    5.   To administer the sacraments.

The best estimate of just how much of the Cathedral was dedicated is the eastern arm, crossing and transepts, together with the eastern three or four bays of the nave to form an abutment for the construction of the centre tower.

The manner of a consecration covers many pages in Durandus. Bishops, clergy and people processed round the Church; prayers and litanies were intoned; and various parts of the building marked with the sign of the cross. Holy Water was used to signify the purification of the Church. The Bishop, representing Christ, struck the door of the closed church three times and was admitted by the sole deacon left in the Church. So Christ came into his own, the altar was consecrated and the whole interior sprinkled with holy water, lamps lighted and Mass said.[8] An impressive piece of architecture had become a living cathedral.

The Actual Building

The question is often asked — are there any accounts or plans of the actual building of Winchester Cathedral? So far none have been found. From a slightly later date it is possible to learn something of what the site must have looked like during the building construction. One of the nearest accounts in time and place which throws light on the building operations at Winchester comes from Chartres in Robert of Torigni's *Chronicle* (1145):

> "In that year, men at Chartres began to drag carts, harnessed to their own shoulders, laden with stones and wood, corn and other provisions, needed for the new church, whose towers were being built at this time . . . you would see men and women dragging carts through marshes . . . . everywhere miracles daily occurring, jubilant songs rendered to God."

Abbot Suger of Paris (in the late 1130s) speaks of stones being hauled "by our own people, and neighbours, both common folk and nobles, acting as draft animals." The Metrical Life of St. Hugh of Lincoln relates how St. Hugh "with the sweat of his own brow... oftentimes bore the hod-load of hewn stone . . ."

These accounts are infused with a strong religious sense. At Winchester the undertaking may well have been more prosaic. Nevertheless, the moving of the large amounts of stone and timber must have meant immense physical effort by horses and men to drag the carts, say from the river Itchen to the Cathedral site if, for example, the stone had been brought by barge from the Isle of Wight, the home of much of the stone used at Winchester. Later records tell of stone being brought to Winchester from Selborne. The work involved in such transport when there can only have been rough cart tracks must have been enormous. Hauling timber from Hempage wood was no small task.

When the materials reached the site masons and carpenters would be required. Martin Biddle and Dr. Keene in *Winchester in the Middle Ages* give statistics of those engaged in the building trades in Winchester early in the twelfth century. They note that while the properties of building craftsmen were widely scattered in 1148, some of them were grouped in the neighbourhood of the Cathedral "there would probably have been a steady demand for masons as well as carpenters." The numbers of such men in Winchester would appear to be insufficient for the tasks on which they were involved and outside labour would seem to have been necessary. This was certainly the case when the Castle was being built in 1222. A fragment of a roll of wages for that year mentions 34 masons. Some lived in and near Winchester but others came from as far afield as Cornwall and St. Albans. We read too of carters of stone among the work force. (see H. M. Colvin *The Building Accounts of Henry III.* pp. 99 . . .)

The Crypt

A hint of the overall supervision occurs in a sermon of the Dominican friar Nicholas de Biard who says: "In such great buildings there is wont to be one chief master who only ordains by word and rarely or never sets hand to the work: yet he takes higher pay than the rest". This custom no doubt stretched back to Hugh of Chilcomb.

Building Plans

It is unlikely that any plans used on the site could have survived the use to which they would be put. Nevertheless, Villard de Honnecourt in northern France produced an album of drawings about 1240 for architectural styles of his own day and made drawings of machines used in building. His plan of the choir chapels at Rheims reminds us of the architecture of the retro-choir of Winchester.

Honnecourt also give technical drawings of the piers and responds of Rheims. He used full sized templates for his work.

Honnecourt also gives drawings of the necessary machinery: a water powered sawmill; a screw-jack for lifting great loads; a method of attaching spokes to a wheel without cutting the axle; how to shore up a leaning framework back to an upright position; how to construct a floor with timbers too short to span the required distance. one drawing of particular interest to those concerned with Winchester is a saw for levelling heads of underwater piles. This must have been extremely useful at Winchester where the Cathedral is built upon water. A minor point is his drawing of an eagle for use as a Gospel lectern with moveable head. This type of lectern is still in use in the Quire of the Cathedral.

The Benedictine Rule.[9]

The observance of the Benedictine Rule continued unbroken. On one day it was followed in the Old Minster: on the next day in the present Cathedral. In all the Rule was observed unbroken from c.964 to 1538 when it was forcibly suppressed.

Opposite: Interior of the Choir chapels at Rheims, drawn by Villard about 1240.

Walkelin was fortunate to see the substantial completion of his projected cathedral. The relics of St. Swithun were transferred to the new building and the dismantling of the old set in hand immediately. More building was needed before the whole Norman Cathedral was completed. The central tower collapsed in 1107 and had to be rebuilt. There are those who claim to be able to see which part of the structure near the central tower ante-date the collapse and which post-date it. In addition, the building was lengthened towards the west where two towers were constructed. The foundations of these were seen again during the excavations of the 1970s. The full length of the building can be realised on looking at the north wall of No. 11, The Close, where there is a tablet some forty feet further west than the present west front. It reads:-

HAVE IN MIND WILLIAM WALKELIN
BISHOP OF WINCHESTER 1070-1098
WHO PLANNED THE CATHEDRAL CHURCH
THIS STONE MARKS THE WESTERN
LIMIT OF THE SOUTH WALL

Besides St. Swithun, the remains of St. Athelwold were transferred, probably about 1111 to the *feretrum,* i.e. that part of the Cathedral behind the present High Altar, which carried *(fero)* the remains of the saint. In all the building took just over forty years to its completion from 1079 to about 1122.

Opposite: Villard's machines: saw for levelling heads of underwater piles (plumb-rule); method of attaching the spokes of a wheel without cutting the axle; stay with levers for restoring a leaning framework to the upright; construction of a floor with timbers too short to span.

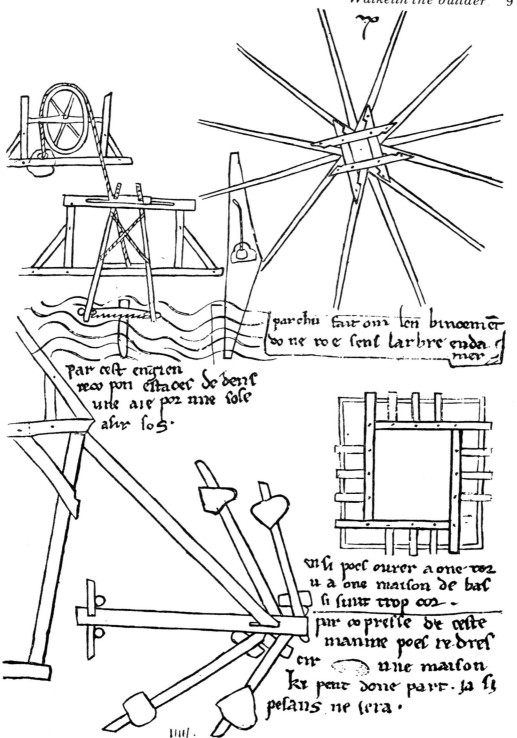

par chu fait om len binoemēt
vo ne vo e senl larbre enda q
mer

par cest engien
reco poi estacer de bent
une ais por nme sole
aur sos.

vn si poes ourer a one voz
u a one maison de bal
si sunt trop cos.

par co presse de ceste
manine poes redres
en une maison
ki peut done part. ja si
pesans ne sera.

IIII.

The Subsidiary Arts

With the shell of the building complete and the saints' remains transferred to the new building and provision made for the due celebration of the Mass, the adornment of the cathedral could be contemplated.

Again there was a vast body of organised knowledge, committed to writing by c.1125 by one Theophilus in his work *On Divers Arts*.[10] The three arts to which he refers are illumination of manuscripts, metal work and glass work. We shall come to the illumination of manuscripts when we examine the great part played by Henry of Blois in his patronage of the arts in the middle of the following century. Traces of early glass have long since disappeared, no doubt due to its very brittle nature. But metal work (which, for Theophilus, included organs) may still be seen in the relics of the grille that once protected St. Swithun's shrine. The skill of the metal worker is remarkable as the illustration opposite indicates. Almost certainly this was completed and put in place before Walkelin died.

Tradition has it that the massive wooden bench in the south transept dates from this early period and that the smaller curved bench in the south-east corner of the south transept dates from this period. The latter bench may well have been part of a series of seats for the Bishop, Prior and monks and which was situated against the inside apse at the original east end of the building.

The curved bench that may originally have been situated in the apse.

Part of metal grille which once protected the shrine of Saint Swithun (late XIth century)

Walkelin's Death

When Walkelin died in 1098 his Cathedral looked like the engravings of the south transept made early in the 19th century. It was Norman throughout with an open roof in nave, quire and transepts revealing the massive timbers which supported the outside roof. The Crypt also reveals the strength of the Norman building. The nature of the outside roof we can only conjecture. A wall painting behind the shelves in the Library suggests that the roof may have been tiled.

The interior decoration of the building was still at an early stage. The most important need was to protect the shrine of St. Swithun, patron saint of the Cathedral, and this seems to have been the first embellishment within the Cathedral. Wall paintings followed. Storage of treasures soon had to be provided. But altogether within a short time a huge Norman Cathedral had been erected and although, as it neared completion, it was excelled by Cluny in France, it was one of the wonders of the civilised world. As was fitting, Walkelin was buried in his Cathedral. We learn that he was buried before the rood loft:

Praesul Walklynus istic requiescit humatus
Tempore Willelmi Conquestoris cathedratus.

Bishop Walkelin rests, buried here
He was enthroned bishop here in the time of
William the Conqueror.

So far the remains of the Bishop have not been found.

William Rufus

Two years after Walkelin's death William Rufus was shot dead in suspicious circumstances while hunting in the New Forest. His body was brought to the Cathedral for burial. There was no sorrow for his death and when the tower collapsed in 1107 it was said that to have buried so evil a man in so sacred a place was to invite the vengeance of God. It was no wonder the tower collapsed.

Prior Godfrey

In the same year there died the Prior who had presided over the monastery's building for a quarter of century. Nothing is known of his administration or his practical gifts. But Prior Godfrey is known for his writings, in Latin, which, according to their editor, are much superior to what we might expect, and their interest is greatly increased by the circumstance that a certain number of them are devoted to persons of great historical importance, who lived in Godfrey's time, such as king William (the Conqueror), queen Matilda...and others.' Amongst the others is a poem on Walkelin. He writes of him as a corrector of youth, a servant of the aged, feet to the lame and light to the blind, helping those who are sick and raising them that are fallen. He spoke for the people and had the ear of the King. One could wish that someone combining the gifts of scholarship and poetry that are needed would turn Godfrey's Latin verse into English verse.

In 1111 the relics of Aethelwold were taken and placed in a new shrine in the presence of the Queen of Henry I.

Less pious was the struggle that raged between the monastery and the Bishop, William Giffard. The issue at stake was the revenues of the monastery which the monks alleged were wrongfully taken away from them by the Bishop. To register their protest they "went in procession, barefooted, and contrary to the course of the sun and to the custom of the Church; to imply that, as the Bishop had contrary to the canonical decrees, deprived those who had served God in his Church of their proper dues, so they would serve the Church in a way opposed to law and contrary to ecclesiastical decrees. The King sided with the monks, thus prolonged his dispute with the Bishop, though the principal nobility of the realm sided mainly with the Bishop.

At last Bishop and monks were reconciled in 1124. The Bishop took the Monastic habit and lived in the greatest harmony with the monks. He died in 1128 and was buried in a grave (now lost) near that of Walkelin. It bore the epitaph (in Latin)

William Giffard, the bishop lies buried here
He took the monastic habit while still alive.

The Laws of Henry I
"A minor ecclesiastical official', says the latest editor of the Laws of Henry I, was their author and the likeliest place of composition is Winchester between 1110 and 1118.[11]

Stavanger[12]
In 1125 the monk Reinald crossed the North Sea to found the city and cathedral of St. Swithun Stavanger. He took with him an arm of St. Swithun as a holy relic.

NOTES

[1] T. Wright, *The Anglo-Latin Satirical Poets and Epigrammatists of the twelfth Century*. London, 1872. pp.103-155.

[2] H. R. Luard: *Annales Monastici* Vol. ii. London, 1865. p.35.

[3] J. Harvey. *The Mediaeval Architect*. London, 1972. p.61.

[4] Vitruvius *On Architecture*. (Loeb Classics) London, 1970. Vol. 1. book V. ch. 1.

[5] Dom Claude Jean-Nesmy. *Saint Benoît-sur-Loire*. Édition Zodiaque, 1972. p. 5.

[6] For Aethelwold's and Abingdon's links with Fleury see J. Stevenson *Chronicon Monasterii de Abingdon*. 2 Vols. London, 1858. Vol. 1. p.129 & p.344. Vol. 2. p.259 and p.278.

[7] H. R. Luard. *op. cit.* p.37.

[8] William Durandus. *The Symbolism of Churches and Church* A translation of the first book. J. M. Neale and B. Webb, London, 1906.

[9] J. McCann. *The Rule of Saint Benedict in Latin and English*. London, 1952. In addition, the *Regularis Concordia* drawn up in Winchester c 970 and edited by T. Symons, London, 1962 should also be consulted.

[10] Theophilus. *On Divers Arts*. Translated by J. G. Hawthorne and C. S. Smith. Chicago, 1963.

[11] L. J. Downer. *Leges Henrici Primi, Oxford, 1972*. p. 35.

[12] C. Hohler. *The Cathedral Church of Stavanger in the Twelfth Century* Journal of the British Archaeological Association. 3rd series. 27. (1964) pp.22-118. Plates XVI-XXV.

FURTHER READING

M. Biddle (Ed.). *Winchester in the Early Middle Ages*. Winchester Studies Vol. 1. C.P. 1976.

R. A. Brown, H. M. Colvin and A. J. Taylor. *The History of the King's Works*. Vol. 11. The Middle Ages. pp. 854-864. H.M.S.O., 1963.

H. M. Colvin. *Building Accounts of Henry III*. C.P., 1971.

G. C. Coulton. *Life in the Middle Ages*. 4 Vols. C.U.P. 1928-9.

D.N.B. s.v. *Godfrey; Walkelin*.

A. W. Goodman. *The Winchester Chartulary*. Winchester, 1927.

J. Harvey. *Mediaeval Craftsmen*. London, 1975.

G. Henderson. *Chartres*. London, 1968.

S. Lindsay. *An Anatomy of English Wrought Iron*. London, 1964.

C. H. Moore. *The Vaults of Winchester Transepts*. R.I.B.A. 1916.

T. Rudborne. *Annals of the Church of Winchester from the year 633 — 1277*. Trans by J. Stevenson. London 1856.

Latin Text. H. Wharton. *Anglia Sacra*. 2 Vols. London, 1691. Vol. 1. pp.287 — 314. See also pp.179 — 286.

Villard de Honnecourt. ed by Hans R. Hahnloser. Graz, 1972.

R. Willis. *The Architectural history of Winchester Cathedral*. Proceedings of the Annual Meeting of the Archaeological Institute . . . Winchester, 1845. London, 1846. pp. 1 — 79.

Chapter II

Henry of Blois
Patron of the arts

About two years after the death of Walkelin, Henry of Blois was born, son of Stephen Count of Blois and Adela, sister of William the Conqueror. He was brought up in Cluny and in 1126 was invited to England by his uncle, Henry I, to be abbot of Glastonbury. Three years later, and not yet twenty-nine years of age and below the canonical age for ordination as a bishop, he was promoted Bishop of Winchester. Learned, noble, rich, liberal and magnificent, he soon became the most powerful of English bishops. His tenure of office was eventful in the extreme. In 1135, his brother, Stephen, came to the throne. Three years later Henry started to build his castle of Wolvesey where he later received Queen Matilda, 'mistress of the English.' His ecclesiastical ambition was to make Winchester an archbishopric.

Civil war between Matilda and himself raged in the city. When the fighting eventually ceased, he concerned himself with the Cathedral, causing the relics of Saint Birinus and the early kings of the West Saxons to be brought into the Cathedral in 1150. Their first resting places were leaden sarcophagi.

In 1162, Henry consecrated Thomas à Becket in Winchester as Archbishop of Canterbury; and in extreme displeasure summoned the King to his bedside when he learned of the murder of the Archbishop. His career, therefore, was influential and colourful. He was also, in the understanding of his own day, somewhat of an eccentric. John of Salisbury tells how he was known in Rome to collect ancient statues so that his critics could quote Horace against him:

Insanit veteres statuas Damasippus emendo
Buying old statues is Damasippus' craze. [1]

This eccentricity we recognise in the Cathedral because of its manifestation in the encouragement of the arts in such manner as made the Winchester School pre-eminent, particularly in the field of manuscript illumination and wall painting. The Cathedral also benefitted from his encouragement of architecture and other arts. Beyond the Cathedral and still in Winchester was his building of the Hospital of St. Cross. Winchester owes much to Bishop Henry. Here we are concerned with the Cathedral.

The Winchester Bible

First and foremost among the works for which Henry is remembered is the *Winchester Bible*. It is the culminating achievement of the 'Winchester School' which dates back to about the time of the end of the reign of King Alfred. Outstanding achievements of the school are the *Benedictional* of St. Aethelwold (c. 970) and thereafter a series of manuscripts, plain and illuminated. Among them was *The Winchester Bible*, originally in two volumes.

The brilliance of the colours and the technique of the artists is awe-inspiring. We have already referred to the fact that Theophilus had produced a book entitled *On Divers Arts* which showed that well organised information was already at the disposal of the artists. A few chapter headings will indicate the range of that section of the book dealing with the art of illumination:-

  First shadow pigment
  Hair of boys, adolescents and young men
  Gold leaf
  Translucent paintings
  Spanish Green

In all there are nearly forty such chapters shewing that the artists at Winchester were backed by considerable organised knowledge.

There is more than artistic skill. There is the thought-world of the 12th century which lies behind the work of the artists. The 'Masters' reflected the thought of their day, possibly the events of their day. A glance at a few initials only is possible.

The Beatus Initials

Artist: The Master of the Genesis Initial and The Master of the Leaping Figures.

The Latin word *Beatus* means blessed and refers to the opening word of Psalm 1: Blessed is the man . . . . The first feature to note, and this is peculiar to the Psalms, is that the head of the book has not just one

The Beatus Initials. Psalm 1.

illuminated initial which is the general custom, but two. The opportunity to have two arises from the fact that the Psalms are written in two versions known as the Vulgate (i.e. popular) and the Gallican. Both versions are by St. Jerome. The Gallican is a revision of the Vulgate and became especially popular in France or Gaul, as it was called. Hence the name of the version. The Vulgate is on the left side and the Gallican on the right.

Each letter 'B' is about the size of an ordinary post card. The one on the left has in the two loops of the letter two scenes from the life of David: the slaying of a bear and the slaying of a lion. Both events are recorded in 1 Samuel Chapter 18 verses 34 and 37. On each occasion David the shepherd rescues one of his sheep. In the right hand letter the two loops shew the Son of David rescuing His sheep by driving out an evil spirit (as recorded in St. Mark 9.17) and in the lower loop rescuing His sheep from Hell itself (1 Peter 3.18). This was a favourite mediaeval theme, known as the Harrowing of Hell. In the artist's mind was the typological belief that the Old Testament foreshadowed the New.[2] What was true of David was true in an even more important sense of the Son of David.

The Genesis Initial
The Master of the Genesis Initial

This initial also gave the artist an opportunity to express his ideas. The first words are: *In the beginning*. In Latin the first word is the same . . . *In*. The artist, therefore, had an opportunity to illuminate a large letter 'I' as long as the folio itself, nearly two feet. He used this opportunity to make a statement in art form about his concept of the creation. He did so by painting seven roundels within the letter. Beginning from the top they represent:-

The Creation of Eve
Noah in the Ark
The Sacrifice of Isaac
The Giving of the Law on Sinai
The Anointing of David by Samuel
The Nativity of Christ
The Risen and Ascended Christ at the Last Judgement, seen through the Cross.

To him, creation was thought of as a process stretching from the very foundation of the world to the final judgement of man. It was not, to his way of thinking, a once for all event. Equally it was not a 'scientific' event or series of events. It was a process involving the judgement of man.

Further insight into the ideas of the artist can be gleaned from contemporary writers. Hugh of Saint Victor[3] in Paris (1096 — 1142), himself an English scholar, gave a whole course of lectures *De Arce Noe*, On Noah's Ark. The lecturer's understanding is not ours. He attempts no historical or archaeological understanding. The dove, for example, typifies three forms of contemplation. It has two wings since there are for Christians two kinds of life, the active and contemplative. The grey-blue feathers of its wings show heavenly thoughts. The changing colours of the rest of the body, like a troubled sea, symbolize the sea of human passion, on which floats the ark of the Church. Why are dove's eyes golden yellow? Because yellow, the colour of ripe fruit, is the colour of experience and maturity. The yellow eyes of the dove symbolize the glance of wisdom which the Church casts on the future. Finally the dove has red feet for the Church progresses through the world, her feet reddened by the blood of the martyrs.[1]

INCIPIT
LIBER GE
NESIS ·;
IN PRIN
CIPIO CRE
AVIT DEVS
CELVM ET TERRAM.

Terra autem erat inanis &
uacua · & tenebrę erant
sup faciem abyssi · & spi
dei ferebatur sup aquas.
Dixitq dŝ · Fiat lux · Et
facta est lux · Et uidit dŝ
lucem quod ēē bona · &
diuisit dŝ lucé a tenebris.
Appellauitq; lucé dié · &
tenebras nocte · Factúq;
est uespe & mane dies unʹ
Dixit quoq; dŝ · Fiat firma
mentum immedio aquarū ·
& diuidat aquas ab aquis ·
Et fecit dŝ firmamentū ·
diuisitq; aquas quę erāt
sub firmamento · ab iis
quę erant sup firmamcū ·
Et factum est ita · Voca
uitq; dŝ firmamentū cę
lum · & factū est uespe &
mane dies secundus ·
Dixit uero dŝ · Congre
gentur aquę quę sub
cęlo sunt in locū unum ·
& appareat arida · Fac
tumq; est ita · Et uocauit
dŝ aridam terra · congre
gationesq; aquarū appel
lauit maria · Et uidit dŝ

The Genesis Initial.

Ezekiel and the Building of Chartres
Artist: The Master of the Morgan Leaf.

An interesting suggestion about this initial comes from Professor G. Henderson.[4] Recalling the words of the Chronicler Robert of Torigni, who described the building of Chartres (see p.34f), he adds a further comment of the Chronicler: . . .You would say the prophecy was fulfilled: "Then the Spirit of the living creatures was in the wheels." The Chronicler is quoting the words of Ezekiel 1.20: 'The Spirit of the living creatures was in the wheels.' These wheels with the living creatures are part of the illumination at the head of the book of Ezekiel and are part of his vision. There is a representation of the River Chebar (Ezekiel ch. 1. v. 1) at the foot of the painting where the prophet dreams.

The Ezekiel initial

Christ Pantocrator: Cefalu

Cefalu and Monreale in Sicily

These three examples must suffice from among many that could be so treated. We turn now to another aspect of the Bible: its connection with Sicily. This apparently surprising connection is due to the circumstances of the day. In 1154, Henry II succeeded to the throne. His daughter, Joan, who came to Winchester, married William, King of Sicily, who was responsible for the building of the dazzlingly brilliant Church of Monreale. The Byzantine style of painting which is visible in the Book of Lamentations in the Bible (and also in the Holy Sepulchre Chapel) links Winchester with the similar style found in the mosaics of Monreale and Cefalu with their splendid representations of Christ *Pantocrator* (the Almighty). The links are due to the personal ties between the two countries in the 12th century. The royal patronage exerted upon craftsmen meant that these craftsmen worked in both countries. Englishmen held high ecclesiastical office in Palermo and Messina and it is noteworthy that Thomas à Becket, within a decade of his martyrdom, figures prominently in the mosaics of the apse of Monreale, in the year 1182.

Sigena and the Artists of the Winchester Bible

Dr. Oakeshott has used this title to indicate the links between Winchester and Catalonia.[5] The Convent in Spain was a royal foundation and once again it looks as though artists under patronage worked in several countries. Sigena is a convent inland from Barcelona with mural paintings which have affinities with the artists of the Winchester Bible. These were photographed in the 1930's, just before the Spanish Civil War. Unhappily the originals were largely destroyed during the war but an imaginative attempt has been made to reconstruct them in the Catalan museum in Barcelona where the reconstructed paintings can now be seen and their affinities with Winchester have been examined in detail.

The Crusades

Towards the end of the 12th century, about the time the Winchester Bible was finished, there was in the monastery a certain monk named Richard of Devizes. His editor says that he was particularly well placed to record the annals of his day.[6] He writes about the events in the reign of Richard I including his campaign to the Holy Land. The *Annalist,* who could be Richard of Devizes describes how the Patriarch of Jerusalem was received in the Cathedral in the presence of the King in 1185.[7] There is no doubt, therefore, that there were links between Winchester and the Holy Land.[8]

The Subsequent History of the Bible

The biographer [9] of St. Hugh of Lincoln tells how Henry II visited Hugh when he was Prior of Witham, Somerset, before he became bishop, and asked if he could help with the production of a Bible. Hugh was grateful for the offer and for the generosity of the King. Consequently, the King ordered a Bible to be sent from Winchester to Witham. It has been suggested that what we now call the *Winchester Bible* was sent to Witham. More recently, however, another Winchester Bible (now in the Bodleian) has been thought to be the Bible which was taken to Witham. This second Bible remained in the Library when returned from Witham, until about 1600 when one of the Canons sent it to Oxford to help in the enrichment of the Bodleian Library.

In 1622, the Bible is mentioned in the manuscript catalogue of the Winchester manuscripts made by Sir Patrick Young, brother of the then Dean and Librarian to James I [10]. In the catalogue, it is referred to as *Biblia Latina 2 vol.* It has thus survived the upheaval of the Reformation and was to survive the ordeal of the Commonwealth for it is mentioned in a printed list of manuscripts published towards the end of the 17th century.[11]

Christ Pantocrator: Winchester Bible.

Lamentations.

Under the reforming zeal of Dean Rennell and Prebendary Nott, the two volumes were re-bound, rather illogically, in three volumes early in the 19th century. No trace of the original binding remains. The 19th century binding was a strong, workmanlike binding of boards covered with green leather: the edges were trimmed and gilded, much to the consternation of later scholars.

The Second World War was a threat to the security of the Bible. It was, therefore, taken to safety. The Bible returned in triumph with police escort on St. Swithun's Day, 1945 from the British Museum Repository near Bradford-on-Avon to its original home in the Cathedral Church of St. Swithun where it had first been written nearly eight hundred years earlier.[12]

The return of the Bible coincided with the publication by Dr. Oakeshott, Headmaster of Winchester College, of his *The Artists of the Winchester Bible*. This has proved the foundation of all subsequent study of the Bible. It has led to world wide interest in the manuscript. A particularly important step was taken when he decided, with the practical co-operation of Miss Beatrice Forder, eminent for her calligraphy and bookbinding, and Assistant Librarian of the Cathedral, to rebind the Bible in four volumes. Thus the illogical division of the 19th century gave way to the more logical binding of the original volume 1 into two parts and the original volume 2 into two parts. The work was handsomely completed in 1948. The present exhibition room which had previously been a rather crowded addition to the Library was cleared and made into a well laid out room where the Bible is suitably displayed offering four openings to the visitor. Thus what was written over eight hundred years ago within the confines of the monastery is still in its original home and gives pleasure, awe and wonder to thousands who see it every year. When Miss Forder died in 1976 it was decided to add an inscription on the case holding the four volumes of the Bible which she had so well bound:

Remember Beatrice Forder who rebound the Bible in 1948.

The Obadiah Initial

By a remarkable coincidence, just as the Bible was being rebound, the combined scholarship of Dr. M. R. James and Dr. Oakeshott, now Honorary Librarian of the Cathedral, discovered in a Yorkshire sale of books an illuminated initial from the Book of *Obadiah*. It proved to be one missing from the *Winchester Bible*. Not only does the initial fit but the words of the text on the reverse of the initial also fit. With outside financial help from the National Art Collections Fund, the Dean and Chapter were able to recover the initial and Miss Forder sewed it in place.[13] There are still initials missing and it would be pleasant to think that the wider knowledge of the Bible will finally reach those who possibly still have missing initials in their keeping and would return them to their original home.

An example of 12th century Winchester bookbinding.

The Morgan Leaf

The most important missing part of the Bible is a folio known as the Morgan Leaf which is in the Pierpont Morgan Library in New York Originally it served as a frontispiece to 1 Samuel. Dr. Oakeshott first thought an appropriate title for the artist was the Master of the Morgan Leaf but has more recently suggested The Master of the Apocrypha Drawings, as there are two full page drawings in the *Aprocrypha (Judith* and *1 Maccabees,* both uncoloured). The date is c 1180. Something of the magnificence of the illumination can be seen in the coloured reproduction facing the Foreword in C. M. Kauffmann's *Romanesque Manuscripts 1066 — 1190,* London, 1975. The whole volume is valuable for any who are deeply interested in the background from which the Winchester Bible sprang and indicates the wealth of artistic skill and fertile imagination that marked the 12th century.

Bookbinding

While we do not know what the binding of the Winchester Bible was like in the 12th century there is in the Cathedral, returned in 1947 by the generosity of the late Mr. Dyson Perrins, the 12th century copy of Hegesippus Church Historian of the second century. It is covered by a Winchester binding of the 12th century. Three such bindings survive: two in London and one in Winchester. A glance at the illustration will reveal at once its handsome nature. It was bound in wooden boards, covered with calfskin.[14].

The Winchester Psalter

There is another outstanding manuscript from the age of Henry of Blois: *The Winchester Psalter.*[15]. This was sometimes called the St. Swithun's Psalter, or the Psalter of Henry of Blois. It has even been suggested that it was his own personal copy, particularly because of a prayer that it contains, the Latin of which may be turned into English broadly as follows:-

Blessed Swithun, thou art now at rest and filled with all blessedness. Once thou didst yearn for Christ. Now thou art with Him in the company of His saints. As for me, miserable sinner, I have sinned in thy courts by my evil life and wicked deeds. Help me, with all Thy saints whose bodies rest beside thee and whose remains lie within this Cathedral and in this City and in this Court

Opposite: The Winchester Psalter.
Note the title of the folio in Norman French

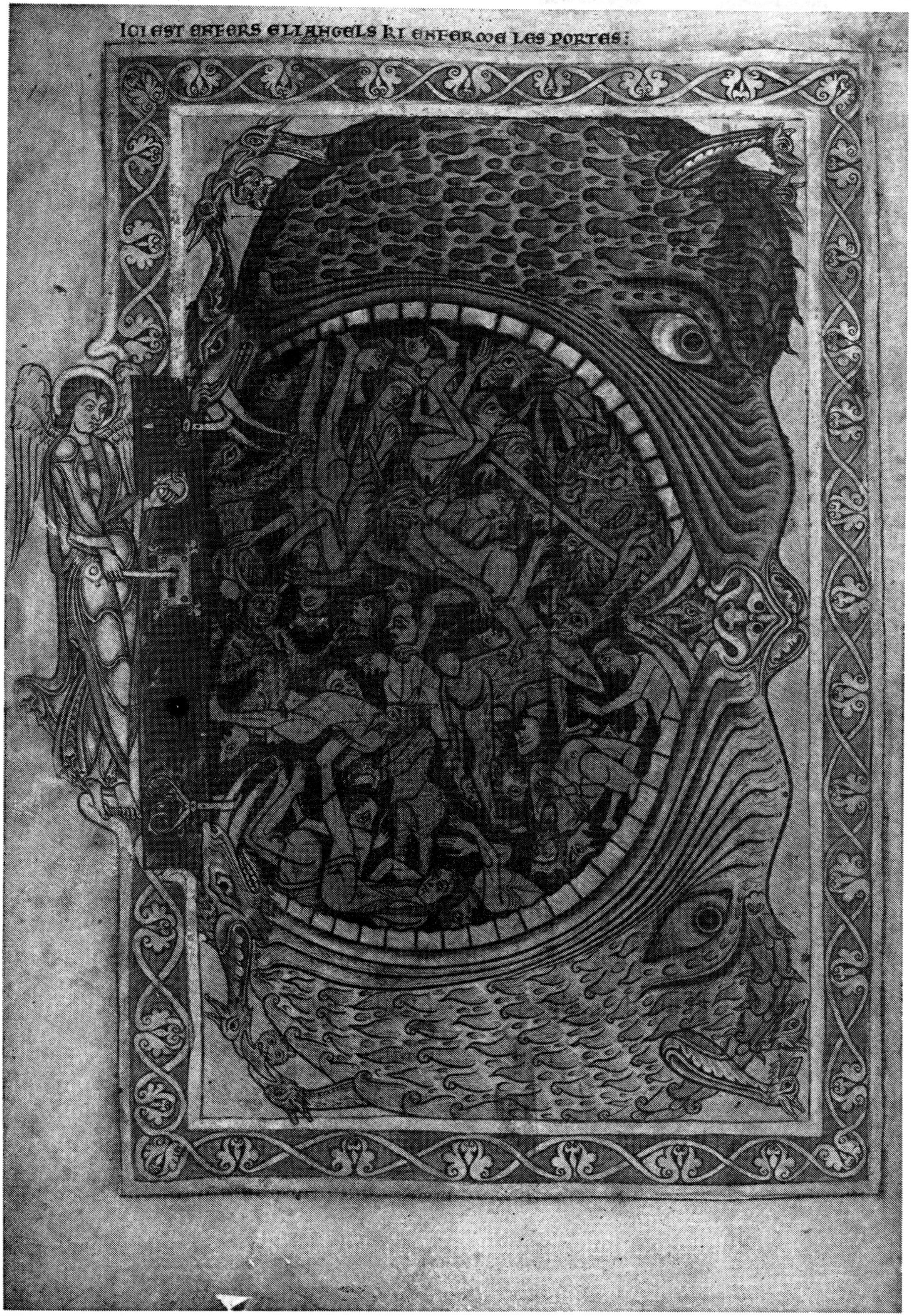
ICI EST ENFERS E LI ANGELS KI ENFERME LES PORTES:

The Psalter is not quite so finely executed as the Bible as a comparison between the *Beatus* initials in each book shows. There is a small amount of illumination suggesting the presence of a Byzantine influence. In addition there are numerous illustrations headed with captions in Norman French, the language of 12th century Winchester. The vivid illustrations of the Life of Christ may well be drawn from the persons who took part in the mystery plays of the time. Thus the entry of Christ into Jerusalem could well depict an appropriate drama enacted by the citizens of Winchester as they entered in by the West Gate of the City. The artist was not aiming at a correct historical representation of the events of Palm Sunday. He was shewing its contemporary meaning to the men of his own day in Winchester. Illustrations have Norman French titles as the representation of the angel closing the gates of Hell shows.

One final feature of the Psalter must be mentioned and that is the Litany which refers particularly to the saints connected with Winchester: Judoc, Boniface, Birinus, Swithun and Aethelwold.

Wall Paintings

From manuscripts and their illuminations it is a natural step to a consideration of the wall paintings of the Cathedral. Those particularly associated with this period are to be found in the Holy Sepulchre Chapel. It is now thought that there is an artistic link between the Master of the Morgan Leaf and the Artist or Artists responsible for the Holy Sepulchre paintings.

At one stage, perhaps in the days of the Puritanical Bishop Horne in the 16th century, the wall paintings were covered. But for more than a century now they have been known, and the subject of several studies. Noteworthy among earlier writers are Professor Willis and Professor Tristram. More recently Professor Baker has worked on the paintings. In particular she removed the top painting of the east wall of the Chapel and placed it on the west wall. This was a process calling for much skill and great delicacy of treatment. We now have a glimpse of the original paintings of the chapel, particularly over the altar with which alone we concern ourselves here. What we now see is a painting appropriate for the Holy Sepulchre: a deposition of Christ from the Cross. Nicodemus is extracting the nails from the feet of Christ. Joseph of Arimathaea holds the dead Christ in his arms while the hand the Virgin Mary, in a gesture of supreme compassion, touches the shoulder of Christ. Below this deposition we see the entombment

Opposite: The wall painting in the Holy Sepulchre Chapel.

of Christ. His body lies in the tomb and the crowned figure of the Virgin stands behind holding the left hand of Christ in both of hers. Joseph of Arimathaea anoints the body of Christ while a bearded figure wipes his feet. An angel above carries his censer while on the left we see the three Maries and the Angel by the tomb. To the right we see Christ holding the staff of Resurrection and the dead rising from their graves.

When we look up to the vault we see a Byzantine style Christ holding a book bearing the words, I am the Salvation of the People:

S A	L U S
P O P	U L I
E G O	S U M

It is a tradition that in olden days the pilgrims came here on entry to the Cathedral to say their prayers before visiting the shrine of St. Swithun. Now the Chapel is used each Saturday, the day when Christ rested in the tomb, and we remember especially the departed, risen with Christ. Tradition also has it that from here began the processions on the eve of Easter when the words going back to the days of St. Aethelwold and recorded in the *Regularis Coxncordia*[16] were used (and still are) during the period of Easter:-

V. Whom seek ye in the Sepulchre, O worshippers of Christ?
R. Jesus of Nazareth who has been crucified.
V. He is not here. The Lord is risen. Alleluia.

The present version differs slightly from that of the *Concordia*.

The Font

Usually associated with Henry of Blois, though occasionally with his successor Richard Toclyve, is the Font which comes from Tournai in Belgium. This is one of very few of this style in Britain. It is a style found in many places in western Europe where access was possible by sea or river. The transport of so heavy a piece of work would require this and a map of the distribution of fonts throughout England, France, Belgium and Germany indicates that this is so. The most famous of these fonts on the Continent is at Zedelghem near Bruges. Besides having emblems of the Holy Spirit and the Sacraments, the theme round the sides of the Font is the life of St. Nicholas. These carvings excite the interest of specialists in different fields. The historian of shipping is interested in the rudder: the ecclesiastical historian and artist is interested in the peculiar shape of the mitre.[17]

The Font which is over 800 years old.

The Treasury

The last remaining part of the Cathedral associated with the Bishop is the Treasury abutting on the west side of the south transept. It is a part of the Cathedral now used as a Choir Vestry. The previously existing Norman arch was filled in by a wall in which are two later Norman pointed arches. There is a long list of items which Henry himself bequeathed to the Treasury. Here are just a few:-

6. Processional cross, all in gold, in which are 56 sapphires, 10 topaz, 7 pomegranates and 10 emeralds and 257 oriental pearls. All the stones are precious and of great price.
16. Two golden candelabra
30. A silver vessel for sprinkling water at dedications
36. Golden cope with morse made of gold
42. Two stoles from Germany with maniples of great price
52. Two mitres
53. . . . . the hoof of a griffon [18]
60. Four candles to be kept burning continually
62. A corona which hangs in the Quire splendidly adorned in gold, silver and brass. [19]

For a time the Domesday Book was kept in the Treasury. [20] Thomas Rudborne, a monk of Winchester (c. 1460) also tells us that the Axe of Colbrand was kept there in his time. [21] It remained well stocked until that day in September 1538 when many of the treasures were removed.

Saxon Kings and Bishops

Bishop Henry brought into the Cathedral from the minster of St. Aethelwold the relics of the Saxons Kings and Bishops of Wessex and indeed of England. The remains are now on the top of Fox's Presbytery screens erected in the 16th century. Their earlier disposition is difficult to ascertain. One suggestion is that they were situated over the 'Holy Hole' behind the Reredos. Whatever their actual placing in the building, their identity is worth recording. On the south side, beginning from the High Altar we have:-

1. King Kynegils, died 641. Founder of the Saxon Cathedral.
   King Ethelwulf, died 857, a benefactor of the Saxon Cathedral.
2. King Edred, died 955. Grandson of Alfred the Great.
3. "In this chest and in the one opposite are the remains of Cnut and Rufus, kings: of Emma, queen; and of Wina and Alwyn, bishops" (So runs an inscription of 1661).

On the north side, beginning again from the High Altar we have:-
1. King Edmund, son of Alfred the Great.
2. King Kenulph who died in 714.
   King Egbert, usually considered to be the first king of England, who died in 837.
3. The same inscription as no 3. above.

Thus, whatever the original disposition of the relics, their preservation is due to Henry and gratitude must be recorded for his preservation of some of the most important relics of the country's earliest history.

When Thomas Rudborne,[22] who wrote a brief history of Winchester in the 15th century, came to sum up Henry's career he wrote: "Henry, bishop of Winchester, than whom never was man more chaste or prudent, more compassionate, or more earnest in transacting ecclesiastical matters, or in beautifying churches, departed to the Lord" (August 8th., 1171). He was buried before the High Altar.

NOTES

1 M. Chibnall. *John of Salisbury's Memoirs of the Papal Court*. London, 1962. p.79.
2 For a detailed account of typology' see *E.R.E.* Vol. XII. pp.500 — 504.
3 Hugh of St. Victor. *Selected Spiritual Writings*. London, 1962. p.79.
4. G. Henderson. *Chartres*. London, 1968. pp.34 __ 37.
5 W. F. Oakeshott. *Sigena and the Artists of the Winchester Bible*. London, 1972.
6 J. T. Appleby. *The Chronicle of Richard of Devizes*. London, 1963. p.xi.
7 H. R. Luard, *Annals Monastici*. Vol. 11. Rolls Series. p.62.
8 The representations of the Temple in Jerusalem in the Winchester Bible are the same as those in the twelfth century maps of Jerusalem which reached the West at this time. Z. Vilnay. *The Holy Land in Old Prints and Maps*. Jerusalem, 1965. p.54.f.
9 D. L. Douie and Dom H. Farmer. *The Life of St. Hugh of Lincoln*. 2 Vols. London, 1961. Vol. 1. pp.84 — 88.
10 Winchester Cathedral MSS. XIX. 1622.
11 E. Bernard. *Catalogi Librorum Manuscriptorum Angliae*. Oxford, 1697.
12 *W.C.R.* 1946. p. 2.
13 *The Illustrated London News*. January 24th., 1948. p.109.
14 E. A. Savage. *Old English Libraries*. London, 1970. p.107.
15 F. Wormald. *The Winchester Psalter*. London, 1973.
16 Dom T. Symons. *Regularis Concordia*. London, 1953. p.50.
17 J. O. Andries. *Monographie des Fontes Baptismaux de Zedelghem*. Bruges, G. C. Dunning. *The Distribution of Black Tournai Fonts*. The Antiquaries Journal. Vol. XXIV. 1944. p.1.f. C. H. Eden. *Black Tournai Fonts in England*. London, 1909.
18 In Christian iconography a griffon stood guard over treasure. The fact that there is the hoof of a griffon on folio 1r of the Winchester Bible might be taken to indicate that it was placed there to assure its future safety. (I owe this suggestion to Dr. Oakeshott.)
19 E. Bishop. *Liturgica Historica*. C.P., 1918. pp.392 -- 401.
20 H. Ellis. *A General Introduction to Domesday Book* 2 Vols. London, 1971. Vol. 1. p.353.n.2.
21 H. Wharton. *Anglia Sacra*. 2 Vols. London, 1691. Vol.1.p.212.
22 *D.N.B.* s.v. Rudborne T. J. Stevenson. *The Church Historians of England*, Vol.IV Pt.1. London, 1856. pp.347 — 384. (see p. 365).

FURTHER READING

L. Ayres. *The Work of the Morgan Master at Winchester and English Paintings of the Early Gothic Period*. Art Bulletin. California, 1974. lvi.2. 201 — 233.
R. W. Eyton, *Court, Household and Itinerary of King Henry II*. Hildesheim, 1974.
D. Knowles. *Saints and Scholars* C.VII. Henry of Winchester. C.U.P. 1963.
W. F. Oakeshott. *Artists of the Winchester Bible*. London, 1945.
Theophilus. *On Divers Arts*. Tranlated from the Medieval Latin. J. G. Hawthorne and C. S. Smith, Chicago, 1963.

Opposite: Plan of the Cathedral at the time of the death of Henry of Blois.

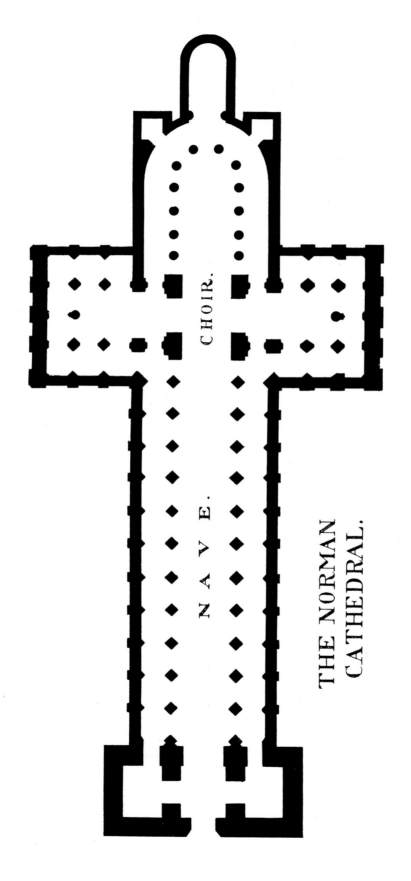

CHOIR.

N A V E.

THE NORMAN
CATHEDRAL.

William of Wykeham

Chapter III

Later Mediaeval Craftsmen

The word mediaeval is one often used but rarely defined. Generally there is the impression that the word must always have existed to refer to events vaguely thought to be in the 'middle ages.' Like so many terms we think ancient, it is, in fact, quite modern. The word was not coined until the last century and seems first to have been defined by Ruskin: 'the period which extends from the fall of the Roman Empire to the end of the 15th century.'[1]

During the last three centuries which fall within this definition, two Winchester names stand out pre-eminently: William of Edington (1346 — 1366) and William of Wykeham (1366 — 1404). While concentrating on these two names it is not suggested that there was no other builders. Indeed the building of the Cathedral never ceased. The former Cathedral Architect, Wilfred Carpenter Turner, indicates that it was early in the 14th century, about 1315, that the Presbytery was re-shaped and the original Norman apse replaced and the walls of the Presbytery added. To do this the walls had to be slightly canted in order to find a secure foundation. The aisles of the presbytery probably still retained their Norman appearance. Work on this area of the Cathedral continued till Edington's time and was only finally completed in the days of Bishop Fox.

William of Edington

By the middle of the 14th century attention focussed upon the west end of the Cathedral. Up to that time there had been two towers which extended some forty feet further west than the present west end. In Edington's time these had become insecure or had actually collapsed so that re-building was essential. Unfortunately, the crisis could not have come at a worse time for it was the period of the Black Death. John Harvey, an authority on Mediaeval

Architects, considers that the crisis meant that Edington had at his disposal less competent builders than might otherwise have been the case. They were men, he thinks, used only to smaller building than the scale the Cathedral required. Whatever the precise truth, it was in Edington's time that the present west end was erected and the windows on the north and south side at the west end of the nave constructed. A single glance reveals that they are of different style from the more easterly windows built by Wykeham. In his will, Edington left instructions that part of his wealth should be spent on the completion of the reconstruction of the nave which he had begun (Wharton: *Anglia Sacra* 1. 317).

William of Edington

Edington also requested that his chantry should be erected near the place where the monks entered the Cathedral from the cloisters to begin their processions.[2] This was done. In 1366 access to the south aisle was from a door at the east end of the nave. It is still clearly visible from the outside, though access is not now possible. So the chantry was erected with a figure of Edington sculptured over the tomb. Edington is also remembered as the first Prelate of the Order of the Garter, an office since then always held by the

Bishop of Winchester.

Round the edge of the tomb is an epitaph on a strip of blue enamelled brass which may be translated as follows:-

William, born at Edington, is here interred.
He was a well-beloved prelate, and Winchester was his See.
You who pass by, remember him in your prayers.
He was discreet, and mild, and of much sagacity.
He was a watchful guardian of the English nation,
A tender father and protector of the poor.
To 1,000, three hundred, add 50,10,5 and 1(1366)
Then the eighth of October will mark the day of his death.

William Wynford —
William of Wykeham's
brilliant architect. His
picture can be seen in
Winchester College.

William of Wykeham and William Wynford

The most celebrated of all the builders of Winchester Cathedral is William of Wykeham (1366 — 1404). His work is famous not only in the Cathedral and the College at Winchester, but also in Oxford and Windsor. In the Cathedral he completed the work on the nave set in hand by his predecessor. His windows are different in shape. The Norman columns were surrounded by shafts of masonry and so converted into a perpendicular style, while the Norman arches were converted into the present pointed arches giving a new strength and effortless majesty which characterises the nave. All was covered by a stone lierne[3] vaulting below the original Norman timbers. It is Wykeham's nave we see as we enter the Cathedral to-day, more than five centuries later. The passage of time leaves it almost unrivalled among the achievements of ecclesiastical architecture anywhere in the world, both for style and scale. Wykeham's architect was William Wynford.

Indeed when speaking of what Wykeham built we mean in effect that Wynford built. Wynford's earlier work[4] was at Windsor and Wells and Abingdon. He worked too at Corfe Castle, Southampton and Oxford. Finally he did much work for Wykeham both at the College and the Cathedral at Winchester. In connection with the Cathedral, Wykeham, in his will, arranged for Wynford to have the *"dispositio et ordinatio'* (the disposition and ordinance)[5] of the work Wykeham projected. So Wykeham's nave is really Wynford's nave. Wykeham made it clear in his Will that upon his death 2500 marks should be set aside for the completion of the nave, and that Wynford could call in "other sufficient and discreet persons", such as Simon Membury the surveyor, as he deemed fit. A further 500 marks was earmarked for the windows and the Prior and Convent were to produce the scaffolding.

The honour in which Wynford was held can be deduced from the facts that he should daily, as long as he lived, be free to eat "at dinner and at supper in the Prior's Hall at the Prior's own table unless the multitude of people or the presence of important and distinguished magnates of the country should prevent it." Each year he was to be fitted out with a suit of one of the Prior's esquires, furred with lamb, and a robe for his servant. He was entitled daily to half-a-gallon of the best convent ale and during the winter, from the feast of All Saints to the feast of the Purification, to two candles in his room. He was also entitled to a horse for himself and for his servant. Spiritually he was taken into the special fraternity of the Chapter, to participate in the benefits of their masses and prayers, both during his life and after his death.

The precise nature of Wykeham's achievement can best be envisaged with the help of a drawing made by Professor Willis for the meeting of the Archaeological Institute at Winchester in 1845 (opposite).

INTERMEDIATE STATE   PRESENT STATE.   ORIGINAL STATE.

R. WILLIS *del*

DELAMOTTES NEAVISIDE sc

The alterations to the arches of the nave

Wykeham's Chantry

Wykeham bequeathed to the Cathedral its best known chantry. It was planned and dedicated during his life time and he was buried there on September 27th, 1404. He planned the chantry at the place where, as a boy, he had attended Mass celebrated by one of the monks, Richard Pekis.

The inscription round the edge of his tomb may be rendered as follows:-

Here, overthrown by death, lies William surnamed Wykeham.
He was Bishop of this church, and repairer of it.
He was unbounded in hospitality, as the rich and poor can equally prove.
He was an able politician and councillor of the State.
His piety is manifest by the colleges which he founded,
The first of which is at Oxford, and the second at Winchester.

The achievements of Wykeham[6] are so massive that it is pleasing to mention some smaller provisions that he made indicating Wykeham the man as distinct from the great prelate. He issued letters patent to reserve for the bishop a private right of way from Wolvesey to the Cathedral so as not to disturb his contemplations, his devotions or his prayers.[7] Very practical was his monition against stone throwing and ball games in the grave yard of the Cathedral to avoid the breaking of the windows.[8]

Beaufort's Chantry

Beaufort and Waynflete both wished to be buried as near as possible to the shrine of the Cathedral's patron saint. And so we find Beaufort's Chantry on the southern side of the place where Swithun's shrine was situated. In his will[9] he directed that his body be buried (1447) 'in my Church at Winchester in the place I have appointed. I will that every day three masses be celebrated for my soul by three monks in that Church in the Chapel of my sepulture. And that the name of Henry Cardinal be pronounced, and that in celebrating, the souls of John Duke of Lancaster and Katherine his wife, my parents, the souls of Henry IV and Henry V Kings of England . . . be especially remembered.' Again financial provision was arranged and vestments and furnishings provided. The inscription round the tomb reads: 'I should be in anguish, did I not know Thy Mercies.' The present figure of the Cardinal was apparently added in the reign of Charles II and the chantry restored by Henry Charles, Duke of Beaufort, in 1819.

Beaufort is remembered for his association with the trial of Joan of Arc and because of a scene in Shakespeare's *Henry VI* in which the Earl of Warwick says:-

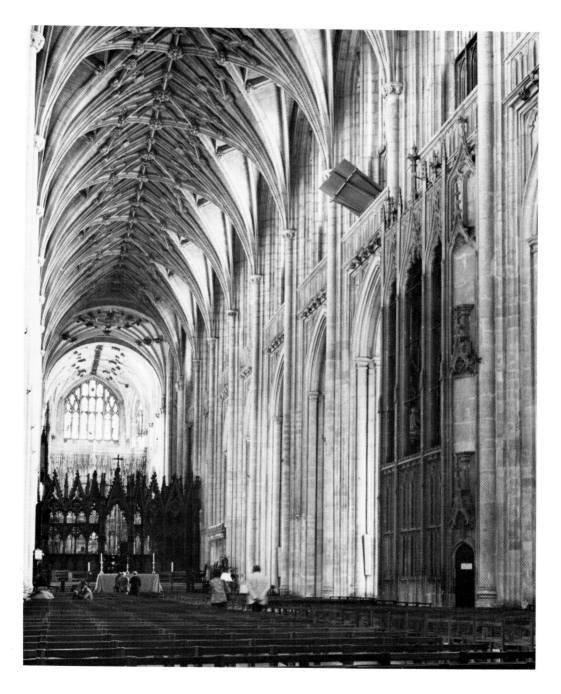

The arches created by Wykeham

'Lord Cardinal, if you think'st on heaven's bliss,
Hold up thy hand, make signal of thy hope.
He dies, and makes no sign. O God, forgive him.

To this Warwick adds:

So bad a death argues a monstrous life.

But the King answers:

'Forbear to judge, for we are sinners all.
Close up his eyes, and draw the curtain close;
And let us all to meditation.

Thirteen years after Beaufort's death we find the Prior and monks binding themselves to observe the injunctions of his will. To-day his *obit* is annually observed on April 8th.

Waynflete's Chantry

Waynflete, Bishop of Winchester from 1447 to 1486, is shown as dressed in full pontificals; his hands clasped in prayer. The inscription which once ran round the tomb has disappeared. Among his achievements is the foundation of Magdalen College, Oxford which has generously kept an interest in the chantry during the present century, assisting more than once in its maintenance. It was restored and rededicated by Archbishop Cosmo Gordon Lang on July 5th, 1924. The chantry itself has a number of noticeable features. It has a ceiling of surpassing beauty. Even the detailed work of the chantry such as the lock on the door is the original iron lock-plate of Waynflete's time.

Among the Cathedral archives is a document of King's College, Cambridge, which affirms that the Provost and Scholars of that College bind themselves to pray for him and when he died they will celebrate his obsequies and on the anniversary of his death they and their successors will keep a yearly obit for his soul.

A striking feature of Waynflete's effigy is the fact that he is holding his heart between his hands. This is doubtless a reference to the words in *Lamentations* c. 3. v. 41: *'Let us lift up our heart with our hands unto God in the heavens.'* It could also be a reference to the more liturgical phrase, *Sursum corda,* Lift up your hearts.

The Dean and Chapter observe the Bishop's *obit* each year on August 11th.

Superb stone canopy above the effigy of Bishop Waynflete in the bishop's chantry. The angel displays the bishop's arms which are also those of Waynflete's foundation of Magdalen College, Oxford.

Langton's Chantry

Bishop Langton, bishop from 1493 to 1500, is particularly remembered because he took care to train youths at his own charge 'in grammar and music' (which he infinitely delighted in) in a school which he set apart in the precincts of his house. He observed that 'the way to increase virtue was to praise it.'[10] In 1500, he was elected Archbishop of Canterbury but died before he could be enthroned. His large altar-tomb almost fills the chantry. The metal work upon the tomb disappeared long ago. To-day the chantry is noteworthy for its fine wood work and for the wealth of heraldry in the roof. There is ample scope for this for besides being archbishop designate of Canterbury he had been bishop of St. David's, Salisbury and Winchester. The chantry is in the south-east corner of the Cathedral.

In recent years there has been added, on long loan from Basingstoke Parish Church, a Dutch triptych of the sixteenth century depicting the nativity.

Langton's nephew was Cardinal Bainbridge, well known in Rome between 1509 and 1514, who was Provost of the Queen's College, Oxford (1495). He left a provision in his will 'for a priest of good and honest conversation to sing divine masses perpetually for the soul of the Rev. Father in God Thomas Langton bishop of Winchester and for the souls of the Father and Mother of the same Bishop! In 1512 in Rome he supplicated that all the faithful who visited the chapel of Thomas, bishop of Winchester, in Winchester Cathedral and said a prayer there might receive an indulgence.[11] In recent years the Dean and Chapter have resumed the observance of Langton's anniversary on January 27th each year.

Monuments to Bishops

Edington and Wykeham are the foremost builders of this mediaeval period. The chantries of Edington, Wykeham, Beaufort, Waynflete and Langton are the most conspicuous memorials. But there still remain other memorials to bishops and priors of great interest. The earliest is that of Godfrey de Lucy facing the entrance to the Lady Chapel. Early historians confused him with a certain King Lucius who was alleged to have brought Christianity to Winchester. In actual fact he was bishop of Winchester from 1189 to 1204 and is connected with the building of the retrochoir. His memorial is very plain, seven matrices in which candles were placed on the tomb can still be seen. They are in the form of a cross. The monk whose duty it was to recall anniversaries saw to it that these candles were lit on the anniversary of the bishop's death and that bread was given to the poor.

The earliest episcopal statue is that of Peter de Rupibus[12] in the north presbytery aisle (died 1238).

Looking at the Guardian Angels Chapel, there is on the right a figure of Bishop Aymer or de Lusignan who died in Paris in 1260. He left instructions that his heart should be brought to Winchester and buried in the Cathedral. For centuries its location was unknown until it was re-discovered in 1912, in a leaden box which in turn had once been in a golden cup. His monument is of particular interest because it bears the oldest known coat of arms in the Cathedral.

Henry Woodlock, Bishop

Bishop Woodlock

The corbel in the Quire is thought to be a portrait of Bishop Woodlock. His career is of special interest because he was both prior and Bishop of Winchester, in succession. His *Register* (1305 — 1316) also survives in which he has left us vital information about the Quire stalls.

Monuments of Priors

Only one monument to a Prior can be definitely established. It is the one commemorating William of Basing, prior from 1283 to 1295. He was buried originally in the south transept. To-day his tomb is slightly west of Beaufort's Chantry. Round the edges of the tomb runs a Latin inscription which says: Here lies William of Basing, formerly Prior of this Church, on whose soul may God have mercy: and whosoever shall pray for his soul shall obtain an indulgence of three years, one hundred and forty five days.

It is noticeable that Prior William of Basing is wearing, somewhat surprisingly, a mitre as though he were a bishop. A corbel in the south east of the Quire shows another Prior, thought to be William of Taunton, also wearing a mitre. This privilege was accorded to the priors of Winchester in 1254 by Pope Innocent IV and conferred upon them the privileges of wearing the ring, and carrying the pastoral staff, and wearing the mitre, dalmatic, gloves and sandals. They could bless chalices, altar palls, and other Church ornaments. They could give the first tonsure and confer minor orders (doorkeeper and reader) and give the full benediction in divine office and at table. [13]

The Gaveston Monument

The only monument to a layman before the Reformation which survives in the Cathedral is that to Sir Arnald de Gaveston. Originally in the north transept it was moved to the retro-choir behind the High Altar in the 19th century. Later it was moved in the 1930s to its present position. There used to be a slab on the side of the monument, with five coats of arms. This is now under the east window of the Guardian Angels' Chapel. Originally the monument seems to have been in the west aisle of the north transept. Gaveston died c. 1302. His home was originally in Gascony. His son, Piers Gaveston came to a violent end in 1312. [14]

St. Swithun's Shrine

The feature which the medieval worshipper and visitor would seek above all else was the shrine of St. Swithun. Unhappily it is the feature about which least is known. We know of its destruction in 1538 but what it was like prior to this time, when it was second only in popularity to the shrine of St. Thomas of Canterbury, we can only conjecture. Taking into account what is known of shrines at Westminster, Canterbury, Bury St Edmunds, St Albans and elsewhere it would appear that it stood from about 1200 onwards in the retro-quire and that in due course it was flanked by Beaufort's Chantry on the south side and Waynflete's on the north. Its existence is occasionally mentioned in the Obedientiary Rolls, the last reference being in the roll of the Clerk of Works in 1532-3.

SCALE OF FEET

Based on a sketch by Mr. D. H. M. Carter.

Conjectural reconstruction of St. Swithun's Shrine. [15]

The Quire Stalls, 1308

During this period the Cathedral was embellished with a great deal of woodwork of great importance and beauty.

It was not until 1927 when the late Canon Goodman[16] was editing the Register of Bishop Henry Woodlock (1305 — 1316) that a precise date could be given to the construction of the Quire Stalls. The register includes a letter from the bishop to the bishop of Norwich which translates as follows:-

Brother Henry &c. to the worshipful Father in Christ, the Lord John by the grace of God, bishop of Norwich: William of Lynwode, carpenter, a tenant of your manor of Blofield, has already begun a piece of work belonging to his craft in the quire of our cathedral church of St. Swithun, Winchester, and his continual presence is needed for its satisfactory accomplishment. Relying upon your sincere friendship, we earnestly request, that so far as you fairly may, you will excuse the absence of your tenant from doing suit to your court for a year from the feast of St. Michael next ensuing until he has finished the said work, and that you will give instructions to your steward and bailiffs not to trouble or disturb him in this behalf. In reply to this write to us your wishes, and rest assured that we will fulfil them. May the Most High have you in his keeping and prolong your days.

This letter gives us the exact date of the stalls as 1308. There are sixty-eight of them in number, thirty-one in the upper row on either side of the Quire, and three each in the lower rooms at the entrance to the Quire. Sixty six of the sixty-eight misericords originally carved still remain. The carvings are all of a secular nature and are listed in detail by G. L. Remnant in his book: *A Catalogue of Misericords in Great Britain* (Oxford, 1969). Only two cathedrals have longer series of such stalls: Salisbury with 105 and Lincoln with 90.

A brief description of just a few of the misericords give an idea of the whole range:-

Foliage. Supporters: left and right, leaf.
Large cat's head. Supporters: l. & r., leaf.
Grotesque human-headed monster, Supporters l. & r., leaf.
Hooded figure with gauntlets on hands, laughing, with right

Opposite: Winchester Cathedral Quire Stalls

eye closed in wink. Supporters: l. woman's head in wimple and gorget; r. man's head in hood with wagging tongue.

A misericord is defined as follows: a shelving projection on the under side of a hinged seat in a quire stall, so arranged, that when turned up, it gives support to one standing in the stall.

Another aspect of the Quire Stalls (possibly, though not certainly of this date) was a series of features above the stalls which are described for us by a visiting officer from Norwich (be it noted) in 1635.[17] Over the stalls of the Dean and Prebends he writes are 'remarkable, artificial and rare postures ravishing the eyes of the beholders . . . a lively woody representation, portraits, and images from Creation to the Passion. On one side there were 35 such scenes from a representation of the Trinity to the appearance of the Angel to Zacharias.

The list evokes several comments. Number 31 is missing and number 35 carries us over into the New Testament, testifying to the unity of both testaments, a universally held belief at the time. Much of the iconography suggests a link with the *Winchester Bible,* due no doubt to the representation of the main events of the Bible itself. But a more direct influence cannot be ruled out early in the 14th century when craftsmen would need the help of accessible illustrations for work of this kind unless they were to carve from life as they did elsewhere in the stalls where, for example, they carved the figure of a falconer.

On the other side 26 scenes are depicted from the New Testament.

These range from the Salutation of the Angel to Mary to Christ's Ascension, with two angels appearing in white garments, answering those who stood gazing. It is interesting to note that in the third of these carvings the author speaks of Joseph as the Father of John the Baptist (and not Zachariah) being dumb. Another description suggests that the original craftsmen left the Biblical text for a work which is described as John preaching in the Wilderness to the people, '*the ffowles and beasts*'. It reads as though some recollection of the early Franciscans had crept into the Gospel story.

Since these carvings were destroyed that particular area has been painted red at one time; green at another. In each case lead stars, painted gold, were affixed. More recently all paint has been removed, save in the north-west corner of the stalls where a small area has been left so that our successors may see what earlier painters did.

Beneath the biblical scenes there is much fine woodcarving.

Above: Misericord.

Opposite: Quire stalls detail.
A Falconer.

The Pilgrims' Hall,[18] where mediaeval pilgrims are believed to have stayed during their pilgrimage to St. Swithun. The roof beams were probably built by Thomas of Witney in 1325.

The Roof Beams

In recent years C. A. Hewett has pioneered a new study in connection with cathedrals. He has paid particular attention to the roof beams that support the external roofs of the cathedrals. In his study, he examines the position at Winchester and dates the earliest surviving roof work from this period. Writing of the roof work that surmounts the Presbytery he dates it between 1315 and 1360 and believes the architect to have been Thomas of Witney, who died in 1342.[19]

The Lillebon Panel

The late Roger Quirk subjected the Lillebon Panel, now under glass in the north Quire aisle, to a detailed study *(Winchester Cathedral Record, 1955 pp.17-23)*. He considers that it dates from between 1310 and 1320. It consists of a solid framework of oak about 8 feet long and 2½ feet high. Within that area are twelve sunken panels, ten of which are devoted to religious themes while two depict Lady Anastasia and Sir William de Lillebon who gave the original reliquary chest of which this is the lid. Some have thought that it was once part of an altar. More probably however, it is part of a Reliquary Chest for the keeping of sacred relics to be exposed on certain days; possibly the feasts of St. Thomas the Martyr (December 21st) and St John the Baptist (June 24th). The other panels of painting represent St. John the Baptist, the Crucifixion, and emblems of the Passion, St. George (the shield has St. George's Cross) and St. Peter.

St. George and St. Peter.

The Great West Window

Another achievement of the period is the great west window. It was extensively damaged during the early days of the Civil War, so that precise knowledge of the original is largely conjectural. Addressing the Royal Archaeological Institute at Winchester in 1924, J. D. Le Couteur, a well known writer on stained glass, considered that the original was glazed about 1380, apparently by a firm of the Oxford School of glass painting. His reconstruction is as follows:-

'. . . something in the nature of a great triptych with scenes in the life of Christ in the middle; and figures of apostles and prophets at the sides: the six upper main side lights contained the twelve apostles, in two rows; . . . in the six lights below were twelve prophets . . . . . .

Of the middle scenes, the Resurrection still exists in a much-shattered condition . . . fragments of the Annunciation . . . are in lights 1 and 2, and of the Entombment in light 21.

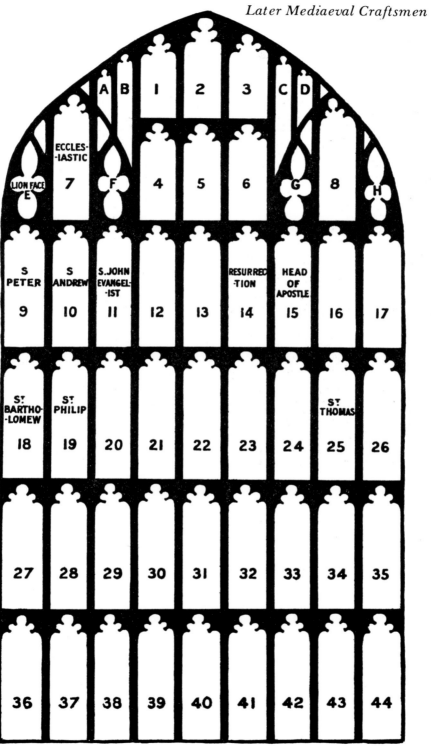

Diagram of the West Window

Edington Glass

The Great West Window is the dominant feature when considering the glass of the Cathedral. Other early glass there was in the Cathedral but little has survived. In the western window on the south side of the nave are four figures, all of musicians, which are attributed to the time of Edington. Being so high they have escaped the attention of despoilers throughout the centuries. Le Couteur describes the four figures as angels in white robes, with coloured wings. Each figure has a different instrument. A possible date is 1365.

Wall paintings

Guardian Angels' Chapel, 1241

Henry III, baptised in the Cathedral in 1207, had a great love of Winchester and sent his Master William to paint the vault of the Guardian Angels' Chapel in 1241. The roof has twelve small angels in roundels and eight larger ones. Professor Baker thinks that the decorative background work was added some forty years later and detracts from the earlier work. The original conception was of the angels peering through dome of heaven against a dark sky studded with stars. The work has avoided being covered with white wash which has been the fate of many other early wall paintings. It was restored in Prebendary Nott's time, early in the 19th century and again by Professor Tristram. It was last restored in 1956.[20] (See p.xiii).

Wall Paintings in the Lady Chapel

The last mural paintings to be added to the Cathedral were added in the Lady Chapel by Prior Silkstede between the years 1498 and 1524. The paintings line the north and south sides of the chapel and depict legendary scenes from the life of Our Lady. They are now faint and difficult to see. At one stage they were covered with whitewash. Writing about them towards the end of the 18th century, Milner says: "I do not find any person who can remember the paintings being much less visible than they are at present". Drawings of them were made in 1784 and engravings of them in 1845. In 1937 they were covered, after work by Professor Tristram, by hinged boards on which an attempt was made to paint resemblances to the original wall paintings. These protective boards were painted and presented to the Cathedral by the generosity of Lady Northbrook in memory of her husband.[21]

WINCHESTER LADY CHAPEL SOUTH WALL

EAST   WEST

Prior Silkstede	I Betrothal to Image	III The Jew of Bourgos	V The Image as Hostage	VII The Columns raised	IX The Drowned Monk	XI A Ship saved
Piscina	II The Priest of one Mass	IV The Vision of S. Angelo	VI The Miracle of Mont S. Michel	VIII The Woman unconfessed	X The wounded Image	XII The Miracle of the Candle

WINCHESTER LADY CHAPEL NORTH WALL

WEST   EAST

III The Rose with Ave Maria	The Annunciation	V The Devil as Steward	VII The Sick Clerk	IX Scene with a Knight
I S. John of Damascus				
IV The Pious Painter	Door	VI St. Basil and Julian	VIII St. George raised by the Virgin	X St. George slays Julian
II The Thief Ebbo				

Plan of Wall Paintings: Lady Chapel

Restoration of stone Altar frontal (c.1260), depicting the Coronation of the Virgin. It is now in the South Treforium of the Cathedral.

Looking back over this particular period it is clear that Wykeham and Wynford dominated it. The work begun by Edington was hampered by the shortage of craftsmen as a result of the Black death. Even so there was much woodwork of the fourteenth century that has stood the test of time, notably the Quire Stalls. The glass has suffered so much that there is little to judge. On the other hand, the tradition of mural painting begun in the 12th century continued, notably in the Guardian Angels' Chapel. Probably much work of the period was blotted out by puritanical fervour in the 16th century so that only here and there do we catch glimpses of painting in the north and south transepts, and behind the book shelves in the Library.

By the year 1500, the Cathedral must have presented a colourful and splendid sight of a great Cathedral greatly enriched. And when we take into account the vestments and silver used for the services, the spectacle must have been breathtaking.

NOTES

1 The *O.E.D.* s.v. Mediaeval.
2 *Registrum Simonis Langham.* C. & Y. 1956. pp. 318 — 323.
3 Lierne. *O.E.D.* s.v. In vaulting, a short rib which .   connects the bosses and intersections of the principal ribs of the roof.
4 *W.C.R.* 1949 pp. 4 — 7.
5 These two terms denote the two main elements in architecture, according to Vitruvius *De Architecture.*
6 R. Lowth. *The Life of William of Wykeham.* Oxford, 1777. Appendix xvii.
7 T. F. Kirby. Wykeham's Register. Winchester, 1896-9. Vol. 2. p.515.
8 *ibid.* 2.409.
9 L. B. Radford. *Henry Beaufort.* London, 1908. pp. 293-295.
10 *D.N.B.* s.v. *Langton, Thomas.*
11 D. S. Chambers. *Cardinal Bainbridge in the Court of Rome, 1509 — 1514.* Oxford, 1965. p.16.f.
12 Lecointre-Dupont. *Pierre des Roches. Tresorier de Saint-Hilaire de Poiters. Evêque de Winchester* Poitiers, 1868.
13 A. W. Goodman. *The Winchester Cathedral Chartulary. Winchester, 1927. p.53.*
14 *W.C.R.* 1937. p.9 and 2 plates. 1953 pp.8 — 11. and four illustrations.
15 J. D. Le Couteur and D. H. M. Carter. *Notes on the Shrine of Saint Swithun formerly in Winchester Cathedral.* London, 1924.
16 A. W. Goodman and T. D. Atkinson. *The Choir Stalls, Winchester Cathedral Archaeological Journal 2nd series.* Vol. xxxiv. pp.125 — 128. 1927.
17 *Camden Miscellany XVI.* London, 1936.
18 J. Harvey. *The Mediaeval Architect.* London, 1972. p. 135 and plate 37.
19 C. A. Hewett. *English Cathedral Carpentry.* London, 1974. p. 38.
20 Professor R. W. and Mrs. E. Baker, *W.C.R.,* 1959 pp.17 — 19. W. G. Constable. *The Paintings in the Chapel of the Guardian Angels.* London, 1929. See also The Central Council for the Care of Churches. London, 1959. *The Conservation of English Wall Paintings.*
21 M. R. James and E. W. Tristram. *The Wall Paintings in Eton College Chapel and in the Lady Chapel of Winchester Cathedral.* London, 1929.

FURTHER READING

T. D. Atkinson. *Mediaeval Figure Sculpture in Winchester Cathedral.* Oxford, 1936
C. J. P. Cave *The Roof Bosses in the nave Aisles of Winchester Cathedral H.F.C.* 1934.
Winchester Cathedral Quire Bosses. Oxford, 1927. *The Roof Bosses of Winchester Cathedral* (reprint) Winchester 1976.
J. D. Le Couteur. *Ancient Glass in Winchester.* Winchester, 1920. *English Mediaeval Painted Glass.* London, 1926.
P. Draper. *The retrochoir of Winchester Cathedral.* Architectural History, Vol. 21, 1978.
Theophilus *On Divers Arts.* Chicago, 1963 pp.45   74.

An Indulgence, 1254

Chapter IV

Monastic Life

To concentrate wholly on the architecture of the Cathedral and its many artistic treasures is to give a partial view of the monastery of St. Swithun. It was a Benedictine Monastery which never exceeded 64 members.[1] And whilst they were, between them, familiar with the aspects already described, they would have asserted that their primary duty lay elsewhere. It was to discharge their task of the daily worship of God. Just what that routine was is not described for us in so many words in the case of Winchester. It does so happen, however, that we have, emanating from another Benedictine house, "the most methodical account known to exist of the life lived by English monks in the period immediately following the Norman Conquest."[2]

Lanfranc, Archbishop of Canterbury (1070 — 1089) in the time of William the Conqueror, played a leading part in the reforming of the old English monasteries and bringing them into line with their Norman counterparts. Along with Worcester Sherborne and Canterbury, Winchester formed a special group and at first it was decided that the monastic character of these foundations should be dissolved. In the end, this decision was reversed and monks were brought over from the continent (both Walkelin and Simeon came from France). To guide these new foundations, Lanfranc drew up his Monastic *Constitutions* They are a conflate production so that they tell of the Benedictine Rule as followed in a general way. Nevertheless, it is sufficiently near the practice of any particular Benedictine House at this time as to be worthy of note. Dom David, in the light of Lanfranc's work, has drawn up what he describes as an *Horarium,* a time-table, which was followed by the monks in their daily lives. This indicates in clear form the way of life followed in Cathedrals for nearly five hundred years:

WINTER	SUMMER

15 Sep. or 1 Oct. to Holy Week
Rise in night habit and shoes
Prayers: *Trina oratio* 1. [3]
      Last 32 psalms
      Prayers and collects

Low Sunday to 14 Sep. or 1 Oct.
Rise in night habit and shoes
Prayers: *Trina oratio 1.*
      15 gradual psalms (120-134)
      Prayers and collects

MATINS *Psalmi familiares* [4]
      Matins for the dead
          (till Feb. 2.)
      Lauds for the dead
      Prayers

MATINS *Psalmi familiares*

LAUDS (said at daybreak)
Psalmi familiares
Suffrages

LAUDS (said at daybreak)
Psalmi familiares
      Suffrages
      Lauds of All Saints
      Lauds of the dead

(October only — bed)
Prayer

      Bed
      Prayer
Trina oratio 11

PRIME
      Psalmi familiares
      Seven Pentitential
      Psalms (6, 32, 38, 51
      102, 130 & 143)

PRIME
Psalmi familiares
Seven Pentential Psalms

      Litany of the saints
      Reading
      Put on day shoes and
      Wash
      Trina oratio 11

      Litany of the saints
      Reading
      Put on day shoes and
      Wash

TERCE
      Psalmi familiares

MORNING MASS

MORNING MASS

      CHAPTER
      Talk in cloister
      Children's breakfast
      Prayer

      CHAPTER
      Talk in cloister

      Prayer

SEXT
> *Psalmi familiaries*
> Talk in cloister
> Processions on
> Wednesdays and Fridays
> Prayer

> HIGH MASS
> Prayer
> Servers' breakfast

NONE
> *Psalmi familiares*

DINNER
> Reading

> Prayer

VESPERS
> *Psalmi familiares*
> Suffrages
> Vespers of All Saints
> Vespers of the dead
> Matins of the dead
>   (Feb. 3 to Easter)
> Change to night shoes
> Sit in Cloister, if light
> Sit in Chapter House, if dark
> Drink in Refectory
> Collation in Chapter House
> *Caritas*[5] in Refectory

COMPLINE
> *Trina oratio III*

TERCE
> Litany of the saints

> HIGH MASS
> Reading
> Children's breakfast
> Servers' breakfast
> Prayer

SEXT
> *Psalmi familiares*

DINNER
> Siesta
> Dress and wash
> Reading
> Prayer

NONE
> Psalmi familiares
> Drink
> Talk in cloister
> Prayer

VESPERS
> *Psalmi familiares*
> Suffrages
> Vespers of All Saints
> Vespers of the dead
> Matins of the dead

> Change to night shoes

> Collation in Chapter House
> *Caritas* in Rectory

COMPLINE
> *Trina oratio III*

Retire to dormitory

This strenuous routine, given local variations, shows how faithfully the scriptural injunction was followed: *Seven times a day do I praise Thee* (Psalm 119. v.164). The strong emphasis upon the recitation of the Psalter, so characteristic of the Benedictines, is clear. No mention is made in the time table for the private masses which were often enjoined upon a monastery; these had to be fitted in as well as they could. The work undertaken by the Benedictines was often an alternative to reading. Finally, it will be noted that no clock time is indicated. Day break was the signal for Lauds. Before that the offices were said during the night hours. It is clear too that Vespers were often said during hours of darkness and Compline too.

As time passed the alternation between reading and work was blurred and some monks became scholars who were excused manual toil. The increasing emphasis upon learning which comes up in the regular meetings of the Black Monks from 1215 led to the selection of the more brilliant men who went to the incipient universities that the monks did so much to foster in the earliest days until at last the institution which they fostered, the University, did much to destroy the parents who created it.

General and Provincial Chapters of the Benedictine Monks

The monks soon began to feel the need to look beyond the confines of their own monastery and from 1215 to 1540 monks from the Benedictine Houses throughout the country met together in some central place, very often Northampton and only latterly in London, to share with one another their worship, their problems and their ideas.[6] From time to time the monks were conscious of a decline from the original ideals and calls were made to observe more strictly the Rule of their founder. The word *'reformacio'* or *'reformatio'* occurs a considerable time before the Reformation. Slowly, at first in ones and twos, the more intellectual of the monks were sent to Oxford to extend their intellectual training. In this way a college system of supervision arose. The foundations of New College in 1379 and of Magdalen College in 1486 have both left their marks upon the Cathedral.

On this wider stage the priors and monks of Winchester played their part. Occasionally a prior presided at the conference; occasionally a Prior or a sub-prior looked after students generally in Oxford before the days of the setting up of a proper college system with its pastoral care over such men. Not only did the priors and representative monks visit the conferences of the Black Monks. At their conferences they appointed some of their number to 'visit' and to report upon particular monasteries. Winchester was, like all the rest, visited in due order. For example on June 10th, 1462 the Abbot of Hyde formally 'visited' the cathedral priory of Winchester. By such means the discipline and cohesion of the Benedictine order was maintained throughout the country

Given the daily pattern of services as indicated by Dom David Knowles further questions arise. Most services would appear austere and sombre, with the monks dressed in black. Lighting was restricted and the temperature was often very cold indeed. In 1243, Pope Innocent IV granted a licence to the Prior and monks to wear caps at divine office as a protection against the cold of winter. Caps were to be suited to their order provided due reverence was observed at the reading of the Gospel and at the elevation of the Body of our Lord Jesus Christ.[7] Another question arises about the form of music used. Here the evidence is singularly minimal. The office of Precentor existed and there are mediaeval references to an organist.[8] If we look at Lanfranc's *Constitutions* again he sets out in detail the duties of the *Cantor*[9]. It was his duty to rehearse those singing any part of service and if the officiant suddenly failed he must be ready to take up that particular part at a moment's notice. He had to stand in the 'midst of the others in the choir.'

On feast days and on other occasions the services were more splendid. A feast was celebrated in copes and 'the sacrist is to choose the required number from among the best copes in use in choir that day.' Hints as to ceremonial occur: bowing when the *Sanctus* (Holy Holy Holy) is sung; incense too was used. Wykeham left the Cathedral thirty copes including his new rich vestment of blue cloth.

Royal Visits

From time to time the feasts of the Church were given added splendour by the presence of the Sovereign. In 1101, Henry I was present in the Cathedral *Coronatus* i.e. wearing his crown, at Easter. This custom continued intermittently for many years. In 1207, Henry of Winchester, later, Henry III, was baptised in the Cathedral.

A highly dramatic royal visit was that of King John in 1213. Austin Poole says of it: it was "a scene where emotion, solemnity, and rejoicing were happily blended, the King was absolved from the ban of the Church; not before, however, he had renewed the coronation oath and promised to maintain the ancient laws of the Kingdom."[10] This act of reconciliation took place in the old Chapter house, remains of which are visible to the south of the South Transept.

Amongst the documents in the *Winchester Chartulary* are two dating from 1307 which would appear to be copies of the instructions received by Bishop Woodlock who deputised for the Archbishop of Canterbury at the Coronation of Edward II. They are entitled: *Manner and form of*

Coronation of a new king or queen. Details of the officers taking part in the ceremony are given and the various prayers to be used for the blessing of the crowns and the hallowing of the sovereign. It may be noted that the oath to be taken by the King is in French.[11]

Not quite a century later, on February 7th., 1403, Henry IV married Joan of Navarre in the Cathedral.[12] The occasion is commemorated in the upper part of the window facing the south door of the Cathedral. A trivial item of information that has survived is the cost of the carpet from the Church door to the high altar: £23.5.8.

From time to time the sovereign took a more than ceremonial interest in the Cathedral. Henry VI rebuked the Benedictines for their slackness and ordered his prelates to undertake reforms. In the case of Winchester he was present for the enthronment of Bishop Waynflete and visited the shrine of St. Swithun in 1447.

Royal Baptism

One of the most splendid royal occasions in the Cathedral was the baptism of Prince Arthur, first son of Henry VII. Had he lived and ascended to the throne, there might have been no Henry VIII. Instead there would have been a King Arthur. There is no doubt that the legendary Arthur inspired the choice of name, and the choice of birthplace. To some, Camelot was Winchester.[13] He was born in Winchester Castle on September 22nd, 1486 and baptised in the Cathedral on the following Sunday. There is a full account of the occasion.[14] The Cathedral immediately celebrated the birth by singing a *Te Deum* and by the ringing of its bells. For the ceremony itself, the body of the Church was hanged with cloth of arras and a special font erected as follows: a stage of seven steps square or round. The font itself was of silver gilt. Over the font a rich canopy. After the birth, the Queen took her residence in the Prior's Great Hall. The Baptism was taken by the Bishop of Worcester (there was a vacancy in the see of Winchester at that date), assisted by the Bishop of Exeter, Bishop Courtenay, who was shortly to become bishop of Winchester. After the child was baptised he was carried to the High Altar and laid upon it by his Godmother. The Chapel Royal sang appropriate music. The child's mother made a gift to the Cathedral in order that the Lady Chapel might be extended to its present size. At a later date the Prior had to write to Prince Arthur, presumably because of the King's absence, on affairs connected with the monastery. The Prince was only sixteen years old when he died.

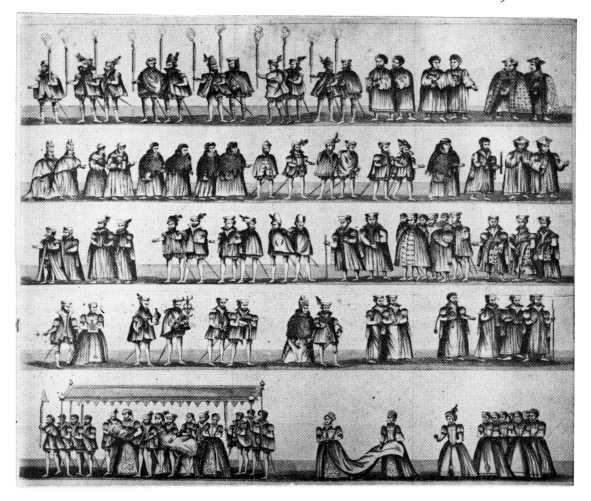

An engraving depicting the royal procession at the baptism of Prince Arthur.

Pope and Patriarch

The Monastery had its links with Pope and Patriarch. Henry of Blois was Papal Legate and, therefore, enjoyed high ecclesiastical influence. In 1267, the monastery was visited by the Papal Legate.[15] Two cardinals are among the mediaeval bishops of Winchester, though Beaufort had more connection with the Cathedral than ever Wolsey had. In 1336, a mandate was transmitted to the Cathedral from John XXII urging that Mass be said in all cathedrals on every Tuesday in view of the forthcoming crusade. A special prayer was to be said and ten days' indulgence promised to every one who used it. It ran (translated from the Latin):

> O God, who by thy admirable providence ordereth all things, we humbly beseech thee, to rescue from the hands of the enemies of the Cross, the land which thine only begotten Son did sanctify with his own blood, and be pleased to preserve it in the faith of Christ.

Money chests were put in all churches (with three keys) to help the crusade.[16]

It should be added that 1270 is usually held to be the date of the eighth and last crusade, undertaken by St. Louis. However, ecclesiastical authorities continued to use the term after this date to describe expeditions which received their blessing in an attempt to drive out heretics and heathens. The Popes of Avignon were obsessed with the idea of a crusade. In this instance, the 'crusade' was the start of the Hundred Years' War between England and France.

More genuine links with the Crusades were the visit of the Patriarch of Jerusalem to Winchester in 1185 and the departure of Richard I from Winchester for the Holy Land after his second coronation in the Cathedral on 17th April, 1194. A Winchester monk, Richard of Devizes, narrated the events of those subsequent years in great detail.[17]

Bishops and Priors

The connection between the bishops of Winchester and the priors of Winchester varied a good deal during the Middle Ages. The fundamental problem was: who founded the monastery? For whoever founded it had clearly the right to appoint the prior. The issue came to a head in the 13th century. Bishop John of Exeter wrote from Viterbo to say that he had been at fault (January 13, 1267/8) in depriving the prior of his office. He admitted that by grant of the Apostolic See and by custom, the monks of Winchester had the right of electing their own prior. The debate is taken a stage further in the Register of Bishop John of Pontissara where it is affirmed that kings founded the church of Winchester and this is made clear in the history of the Church. The Register gives instances of duty rendered to the king.

The conflict flared up again in the time of Bishop Nicholas. He visited the Cathedral but the prior and monks claimed that he had exceeded his rights and, therefore, proposed to protest to the Court of Rome and to the Archbishop of Canterbury. Meanwhile, they added, the bishop must in no way imperil either the temporalities or the spiritualities of the Monastery. The conflict was submitted to arbitration and it was decided, in 1278, that the monastery should have full freedom in the election of its prior. The bishop accepted the ruling, saving the Pope's prerogative. From then onwards the monastery was left practically free to manage its own affairs. The bishop ends the case with a plea for what amounts to mutual tolerance and good will: I have honoured you, he writes, May God honour you. I have written with my own hand what I did not wish to write by means of any one else.

The compromise solution of goodwill was quickly put to the test and in the Register of the same bishop there are instructions that the rules of the monastery be read over at regular intervals so that no delinquent could plead ignorance. This was to re-affirm the Rule of St Benedict. The bishop added a number of requirements:

> That the offices be said regularly.
> That confession be made annually at the least.
> That silence be observed in the customary places and at the customary times.
> That brethren do not leave the Monastery without permission.
> That the brethren do not mix with women outside the monastery.
> That the gates be shut at the appropriate times.
> That juniors respect seniors.
> That they do not sell their victuals.
> That they wear appropriate clothing.
> That they take care of the sick.
> That they be buried within the grounds of the monastery.
> Parents and relatives were to be allowed to visit them.[18]

A few years later when one of Woodlock's successors died and the see was vacant, Archbishop Reynolds of Canterbury visited the Cathedral in 1323 and found all the records satisfactory. Other charges levelled against the monastery were dismissed, provided they observed the discipline of their rule.[19]

The controversy in no way affected the position of the bishop either to be enthroned in his Cathedral; to ordain; or to 'visit' the monastery. There is clear evidence of these acts. A full account of Wykeham's enthronement has been preserved. In this particular instance, although Wykeham had succeeded Edington in 1366, the Pope held up the enthronization for two years. At last on July 9th, 1368 Wykeham adjourned to the Church of St.

Mary Kalendar, made an offering to the Church, changed his shoes and removed his cope, hood, cap and gloves. He was then robed in full pontificals and led to the Cathedral and to the Bishop's throne where he was enthroned by the Archdeacon of Canterbury. 'Embracing him reverently' he said: "By the authority of Christ's Church of Canterbury I induct and enthrone thee, Lord William, duly elected, confirmed, and consecrated bishop of this diocese, into possession of the same, and of its rights, members and appurtenances. The Lord keep thy coming in and thy going out from this time forth, now and evermore". Wykeham's own action was rarely followed and for centuries it was more common for the bishop to be enthroned by proxy rather than in person.

Ordinations

Wykeham likewise conducted a number of ordinations in his Cathedral. Occasions in point are March 12th, 1372/3 and 17th April, 1389. Again Wykeham went further than most of his predecessors and successors in the regularity with which he conferred orders within the Cathedral. One bishop who vied with him was Langton who in the years 1495 to 1500 held fourteen ordinations. On occasion the ordinations were held in the Lady Chapel, at that time resplendent in its new extension and its recent wall paintings. The ordinations included acolytes, sub-deacons, deacons and priests.

Visitations

One power which the Bishop had was his right to 'visit' the Cathedral. The Archbishop too had the right, especially when there was a vacancy in the see of Winchester.

The Scriptorium

The daily life, therefore, was one of regular worship, of work and study. In addition, there were officials who carried on the business of the monastery itself and of the lands which in effect made possible the life of the monastery. And finally there was a scholarly and artistic minority who carried on the scholastic work of the monastery.

The work of the Scriptorium had, as we have seen, already achieved distinction in the 12th century in the time of Henry of Blois. But manuscripts continued to be written here until the invention of printing. Many of these were Biblical texts or psalters, others were liturgical texts, texts of the Fathers and lives of the Saints. Annals were written here and an occasional medical book. To-day these manuscripts are scattered though at first when completed they were taken from the Scriptorium to the Library which has existed ever since 1150. To-day the number of manuscripts still in the Cathedral is greatly reduced. One inherited by the Cathedral is Bede's

The pre-Reformation pulpit installed in the time of Prior Silkstede.

History (c.1000 A.D.). Another, *Promptorium Pervulorum,* has twice been published and is the first Latin English Dictionary in the language.[20] This is set out with the Latin word on the left and with the new-fangled English word on the right. It is pleasant to be able to record that occasionally a manuscript which was written here finds its way back. Within the last generation a 12th century volume of *Hegesippus* has been returned by the great bibliophile Dyson Perrins, while Winchester College has recently returned a manuscript of the lives of saints which evidence, recently come to light, indicates was a companion volume to another volume of the lives of saints within the Library.

Following the Benedictine Rule the monks had, at the beginning of Lent, to take out a book to be read, thus maintaining learning through 'the dark ages.

Preaching

Lanfranc's *Constitutions* have no reference to preaching and it may well be that the stimulus which came from such orders as the Franciscans and the Dominicans prompted the Benedictines within their monasteries to do likewise. Then, besides sermons in the monasteries, there were sermons within the diocese which concerned the Cathedral. During Wykeham's time there were sermons for the maintenance of lights in the Cathedral.[21] Moreover, Thomas Wymbledone, Chaplain to Sir John Sandes, was required not to preach anything 'which might subvert our church of Winchester.'[22]. The most obvious evidence of preaching is the pre-Reformation pulpit installed in the time of Prior Silkstede which is still in regular use for preaching in the Quire. The Prior's name is clearly visible and the craftsman has allowed himself the privilege of carving skeins of silk to adorn the pulpit in order to add detail of interest and relevance.

Besides the pulpit there is the carving of a bishop in the pulpit on one of the bench ends in the Lady Chapel. Originally the bishop is seen holding a cross in his hands.[23]

The final material objects which testify to the practice of preaching within the mediaeval cathedral are to be found in two *incunabula*[24] within the library: *Summa Praedicantium* by John de Bromyarde. Both volumes have an early inscription, unfortunately torn, which identifies the book with some library. Both start *Liber S . . .* The Book belongs to . . . The S. could stand for Sancti Swithuni, but we cannot be certain. We may assume that the books, printed in 1485, came to the monastery at an early date. They were certainly in the possession of the Cathedral before the

PREACHING WITH A CROSS
(Lady Chapel, Winchester Cathedral)

Commonwealth as it evidenced by the numbers on the fore-edge of each volume. Such a *summa* was a compendium for preachers and included the treatment in an encyclopaedic form of an alphabetical list of subjects of interest and concern to preachers and, it was thought, to their hearers. If then Bromyarde was in the Cathedral Library at an early date it implies that some at least of the monks were concerned to have information readily available which they could use in their preaching. A few of the subjects examined will indicate the nature of the work. These are a few headings which are treated: *beatitudo* (blessedness); *damnatio* (condemnation or judgement); *fides* (faith); *justicia* (justice); and so on through the alphabet to *resurrectio* (resurrection).

This aid to preaching was compiled by John de Bromyarde in the 14th century in the time of William of Wykeham. The compiler was a member of the Dominican Order whose special duty it was to preach. He found John Wycliffe among his opponents. When we turn to the Cathedral itself we find that sermons were preached but so far, within the present period, no text of any sermon has come down to us. Early in the 14th century the Bishop gave permission to the Carmelites to preach in the Cathedral after the Domicans and the Franciscans had had their turn "provided that none of the monks wishes to preach in person on that day".[25] All of which suggests that the sermon did play a part within the regular life of the monastery.

The ordinary worshipper

The person in whom we are most interested to-day — the ordinary person — is the one most difficult to discover in the days of widespread illiteracy. The case of young William, later to be the distinguished Wykeham who used to assist regularly at the Mass taken by Richard Pekis must be taken as typical of many who have not left even a foot note in the history either of the Church or their country. Others came to the shrine of St. Swithun seeking a blessing or healing from sickness of mind or body. Others came to seek forgiveness of their sins, as an indulgence found behind the woodwork in the Langton Chantry so clearly indicates. This indulgence, dated 1254, gives the worshipper who visits the altar of Blessed Birinus ten days' indulgence. The indulgence was given by the Bishop of Landaff but was only to be sought with the permission of the Bishop of Winchester. The daily offices, though no doubt heard by visitors to the monastery, were intended for the monks themselves. More affluent lay people could endow a chantry or make provision for private masses to be said for the well being of their souls.

Mediaeval man was aware of the reality of sin and of the need for absolution and forgiveness. From time to time he was summoned to the Consistory Court within the Cathedral (still at the north-west corner of the building) where legal pronouncement was made upon charges laid against him and appropriate penalties of fines and/or penances were exacted.

Monastic Finances

All that has been described of men devoting their life to religion and the glimpses of the life of the monastery either in its more customary daily routine or in its occasional splendour when visited by kings or prelates cost large sums of money. This money came from monastic estates and made Winchester about the sixth wealthiest monastery in the country. In those days wealth consisted of lands and estates. To these we now turn.

NOTES

1 The highest number of monks ever recorded was in 1325. *Wykeham's Register* Vol. 2.p.389.n.1.
2 Dom D. Knowles. *The Monastic Constitutions of Lanfranc.* London, 1951. p.VII.
3 A threefold devotion recited before matins, prime or terce and after compline, consisting of 19 psalms in all with prayers for particular seasons.
4 Psalms for relations and benefactors.
5 A drink of wine given to the monks.
6 W. A. Pantin. *Documents Illustrating the Activities of the General and Provincial Chapter of the English Black Monks, 1215 — 1540.* Camden Society 1931, 1933 & 1937.
7 A. W. Goodman. *The Winchester Chartulary,* 55.
8 Ledger Book 1.
9 Dom D. Knowles. *op.cit.* pp. 80 — 82.
10 A. L. Poole. *Domesday Book to Magna Carta, 1087 — 1216.* Oxford, 1951. p.461.
11 *Winchester Chartulary,* 287 & 410.
12 A. W. Goodman. *The Marriage of Henry IV and Joan of Navarre.* Winchester, 1934.
13 E. Vinaver. *The Works of Sir Thomas Malory.* 3 Vols. Oxford, 1947. s.v. Oakeshott p. 1652. f. and Winchester s.v. p. 1693. See further *The Times Literary Supplement* February 18th., 1977.
14 C. Bailey. *Transcripts from the Municipal Archives of Winchester.* Winchester, 1856. pp.135 — 140.
15 *Annales de Wintonia* p. 105.
16 *Winchester Chartulary,* 108.
17 J. T. Appleby. *Chronicon Richardi Divisensis* (Devizes) London, 1963. (Latin and English).
18 A. W. Goodman. *Registrum Henrici Woodlock, 1305 — 1316.* C & Y 1940-1. p.747.
19 *Winchester Chartulary,* 35.
20 A. Way. *Promptorium Parvulorum.* Camden Society, 1843. A. L. Mayhew, *Promptorium Parvulorum.* E.E.T.S. Extra Series cii. London, 1908.
21 T. F. Kirby. *Wykeham's Register.* H.R.S. 1896 — 1899. Vol. 1 p. 12.
22 G. R. Owst. *Preaching in Mediaeval England.* C.U.P., 1926. p.360.
23 ibid. p.350. (The cross was missing in 1979).
24 Books printed before 1500.
25 F. J. Baigent. Registers of John de Sandale and Rigaud de Asserio. H.R.S., 1897. p.32.f. p.411 & p.422.f.

FURTHER READING

G. E. Aylmer and R. Cant. *A History of Yorkminster* C.P. 1977. c.11.

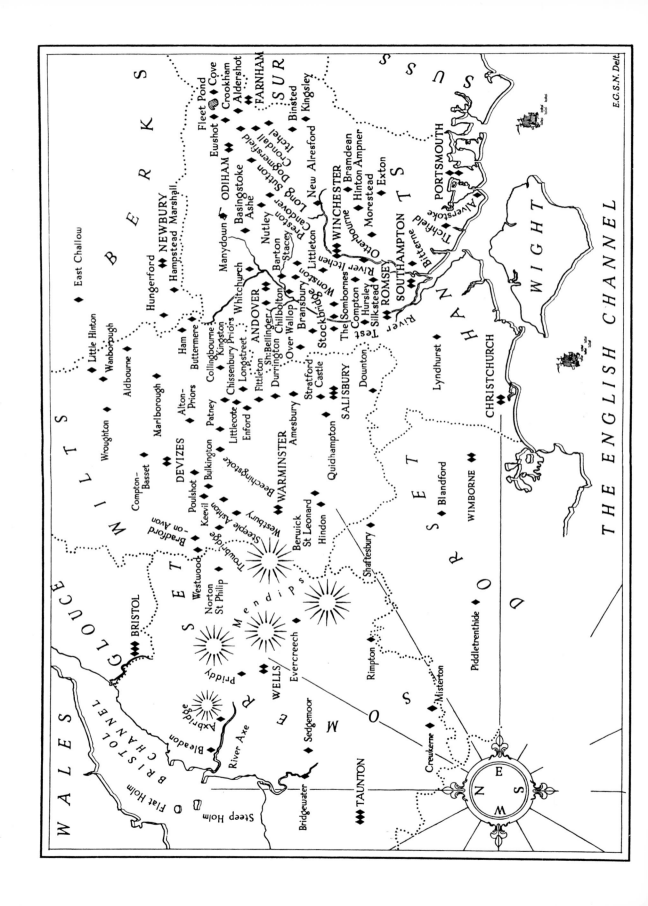

E.G.S.N. Delt.

Chapter V

Monastic Estates

Only comparatively recently has a realistic approach been made to study the maintenance of cathedrals. Too often, and for too long, writers on cathedrals have written as though dissertations about changing styles of architecture or descriptions of artistic treasures fully explain the life of a cathedral. Cathedrals are people with a primary work to do of worship (*opus Dei* . . . the work of God). The accompanying work in building, illumination, glass, music and a number of other activities are really incidental to this central purpose. All these varied forms of work need people and these people can only, in the last resort, be sustained by money or goods.

The early builders of cathedrals were under no illusions. In fact, they would not dedicate a church unless adequate financial provision had been made for its support. The notion of collections and appeals did not arise. True, a monastery sometimes became entangled in its finances and appeals were made to the faithful. But, in the main, it was intended that the buildings and its servants should be supported by the produce of estates. In the case of Winchester, benefactors began to endow the monastery as early as the seventh century. As the centuries passed the administration of these estates became a vast concern and even the surviving records (inevitably many have been lost or worn out or destroyed) present a formidable undertaking to any one who proposes to master their contents. To transliterate, translate and interpret the manorial rolls of just one manor over any length of time is a major work of scholarship. In the case of Winchester where the Cathedral still has its records dating as far back as the year 957, only an outline can be given of their contents.[1] These records may

Opposite: Manors of the Monastery and Cathedral of St. Swithun Winchester

be divided into six main groups:-

1.   Manorial Charters
2.   Compotus Rolls
3.   Court Rolls
4.   Custumales
5.   Obedientiary Rolls
6.   Ledger Books

1. Manorial Charters

In the first instance, a monastery had to be donated land by a king or a great landowner. The gift was marked by drawing up a charter in which, for example, King Edgar gave to the monks of St. Swithun a piece of land in Bleadon, Somerset. They were then to enjoy the fruits of it in perpetuity. In due of course, such a charter could be confirmed or perhaps modified. One such charter will suffice to provide an idea of them all. It dates originally from 975 and was re-issued in 1318. The original runs as follows:

> I, Edgar, King of the English and other surrounding peoples, have given a gift unto God, to St. Peter and the monks of the ancient monastery of the city of Winchester, a certain portion of land, namely . . . of fifteen hides, fifteen carucates . . . with eighteen servants and sixteen villeins . . . in Bleadon for a perpetual possession.

Among the original signatories to the charter were Aethelwold and Dunstan. This particular charter was copied in the reign of Edward II in 1318 and has an introductory and concluding paragraph.

Detailed studies of such charters are highly complex and scholars can find much about which to disagree. Later versions are often viewed with great scepticism. In the present instance, whatever may be the truth about a particular detail, there is no doubt that the manor of Bleadon was given to the monastery and there is equally no doubt that the rents from the manor continued to be given to the monastery and later to the Cathedral until the 19th century when it was taken over by the Ecclesiastical Commission. A glance at the map prefixed to this chapter will suggest just how many charters were necessary to account for so much land given to the monastery between the Bristol Channel and Surrey border.

Opposite: The Winchester Cathedral Charter. Confirmation by Edward II in 1318 of a Charter dated 975 by which King Edgar gave land at Bleadon, Somerset to the Old Minster, Winchester.

2. Compotus Rolls

Once the land had been given, it had to be worked. An account of that work, with the income and expenditure involved, was kept by means of an annual compotus or reckoning roll. About the year 1700 rolls gave way to books and our successors will no doubt return to computors if not to compotus rolls. A very old word has been borrowed for a recent invention. A photograph of one of the oldest compotus rolls provides an idea of what they were like.

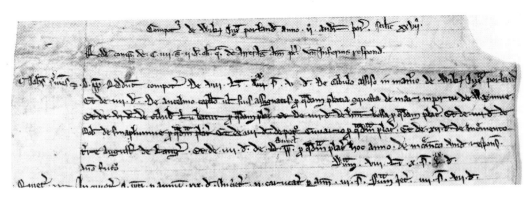

Some readers may be able to make out something of the heading of the roll which comes from Wyke, Portland (in Dorset), dated 1243 with an abbreviation for (Prior) Andrew, who was prior of the monastery from 1241 to 1247. The full translation runs as follows:-

> The account of Wyke near Portland, in the second year of Prior Andrew, viz. the 27th. (year of King Henry III).
>
> The arrears of the preceding year, amounting to 104s 2¾d., are accounted for below
>
> John the Sargeant, and D., the reeve, render account of:-
>
> £8.7.5 from the fixed rents of Wyke, near Portland.
>
> 4d from Anselmus Capellanus or his assigns for a certain piece of land reclaimed from the sea at the port of Weymouth.
>
> 6d. from Gilbert le Batur for a certain piece of land.
>
> 4d each from Henry Bossa, Robert de Knaphuvine(?), and Peter Cooper, for the like.
>
> 12d. from increased rent of the land of Aule de lang.
>
> 4d. from D. Bamel, the reeve, for increase in the rent of a certain piece of land this year, and for which he will be responsible next year.
>
> Total: £8.10.9.

This is just less than three inches of one roll. When it is recalled that there are about 3,000 rolls and some of them thirteen feet long, it will be quickly realised that to master the records of one monastery alone is more than the work of one lifetime.[2]

3. Court Rolls

The Monastery was concerned, and so was the Cathedral for a time, not only with the finances of the manor but also with the behaviour of the people living on the manor. Disputes would arise about the various properties and crimes or misdemeanours were committed. This extract from the records of the Manor of Godbegot (1356) within the city of Winchester is an example:

Court held at la Goudbegete on the Saturday next after the feast of the Holy Nativity of S. John Baptist in the thirtieth year of King Edward the third from the Conquest of England.

Essoin[3] Robert the servant of William Spore against William le Barbour put in an excuse by William Spore in a plea of trespass.

William le Barbour appeared as a plaintiff against Robert the servant of William Spore in a plea of trespass. The aforesaid Robert put in an excuse above and so has a day against the next court, etc.

4. The Winchester Custumale

After conducting the business, both legal and financial, of the manors over a period of years, it was natural that a codification of customs, procedure and business should arise. This was codified for each manor. The first such codification or *Custumale* began in 1280 beginning with the manor of Barton which comprised many farms in and around Winchester itself. On the completion of Barton, twenty-one other manors follow. As time progressed the Custumale was slightly varied. This early one, however, remained the basic document through many centuries.[4]

From such documents it is possible to piece together the life on a manor over a period of years. Mrs. Florence Goodman, who made a special study of many of the early records of the monastery, has written an account of the Home Farm of St. Swithun's, 1248 — 1344.[5] This home farm was the Manor of Barton and was comprised of Chilcomb, Morestead, Wyke, Compton and Winnall. Mrs. Goodman goes into great detail over crops and livestock. Farm buildings and farm equipment had to be maintained as well as the dairy with its pots and pans. As in Godbegot, there were cases to be tried: assault, trespass, breaking of assize and the shedding of blood. Income was derived not only from the animals and the crops but also from timber and dovecotes (the name Culver occurs in Winchester and indicates an ancient dovecote). One of the duties of the Prior and Convent was to give hospitality. Distinguished visitors, even royalty, were entertained by the Prior. Among the most famous was the Black Prince in 1329. The shoeing of his horse was a task for the smith of Barton.

5. Obedientiary Rolls

When finally the income had been collected from the manors it came to the Monastery and was administered by various obedientiaries or officers of the monastery who owed obedience to it and undertook the supervision of different aspects of its life: the sacristan for its services; the anniversarian for the remembering of anniversaries of founders and benefactors, saints and festivals; the almoner dispensed charity; the hordarian (hoarder) looked after the stores necessary to feed the monks; the clerk of works looked after the actual buildings and repairs. An examination of their rolls reveals details of the life of the monastery. We know, for example, how they fed on a particular Sunday in 1492. The total bill that day £1.12.8 and was made up as follows:-[6]

Dominica in Festo Eiusdem

Moile	7	Sub-Prior's entres	5
Burson	4	3rd prior's do.)	
162 eggs	1.3	Hordarian's do.)	10
Nombles	2	Wine for chaplain	6
Sew for supper	6	Courtesy to brethren	
Beef	3.0	in refectory	10.0
Mutton	1.6	Paid to convent	
Valves' feet	3	depositarians	13.4

The Seal of the Chapter of Winchester, 1294.

A roll of the clerk of Works dated 1409 has the following details:-

3000 laths for roofs	16.9	5000 slates	25.0
1000 lath nails	11.8	Tomber bought from	
3000 floor nails	12.0	Bishop	56.8
4000 lead nails		Red Glass	2.6

His total expenditure for the year came to £64.10.5.[7]

These examples, taken literally from hundreds, illustrate how the picture of monastic life can be built up. It continued substantially in this form until the suppression of the monastery in 1538.

The most detailed study of these records over a particular period is that of Dr. Joan Greatrex in her thesis: *The Administration of Winchester Cathedral Priory in the Time of Cardinal Beaufort.* (1405 — 1447), accepted by the University of Ottawa in 1973. Her work may be said to consist of two main examinations — the monastery as landlords and farmers of large estates and then the internal administration of the priory itself. A number of appendices illustrate details of crops, sales of grain and of stock. There is much here for the economic historian interested in this period over a large part of Wessex. There is, in addition, a detailed account of the daily living of the monks, their expenses and their diet. She tells too how monastic officials visited the manors.

Material for further study is already prepared in the invaluable typescript of the late Mr. J. S. Drew who transliterated many of the monasterial rolls of Chilbolton (1945) Michelmersh (1943) and Silkstead (1947). All these transliterations have translations, notes and indexes. There is room here for research. Mr. Drew also left a number of papers on the manors of Compton and Thurmond, though in a less complete state, nevertheless of very great value.

6. Ledger Books

Dr. Greatrex's work made use of the first of the many Ledger Books or Books of the Common Seal as they are sometimes described. These are large folio volumes dating from 1345 and continuing until the second half of the 19th century in unbroken succession and which include copies of documents referring to the properties of the monastery and the Cathedral over a period of more than six hundred years.

The Estates themselves

Going beyond the purpose of the present volume, but arising out of the monastic administration of lands, is the question: what was life like on these estates in the Middle Ages? Untypical is the Manor of Godbegot within the city of Winchester and which is recorded in Goodman's transcription and translation of some of its rolls. Most manors were rural and for a beginner a suitable start can be made in the scholarly reconstruction of a hypothetical manor of Belcome which is undertaken by H. S. Bennett in his *Life on the English Manor 1150 — 1400* (C.U.P., 1937).

Finances of Prior and Monks

It was from a score or more of 'Belcombes' that the monastery drew its revenues. On two occasions it is possible easily to see the whole financial picture. The first occasion is the return made to Pope Nicholas IV in 1281.[8] This does not state the precise sums paid to each office holder but gives the total sum available from the manors for this purpose — £701.0.1. *The Valor Ecclesiaticus* of 1356, which gives financial details of each cathedral (and monastery) on the eve of the suppression of the monasteries, assesses the value of Winchester at £1507.17.2¼.[9] The *Valor* assigns most of the money to the Prior, Henry Broke, £1055.4.3. whilst the remainder is shared between the Sub-Prior, the Hordarian, Precentor, Chamberlain, Clerk of Works, Almoner, Sacrist, Anniversarian, Hospitaller, Gardener, Infirmarian,

Spicerer, Custodian of the Lady Chapel. The balance sheets of these officers during the intervening period are given in G. W. Kitchin *Obedientiary Rolls:*[10] e.g. the Hordarian's Roll for 1406 details an income of £261.3.2 ob.; the Clerk of Works had an income of £67.0.2¼.; the Almoner's income for 1406 was £29.12.8. None of these rolls indicate the Prior's income. It will be seen, therefore, that there is no indication of any payment to the monks unless they were office holders and that such payment as there was accrued to them for the discharge of their duties e.g. as clerk of works or *hordarius*. The Prior, on the other hand, had considerable wealth to uphold his dignity and to enable him to undertake the expensive hospitality which often befel him.

NOTES

1 J. S. Drew. *Manorial Accounts of St. Swithun's Priory.* E.H.R., 1947.
2 The H.R.S. has published the manorial rolls of *Crondal* (1891); and *Manydown* (1895). J. S. Drew has left in the Cathedral Archives typed translations of the manorial rolls of *The Manor of Chilbolton, 1248 — 1433* (1945); *The Manor of Michelmersh*, 1248 — 1331. (1943); and *The Manor of Silkstead* (1947).
3 An allegation of an excuse for non-appearance in court at the appointed time or the actual excuse.
4 The *Custumale* has been transliterated and edited by Mrs. K. A. Hanna in a thesis for the degree of M.A. in the University of London.
5 W.C.R. 1939 pp.10 — 13.
6 G. W. Kitchin. Obedientiary Rolls. H.R.S. 309.
7 ibid. p.209.
8 *Taxatio Ecclesiastica P. Nicholai, 1291.* London, 1802. p.213.
9 *Valor Ecclesiasticus, 1538.* Vol. 2. London, 1814. p.2.f.
10 H.R.S. 1892. p.285.f.

FURTHER READING

D. Oschinsky. *Walter of Henley and other Treatises of Estate Management and Accounting.* C.P. 1971. (13th century treatises.). The author refers to a specifically Winchester method of management and accounting.

The south-east corner of the Cathedral. Fox's flying-buttresses.

Chapter VI

Thomas Dackomb

The Reformation has been described in many ways. It has been described by those who take a strongly religious view and presented as a conflict between religious opinions. In more recent times, the influence of economic and social historians has caused the Reformation to be described in terms of economic and social change.

In this instance, we propose to describe the years of the Reformation in Winchester, so far as that is possible, through the eyes of a man who lived through those years. He was a man of no particular distinction. He was not a great statesman nor a leading churchman. He was Thomas Dackomb, parish priest of St. Peter Colebrook within sight of the Cathedral and for a short time a Minor Canon of the Cathedral. Part of his ministry he exercised in another parish, but still in the diocese of Winchester. All these offices he held between the years 1519 and 1565 when he retired to his native Dorset, there to die in 1572. It is of interest to add that his family has continued to serve the diocese of Winchester right down to the 1970s. During the forty-six years of his active ministry he lived through the reigns of Henry VIII, Edward VI, Lady Jane Grey, Mary Tudor and Queen Elizabeth I. He saw Bishop Fox, Cardinal Wolsey, Bishop Gardiner, Bishop Ponet, Bishop Gardiner duly restored, Bishop White and Bishop Horne. Kings and bishops alternated fairly violently between protestantism and catholicism with Elizabeth striving in her own way to arrive at a 'settlement'. As far as the worship of the Cathedral is concerned it was a Benedictine Monastery with a prior and monks in 1519, observing strictly the rule of St Benedict. In 1538 it was 'suppressed'. In 1541 it re-emerged as a Cathedral governed by a Dean and Chapter, with Thomas Dackomb taking a small part as a Minor Canon.

In 1519 and until the First Book of Common Prayer of 1549 the services he read were written in Latin. From 1549 for a short time he used English. Then, with the accession of Mary Tudor, he had to revert to the Latin of the Sarum Rite. And finally in 1558 he used once again the Prayer Book as amended by Queen Elizabeth in English. He, therefore, lived through many changes which, as an unimportant person, he had to accept with the best grace that he could muster. No doubt his parishioners, as perplexed as he was, did much the same.

The Building

In 1519, as he went about his parish, Dackomb saw the last structural developments of the Cathedral. Fox's flying buttresses were clearly visible from Colebrook street and the statue of the Bishop himself was placed at the top of the eastern gable of the building. Inside the building the roof bosses in the Quire, 91 in number, were resplendent in new colours and the Chantry in which Fox was to be buried was given to the famous architect Thomas Bertie (or Bartie) to erect. On either side of the Quire, screens were erected and on the top of the screens the mortuary chests were placed in which lay the remains of the Saxon Kings of England. In the walls of the southern side were interred Richard of Bernay and the heart of Bishop Nicholas of Ely. A little later, after Gardiner's death, he saw Gardiner's remains walled into place for a 'chapel' to be erected above them. It seems that when Mary Tudor died in 1558 the 'chapel' was incomplete (At the time of writing plans are afoot to make the chapel available for worship, possibly for the first time). In 1558 all building ceased. Bishop Horne is associated rather with neglect and destruction rather than with building and restoration. It seems probable that it was during his time rather than at the time of the suppression of the monastery (the destruction of St Swithun's shrine alone excepted) that the cathedral in general suffered neglect and wanton destruction. [1]

The Destruction of St. Swithun's Shrine

The official report of the destruction of the shrine reads as follows:-

Richard Pollard, Thomas Wriothesley and John Williams to Thomas Cromwell.
Pleaseth your lordship to be advertised that this Saturday, in the morning, about three of the clock, we made an end of the shrine here at Winchester. There was in it no piece of gold, nor any ring, or true stone, but all great counterfeits. Nevertheless we think the silver alone thereof will amount to two thousand marks . . . we intend to sweep away all the rotten bones that be called relics. [2]

When Bishop Horne ascended to the throne of Winchester he issued Injunctions in 1562, while Dackomb was still in Winchester, and in 1571, the year before he died in his retirement. In the first set of Injunctions there is no architectural reference but in 1571 he enjoined that the "rood-loft in the body of the church be mured up and some parcel of scripture be written there . . . Tabernacles of images now standing void in the body of the church may be taken away or filled up and the places made plain . . . all images of the Trinity in the glass windows or other places be put out and extinguished together with the stone cross in the churchyard." The increasing adornment of 1519 had totally ceased and progressive despoliation now became the order of the day. This was the experience of an unimportant parish priest. It was the experience of others of his fellows and of many of the lay people. They had no power to change the policy of those under whom they lived.

Priors and Monks

In 1519 the Prior of St. Swithun's was Thomas Silkested who had come to the Cathedral in this office as long ago as 1498. Already 'reformation' was in the air. Bishop Fox, in a letter to Cardinal Wolsey dated January 2, 1519, speaks of the need for a *reformationem amplioren,* i.e. a far wider reformation.[3] The prior and monks were also summoned by Wolsey to Westminster to consider the *reformacionem religionis,* i.e. the reformation of religion. The wind of change was stirring and it is interesting to note how soundly a catholic word is the word reformation. Fox was fully aware of the need for it. Talking to his brother bishop of Exeter he resolved to leave part of his wealth, not to the endowment of a monastery with 'bussing' monks but to the creation of a new college at Oxford, the college of Corpus Christi where the emphasis would be on the acquisition of the classical learning which was then making its impact in the west and generating the kind of enthusiasm that the discoveries of modern science have evoked in more recent years.

The Death of Bishop Fox

In his will he had requested, in the event of his death at Wolvesey, that he be buried in the afternoon, of the day of his death, "in the chapel which I have prepared within the Church of Saint Swithun". He adds further details: Fifty torches are to accompany his body to the burying and fifty more are to be used on the following day at Mass.[4]

In 1528 Fox died and was buried on the day of his death in the Chantry, already completed, on October 5th. The story of the opening of his tomb will be described when we come to the nineteenth century history of the Cathedral. Fox had ended his days at Winchester, a blind man and very frail. Tradition has it that he used to listen to the offices from the small room behind the chantry. The cadaver below the chantry is not intended as a representation of Fox himself but rather as a reminder of the mortality not only of great prelates but also of all men. In recent years a cast has been made of Fox's statue as sculpted in the 16th century. It is much worn by the passage of time but even now the appearance of the man may still be gathered from the cast now kept in his chantry where his *obit* is faithfully observed year by year on the day of his death.

Cardinal Wolsey

Wolsey added another office to the many he held by becoming Bishop of Winchester in succession to Fox. There is no record that he ever came to Winchester. The monks enacted the ceremony of enthronement by proxy. One of them preached a sermon (somewhat pointedly for an absentee bishop) on the text from *1 Peter 5.2.:* Feed the flock of Christ which is among you. Text and sermon were, of course, in Latin. [5]

Bishop Gardiner

Wolsey soon fell from power and was succeeded by Gardiner who was likewise enthroned by proxy. The preacher this time was the Abbot of Hyde, John Capon or Salcot, though no reference to the text of the sermon has survived. [6] Dackomb would be present on both these occasions as one of the secular clergy of the diocese.

In 1534 a celebrated trial took place in the Cathedral of a certain Robert Cooke of Southampton who denied the presence of Christ in the sacrament. This heretical belief demanded penance and for his penance Cook was obliged to fulfil the required penance both in the Cathedral and at Southampton where the blasphemy was first uttered. Subsequently on Passion Sunday, the Warden of the Friars Observant in Hampton (i.e. Southampton) preached in St. Swithun's Church, Winchester where Cooke was summoned to do his penance. The preacher took his presence as an occasion for speaking of the sacrament of the altar reciting the heresy abjured by Cooke as one of "the olde and damped heresies", exhorting the people to live and die in their faith. He referred to the story of St. Maurice (his church was adjacent to the Cathedral), who refused to execute his prince's commandments which were contrary to God's law, but preferred to suffer martyrdom. He went on to refer to Cooke's heresy about the Pope . . .

"the Pope was no more than a simple curate". The penitent was dressed in white and had to carry a large cross through the Cathedral and had to repeat this same act at Southampton shortly afterwards. Thus until the very eve of the Reformation the old discipline continued.[7]

Another glimpse, of a rather different kind, is the trouble which the prior and monks had in one of their manors, the manor of Godbegot at Winchester. This was in 1535 when "Walter Harman with a showmaker's last did then and there break the head of the aforesaid Simon, against the peace of our Lord the King . . . to the grievous harm of Simon". On the same day a certain Stephen Beddam and others did make forcible entry into the house of Edward Coke within the jurisdiction of this liberty.[8]

Prior Silkested

The Prior, Silkested, kept office until 1524 and signs of his work are still clearly visible. He can be seen kneeling in a panel over the piscina on the south wall of the Lady Chapel. Silkested's mitre is on his prie-dieu. There is also his crosier indicating the high significance of his office. The pulpit in the quire bears witness to Silkested. There is also Silkested's Chapel, now associated with Izaac Walton over which we can still read Thomas S i.e. Thomas Silkested. There is also a fine chest bearing his name in Calbourne Church, Isle of Wight. One can only conjecture how the chest came to be there. One guess could be that it was transported there during the time of the Civil War, as were the Cathedral statues of James I and Charles I.

Priors Brook and Kingsmill

Silkested was succeeded by Henry Brook who soon resigned doubtless due to the mounting pressure against the monasteries. He was succeeded in 1536 by William Kingsmill who seems, very astutely, to have steered the foundation of the prior and monks into the new foundation of a Dean and Chapter between the years 1538 and 1541. When the shrine of St. Swithun was demolished, Kingsmill is reported to have shewn himself 'conformable' and we know that he made a financial payment to one of the King's servants. There were no false heroics about Kingsmill. He made an inventory, as instructed, of the treasures of the cathedral. It was divided into twelve sections:

1. The things that are abroad in the Church.
   This section refers mainly to the furnishings of the High Altar and the Shrine of St. Swithun.

2. The Inventory of the Sextre (i.e. Sacristy)
    The items here are all of gold, crosses, candlesticks, chalices, rings, S. Philip's foot covered with plate of gold, and the four Evangelists written all with gold.
3. Jewels of silver, tables, crosses, chalices, censers, pastoral staffs, five saints' heads, three saints' arms and seven books covered with silver.
4. Copes. About 259 copes are listed.
5/7 Mass vestments.
6. Hangings for altars: eight for the High Altar and twenty one pairs of hangings for the other altars of the Cathedral.
8. Inventory of the Lady Chapel.
9/11. Inventories of the houses of the Prior, the Sub-Prior and the Hordarius.
12. The Refectory of the monks: cups, mazers (i.e. bowls) and thirty seven silver spoons.

The monastery, therefore, had been richly adorned. There is no hint that the monks lived in other than the most simple conditions. The furnishings of the Prior and Sub-Prior are rather more splendid with a good deal of silver and gilt.[9]

Much however still remained of the treasures of the Monastery now become Cathedral. An inventory taken on October 3rd. 1552 indicates that the Cathedral was by no means completely desolate. There were numerous hangings, copes, even "copes for children" (presumably for choir boys) banners, chasubles, albs, cushions, carpet for the Bishop's stall, and altar furnishings. Various items of plate were taken to the Jewel House in Southampton including rings. (Full details are readily accessible in *H.F.C.* 1917 pp. 15 — 19 and p. 39.)

From Monastery to Cathedral

In 1541 there followed in quick succession a number of important documents establishing the Cathedral as a Dean and Chapter instead of a monastery administered by prior and monks. The first such document was issued in March, 1541. Part of it runs:-

. . . the establishment on the site and precinct of the late Monastery, of a Cathedral Church dedicated to the Blessed Trinity, of a Cathedral and served by a Dean and twelve Prebendaries, all Priests, with all ministers needful for Divine Service therein: and Our will and pleasure is that the aforesaid Cathedral Church be the See of Stephen (Gardiner)

(by courtesy of Judges Ltd., Hastings).

Henry VIII presents statutes to Dean Kingsmill, 1541

Bishop of Winchester, and his successors for ever . . . We nominate William Kyngsmill S.T.P., our first original and modern Dean . . . We create this Dean and twelve Prebendaries and their successors for ever a Corporate Body . . . they shall have a Common Seal whereby to bind themselves and their successors henceforth for ever.

And we desire this Cathedral Church to be endowed nobly.

Other documents followed quickly. One dated April 28th., 1541 sets out the stipends of the Dean and Canons and all other members of the Foundation, including Thomas Dackomb. His stipend was to be £10 per annum. It is interesting to note that whereas a Benedictine Monastery was, ideally, to have 70 monks (there were the 70 disciples sent out by Christ), the new Foundation exceeded this number quite substantially. Among the new members were six scholars at Oxford and six at Cambridge.

On May 1st, yet another document appeared setting out the lands with which the Cathedral was to be endowed. These were substantially the same as those which had previously belonged to the Monastery. The Cathedral was indeed nobly endowed and so remained until the reforms of the nineteenth century when the Ecclesiastical Commissioners were established.

The Arms of the Dean and Chapter
And finally on June 1st the promised coat of arms was given:-

The Arms of the Dean and Chapter of Winchester.

That is to say A mynster or churche silver masonede sable, in the yate of the churche the holy Image of the blessed Trynyte golde and sylver Crowned Imperiall with a dyademe golde of the most high and myghtie prince the kynge their foundor,/a canton party par palle gueules and silver, a Rose with the sonne beames celestiall counter-changed of the fyld the sede pomeley gold, with these words of poisie scilicet : Benedicta sit sancta trinitas, as aperith depict in thys margent, To have and to hold unto the sayd Wylliam

(i.e. Kingsmill, the Dean).

There is an explicit account of the dismantling of the shrine. How many other items were removed at the same time we have no means of knowing. Possibly a good many remained if we are to accept the references to the bishops at Mary Tudor's wedding in 'full pontificals'. But whatever precisely happened, Kingsmill ensured the survival of the foundation through the troubled years and while great houses like Glastonbury disappeared and neighbouring foundations like Hyde and Nunaminster, the Monastery of St Swithun continued. The prior became the Dean and the monks became Prebendaries or Canons and Thomas Dackomb became a minor Canon. In 1715 an inscription was still visible in the Cathedral which spoke of:

> William Kingsmill the last Prior
> The First Dean of the Cathedral.

In the Quire one of the panels in the substalls has his initials W.K. In all Kingsmill reigned from 1536 to 1549 so that he saw the suppression of the lesser and the greater monasteries and the abolition of the chantries (1547). He just lived to see the replacement of the Latin Service Books by the First English Book of Common Prayer in 1549. He also had the satisfaction of knowing that his Cathedral was as well manned as ever it had been and that its lands were substantially what they had been on the eve of the Reformation.

Dackomb found himself somewhat torn in these changes. He had his modest place on the foundation of the new Cathedral. He had the pastoral care of Dame Elizabeth Shelley and her nuns, old parishioners of his, when they were driven out of their convent. Abbess and nuns had small pensions. The will of one of these former nuns, Agnes Badgecroft still survives, witnessed by the curate of the parish.[10]

Sir John Mason, Dean

In 1549 Kingsmill was succeeded by Roger Tonge about whom little is known and then, in the same year, by Sir John Mason, the only layman ever to be Dean of Winchester. Mason was more of the 'willow than the oak', being able to adapt himself to the political needs of monarchs as different as Edward VI, Mary Tudor and Elizabeth. Mason held office until 1553 when he was promoted Ambassador to the court of Charles V in Brussels. It is his name which appears signing the minutes of the first extant Chapter Book of the Cathedral (1553-1600).

Sir John Mason

From Latin to English

Through all these changes until 1549 there were no doctrinal or personal changes. The mass continued to be said according to the Sarum Rite. The Bishop remained unchanged. The Prior continued unchanged although now called a Dean and the monks, such as were intellectually qualified, remained unchanged though called prebendaries, or petty canons. The only change was the abolition of the jurisdiction of the Pope. It was not until 1549 that the new English service book appeared though prayers in English had begun to make their appearance. Even in the Latin Service Books the vows between contracting parties in a marriage were in English. The concept of making all the services more easily understood by the ordinary folk was, therefore, no novelty though it was greatly extended. What puzzled Dackomb was that he had no sooner got used to the First and Second Prayer Books of 1549 and 1552 than he was ordered to revert to the Latin of the Sarum Rite. This lasted during the reign of Mary Tudor, 1553 — 1558. In 1559, his new Sovereign ordered a return to English.

Bishop Ponet, 1551 — 1553

To add to Dacomb's confusion was the removal of Gardiner in 1551 and his replacement by John Ponet. A strong diplomatic catholic was replaced by a fervent protestant. Ponet's views are included in his *Apologie* later published in Zurich whither many protestants fled, including some of the future canons of Winchester, during the reign of Queen Mary. The title page of Ponet's book reveals just how different he was from Stephen Gardiner whom he supplanted and who, when Mary ascended the throne, replaced Ponet. With Mary as Queen and Gardiner as Bishop once again, the Cathedral was set for its most colourful spectacle in its long history.

The Prebendaries

If Mary could not tolerate a protestant bishop, she could not endure protestant prebendaries. At this time these were crown appointments and it is noteworthy that in the three months prior to her wedding in the Cathedral, there were many new appointments which packed the Chapter with men of whom she approved. Two good examples are Thomas White and Thomas Harding. Originally Harding was a protestant and a scholar of the College. He became a fervent catholic who drew a stinging rebuke from Lady Jane Grey from her prison: "Sometimes the lively member of Christ, but now the deformed imp of the devil . . . sometime the unspotted spouse of Christ, but now the unshameful paramour of Antichrist". Harding is now best known for his controversy with Jewel whose *Apology for the Church of England* he vigorously assailed when he had fled to Louvain on the accession of the new Queen.

With a sympathetic bishop and a Chapter holding views in sympathy with her own, everything was now ready for the appropriate solemnisation of the Queen's wedding.

Mary Tudor's Wedding

By far the most spectacular event in Dackomb's time was the wedding of Mary Tudor to Philip II of Spain on St James Day July 25th., 1554. In terms of sixteenth century politics this was a European summit. Briefly, there was rivalry between Spain and France as to which nation should be linked by marriage to England. A French success in this matter would have meant the driving of a wedge in the Spanish dominions in Europe. A Spanish success meant the isolation and encirclement of France. In the event Spain proved the successful suitor. France was humiliated and refused to send her Ambassador to the wedding. Taking part in the negotiations before the wedding was Stephen Gardiner. He was Lord Chancellor of England, leader of the house of Lords and especially influential with Mary. It was he who had conducted her coronation. But, traditional churchman as he was he was also an experienced statesman. He recognised fully the art of the possible. Too open a concession to Rome would not, immediately, be acceptable. It was wiser for Cardinal Pole the Papal Legate to remain for the time being overseas. London too had its discontents. The Archbishop of Canterbury was in prison. All in all it seemed wiser to have the wedding not in London but in Winchester. Furthermore it was convenient for Philip who had to sail from Spain and land in Southampton.

Thus, with all diplomatic negotiations completed between the Spanish and English authorities on the royal marriage, Mary and Philip set out from their own homes to Winchester. Mary came in easy stages, staying at the various palaces of the Bishop of Winchester: Farnham, Bishop's Waltham and Wolvesey which she reached on Saturday, July 21st, 1554. Philip had a long sea voyage and an armada was needed to transport his court and chapel royal. Courtesy required the armada to be met by a contingent of the Royal Navy. Courtesy further required Gardiner to go from Winchester to Southampton to pay a courtesy call upon the Prince. Finally, on Monday, July 23rd, and, as befitted an approach to St. Swithun's Cathedral, in the pouring rain, Philip left Southampton for Winchester. He stopped on the way at St. Cross to change into robes more fitting a royal entry. He was met by civic authorities and brought finally to the Cathedral where he was greeted by the Bishop, the Dean and the Chapter and *Te Deum* was sung. Later that night Philip saw his bride to be for the first time at Wolvesey and returned to stay the night at the Deanery. The betrothed couple met again the following day at Wolvesey. Finally, on St James' Day, a day chosen out of courtesy to the patron saint of Spain, the wedding took place. Philip arrived first and Mary a little later. The Cathedral had been richly adorned for the

Philip of Spain.

Mary Tudor.

occasion. Down the centre of the nave ran a long scaffold over three feet high. From scaffold to the hooks still visible inside the nave pillars were suspended twelve Flemish Tapestries, only completed in 1554, which depicted the victory of Philip's Father, the Emperor Charles V, over the infidel at Tunis in 1535. These tapestries, are handsomely woven in gold and silver and silk and are now in Spain in Madrid, Seville and Barcelona. Their history since 1554 is a separate study. Within this handsome setting, with five bishops in full pontificals and the combined choirs of Winchester, the Chapel Royal of England and the Chapel Royal of Spain, the actual wedding took place. There were three stages. The first stage of the actual marriage took place in the Nave. Before the ceremony a herald announced that the Emperor had just created Prince Philip King of Naples. The wedding, therefore, could take place as between equals and not between a sovereign and a prince. Diplomacy could not allow such a discrepancy. The form of service was that of the Sarum Rite with only the vows in English. If we follow

Tapestry hung in the Cathedral at the wedding of Philip and Mary. It depicts Spain and North Africa, including Tunis.

The chair in which Queen Mary sat after her wedding to Philip.

the words as in one of the Sarum Missals still surviving in the Library and which existed at the time of the wedding the vows were as follows:-

I (Philip) take thee (Mary) to be my wedded wife, to have and to hold from this day wafort buttur for wurs, for richere, for porer, in sickenesse and in helte tyll deth us depart, if holi Churche wol it ordeyene: and ther to I plycht the myn trough

Mary too made a similar vow.

In accordance with the directions of the marriage service, and as reported by observers, Philip then took three handfuls of fine gold which the Lady Margaret Clifford (cousin of the Queen) seeing, opened the Queen's purse and the Queen smilingly put the gold into the same. The ring was then produced, "a plain gold hoop", said the Queen," such as maidens have".

Holy water was sprinkled upon it, the ring was blessed and Philip said:-

> With this ring I thee wedde,
> And this gold and silver I thee give:
> And with my body I thee worship,
> And with all my worldly catell (i.e. chattels) I thee honour.

The marriage completed, Nuptial Mass was celebrated in the Quire and then, we are informed, the Queen retired to the Lady Chapel and it is here, so tradition has it, that she sat upon the chair still known in the Cathedral as Queen Mary's Chair. The documentation of the Chair goes back to a will dated in 1610 and thereafter the tradition is unbroken. For years the chair was kept in the Lady Chapel and may be seen to be there in engravings early in the nineteenth century. In later years, because of the wear of the chair it was placed under glass and kept in the unused chapel of Bishop Gardiner, with whom she was so closely associated during her life time. It has to be added that, as in most historical matters, there has been discussion about the chair, its date, its original use and other aspects of it. However, so great a historian as S. R. Gardiner is convinced of its authenticity.

For a few days after the wedding the court remained at Winchester. On 26th July Mary did not appear, following the custom of the time. She did, however, write to the Emperor and tell him that her new husband was "full of virtues." On the following day a more normal routine ensued. A new "stampe" was necessary for sealing state documents which henceforth would be in Latin and Spanish. Saturday was spent quietly. The day began with Mass and a meeting of the Privy Council was held in Wolvesey. The same morning a messenger, who had left Winchester on the Wednesday evening after the wedding, reported in person to the Emperor in Brussels.

After the week end the court broke up and began to return to London, the tapestries continued their interrupted journey to Spain and Winchester, we imagine, returned to its own more normal life.[1][2]

The Martyrdom of John Philpot, 1555

Not only was Archbishop Cranmer in prison awaiting his fiery ordeal but also John Philpot, Archdeacon of Winchester, member of a well-known Hampshire family. He was Dackomb's archdeacon and, because of his protestant convictions, he was burned at the stake at Smithfield in 1555. An engraving of his martyrdom may be found in Foxe's Book of Martyrs which was so soon to be prescribed as a necessary book for the Dean and Chapter to have in their Library.

¶ The Martyrdome of Maiſter Iohn Philpot Archdeacon, with the manner of his
kneeling, and praying at the ſtake.

In the morning the Sheriffes came . . . about viii of the clocke . . . and
he most joyfully came downe unto them . . . and so he went to the place of
execution: and when he was entring into Smithfield, the way was foule, and
two officers tooke him up to beare him to the stake. Then he said merily,
what: will you make me a Pope? I am content to goe to my journey's end on
fotte . . . Then with an obedient hart full meekely he sayd the CVI, CVII,
and CVIII Psalmes . . . . the xviiith day of December (1555) . . . yeelded
his soule into the hands of the Almighty God . . . [13]

The death of Philpot, so well known to Dackomb and members of the
Cathedral Foundation, must have caused an immense shock.

Burial of Stephen Gardiner, 1556

About a month before the death of Philpot, Gardiner himself died.
Being winter, his body was first placed in the Church of St. Mary Overy at
Southwark, near to his London palace, Winchester House. Later his body
was brought to Winchester by easy stages, being appropriately received in
the different parishes (all in his diocese) through which he passed until
finally on 27th February, 1556 he was brought to Winchester and finally on
the following day to the Cathedral. Mass was solemnly sung by the Dean
early in the day and then later a Requiem Mass "executed by the Bishop of
Lincoln (i.e. Dr. White who was to succeed Gardiner as Bishop of
Winchester) and sundry of the canons. The body was then carried to "a
chapell, behind the high altar" and the coffin was placed between two walls
made of brick, a yard high. Dust ('mowlde') was cast upon the coffin at the
words Dust to dust, and ashes to ashes, and officers standing by broke their
staves and rods upon their heads and cast them into the place where the body
lay. A board covered the coffin and over that a rich pall. No ground was
broken for him and he lay there "till such time as a chapell should be made
for him," which was to be arranged by his executors. Apparently this
arrangement continued until Whitsuntide.[14]

It seems, therefore, that there was no chantry awaiting Gardiner as had
been the case with Fox. Indeed we have to remember that legally chantries
had been abolished in 1547 and we note that the word 'chapell' is used. If,
therefore, the chapel was begun after Whitsuntide, 1556 it is beginning to
look as though the chapel was never completed or used by the time
Elizabeth came to the throne in 1558.

Bishop White 1556 — 1560

The death of Gardiner enabled Mary to promote Bishop White of
Lincoln to Winchester where he was already well-known because of his
associations with the College. He was soon in disgrace. At a sermon preached
at Mary's funeral before the new Queen Elizabeth, the Bishop's remarks
caused great offence. He was kept in close arrest and finally committed to
the Tower where he died in 1560. In his will he had expressed a wish to be
buried in his Cathedral but it was not until 1886 that what is thought to be

his coffin was discovered in the Lady Chapel. A stone in the floor tells the story:-

> The Body beneath this stone
> is believed to be that of John White
> Bishop of Winchester 1556 — 1560,
> was suspended by Queen Elizabeth in 1559,
> and died on Jan. 11 1560, when his body
> was brought to Winchester and
> privately buried in the Cathedral.

Bishop Horne, 1560 — 1579

White was succeeded by Bishop Horne, a protestant who had fled to Frankfurt during the reign of Queen Mary. He was a considerable Old Testament Scholar and his initials (R.W. i.e. Robert Winton) can still be seen in the Bishops' Bible at end of the Lamentations of Jeremiah. It is in this version that we have the famous phrase (Jeremiah 8.22) — Is there not tryacle at Gilead instead of the better known rendering: no balm in Gilead. On coming to Winchester he soon made his influence felt for he quickly 'visited' the Cathedral in 1562 and again in 1571 by which time Dackomb had retired but, health apart, he would still be interested in the Cathedral around which so much of his life had revolved. In the first visitation Bishop Horne wanted an end to the old style of music: "no other note be sung but such as every syllable thereby may be both plainly and distinctly pronounced." His 1571 visitation was more far reaching and suggests that the tradition that it was he who allowed much of the cathedral to fall into disrepair or was actually destroyed has in it an element of truth. The injunction about music was repeated and 'the rood-loft in the body of the church be mured up and some parcel of scripture be written there.' Tabernacles of images standing void in the body of the church were to be taken away or filled up and the places made plain. All images of the Trinity in the windows were to be put out and the stone crosses in the churchyard destroyed. There was great emphasis on the scriptures, the catechism of Dean Nowell of St. Paul's and sermons.[15]

Cathedral Music

During Dackomb's lifetime Cathedral music, as we know it to-day, began to take shape. Bumpus begins his book, *The History of English Cathedral Music* with the First Prayer Book of 1549. So far as Winchester is concerned not a great deal is known about the first period. It is pleasing to record that Gardiner used his influence to save the life of John Merbecke in 1544. Merbecke was Master of the Choristers of St. George's Chapel, Windsor. He was also a zealous student of the Bible and his theology led to his condemnation at the stake.

The encounter between two men is told at considerable length by Hunt.[16] Merbecke first came before Gardiner in 1543. Merbecke was suspect for his teaching on the Sacrament, his copying of works of Calvin, and for producing a *Concordance*. He was cast into the Bishop of Winchester's prison at the Marshalsea. Merbecke refused to recant or betray his protestant friends. In due course he came to trial and was condemned to be burned at the stake. At this stage Gardiner intervened and saved Merbecke but not his associates, who perished on the following day.

Foxe records the following conversation between the two men: "What a devil made thee to meddle with the Scriptures? Thy vocation was another way, wherein thou hast a goodly gift, if thou didst esteem it". "Yes", answered Merbecke, "I do esteem it . . . ." "Why the devil", said the Bishop, didst thou not hold thee there?" When Merbecke went on to defend his work on the *Concordance,* Gardiner urged him "not to meddle with the thing which pertaineth not to thee". Gardiner, despite the severity of his questioning, finally released him so that, in Foxe's words, "He is not dead God be praised, and yet to this present singeth merrily, and playeth on the organs".

So it was to the Bishop of Winchester that one of the most important of English musicians owed his life and we owe his music.

Scarcely had it appeared when Edward VI died and Mary Tudor restored the Sarum Use. At the wedding, therefore, of the Queen in 1554 it was the music of pre-Reformation days that was used and also some Spanish music. The Master of the Music during these years (the date of his resignation or death is uncertain) was Richard Wynslade, the first truly Cathedral organist. He was given twelve lay vicars and ten choristers in the foundation deed of 1541. There were also six petty or minor canons whose duty it was to sing the services. Apart from the imbalance of boys' voices, the musical foundation was well served. They seem to have adapted themselves to the changes required by protestant and catholic monarchs between 1541 and 1558.

Part of a setting of Lucem Tuam *by Richard Wynslade, organist of the Cathedral from 1541 to 1572. BM Add. 29.996*[18]

Worth recording is the document, signed by Dean Kingsmill and members of the Chapter, which gave to Richard Wynslade (i.e. some time before 1549) the grant of a revision of a holding at Ibworth in the Manor of Manydown.

Another small glimpse into the members of the Choir of the time occurs in the inventory of the goods made on the death of Henry Stempe who died in 1549. His possessions have no mention of any music or any books referring to music. The only mention which suggests any connection with the Cathedral is:

"A surplise . . . . is."[17]

Bibliophile[21]

Dackomb had lived through many changes, some of which he must have found profoundly difficult. In recent years his reputation as a bibliophile has been growing. A special study has been made of the manuscripts and books which he is known to have had. There are nineteen manuscripts and four printed books. The emphasis of Dackomb on manuscripts, a century after the invention of printing, is of interest and suggests that his mind was of an antiquarian cast. He was probably a lover of the old ways and would probably have subscribed to the words in the Sarum Missal, still in the Cathedral Library and which existed in Dackomb's day which were written by a certain Bartholomew Hussey: "I praye God I may lyve to see the Masse to be saide in England again — for that to see it wolde glade my harte somuch as any thinge in the world." So far no clue to the identity of Bartholomew Hussey has emerged.

Notes on some of Dackomb's manuscripts are worth recording. His most important manuscript is a *Winchester Chartulary*[22] which was in the Cathedral until 1844 when it was purchased by the British Library. Another chartulary passed into the British Library in 1873. Among the printed books the most famous is now in the library of Westminster Abbey: John Lathbury's *Book of Lamentations of Jeremiah*[23] printed at Oxford in 1482. This particular copy belonged to one of the more learned monks of St Swithun, John Avington. The book is annotated both by Avington and Dackomb.

We may imagine him in his closing years finding consolation in his collection which may well have been far more extensive. His mind would run back to the old days of Bishop Fox and, we sense lament (as is the wont of old people) over recent changes. Such was the Reformation for him, rector of an unimportant parish and holder of a minor office upon a cathedral foundation.

Signature of Thomas Dackomb

NOTES

1 W. H. Frere. *Visitation Articles and Injunctions, 1559 — 1575*. London, 1910. pp. 134 — 139 & pp.318 — 323.

2 G. H. Cook. *Letters to Cromwell . . . on the Suppression of the Monasteries* London, 1965.

3 P. S. Allen. *Letters of Richard Fox., 1486 — 1527*. O.U.P., 1929. p. 115.

4 ibid. p.167.f.

5 F. T. Madge and H. Chitty. *Registrum Thome Wolsey*. C. & Y. Society 1926, p.1.f.

6 H. Chitty and H. E. Malden. *Registrum Stephani Gardiner*. C. & Y. Society, 1931. pp.1 — 8. Details of the Abbot of Hyde are available in *D.N.B.* s.v. Capon J.

7 *Registrum Stephani Gardiner* pp. 30 — 34.

8 A. W. Goodman. *The Manor of Goodbegot*. Winchester, 1923. p.35.

9 J. Strype. *Memorials of Thomas Cranmer*. London, 1694. App. XVI. See also Dugdale *Monasticon*. Vol.1.p.202.

10 J. Paul. *Dame Elizabeth Shelley*. H.F.C. Vol. XXIII.Pt.II.1965. pp.60 — 71.

11 *Ledger Book IV:* f.108. Ms.

12 F. Bussby. *W.C.R.*, 1973. pp.40 — 54.

13 J. Foxe. *Actes and Monuments*, 1597. p.1661.

14 J. A. Muller. *Letters of Stephen Gardiner*. C.U.P. 1938.pp.512 — 517.

15 A. Nowell. *Catechismus*. London, 1570.

16 J. E. Hunt. *Cranmer's First Litany and Merbecke's Book of Common Prayer Noted. 1550*. London. pp.29 — 33.

17 *Baigent Papers III*. XVIth Century Wills, II. No. 111.

18 B. Matthews. *The Music of Winchester Cathedral*. London, 1974. P.10. also *Musical Times*, August, 1978 where Wynslade's will is published, (January 13th., 1572/3): "I give to reparations of the Cathedral Church iiis. iiiid.'

19 A. G. Watson. *A Sixteenth Century Collector. Thomas Dackomb, 1496 — 1572*. London, 1963.

20 Codex Wintoniensis B. M. Add. MS 15. 350.

21 F. Madan. *Oxford Books*. Vol. 1. 1895. p.2.f.

FURTHER READING

Acts of the Privy Council. July 28th., 1554.

T., Atkinson. *Elizabethan Winchester*. London, 1963, c. XIII C.A. 1553 — 1600 with Index by E. Foss.

C. Bailey. *Transcripts from the Municipal Archives of Winchester*. Winchester, 1856 pp. 142 — 147. The Marriage of Philip and Mary.

W. Basynge. *Libellus of Hordarius*, 1535. Cathedral MS.

C.C.P. 1500 — 1599. MSS.

D.N.B. s.v. Boxall J., Bridges J., Gascoigne E. (all prebendaries).

J. M. Fletcher. *Sir Thomas Dackomb, Priest 1519 — 1567*. Natural History Society and Antiquarian Field Club, Dorset. 1923.

S. Gardiner. *De Vera Obedientia (On True Obedience*. A translation) Reprint of 1553 edition. Scolar Press, 1966. *A Machiavellian Treatise*. Written in Gardiner's life time but not published until 1975, C.U.P.

R. Hilton *The Marriage of Queen Mary and Philip of Spain*. H.F.C. 1938.

S. Himsworth *The Marriage of Philip II of Spain with Mary Tudor*. H.F.C., 1962.

L.B. 2 — 7. 1496 — 1602. MSS.

C. V. Malfatti *The Accession, Coronation and Marriage of Mary Tudor*. Barcelona, 1956.

Monza and Cantor. *Los Tapices de la Casa Rey Madrid*. Madrid, 1929.

J. Murube. *Alcazar of Seville*. Madrid, 1970. Coloured illustrations of tapestries.

State Papers Spanish and Venetian for the period July 26 to July 28 1554 should be consulted.

Treasurers' Accounts (misc) 1541 — 1561. MSS.

A. J. Willis. *Consistory Court Depositions, 1561 — 1602*. Privately printed, 1960.

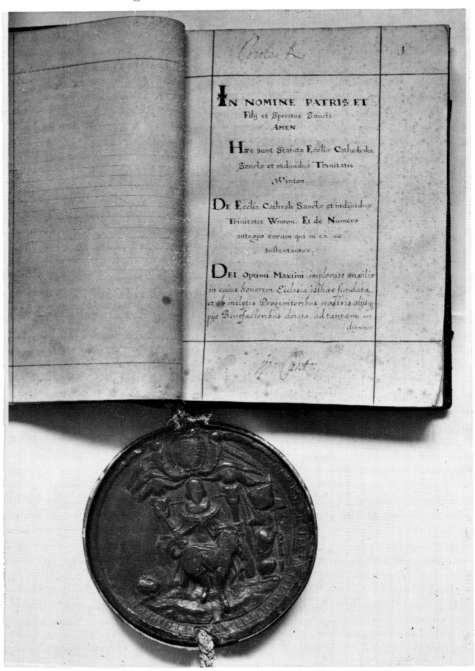

Title-page of the Statutes
The King's signature (Carolus R) is at the top of folio 1. Archbishop Laud's signature (W. Cant) is at the foot of every folio.

Chapter VII

Hassall and Young

The Elizabethan Settlement and the Early Stuarts

Englishmen are not strong on their dates. Those they know are few in number. Among that few is 1588, the year of the Spanish Armada, of Sir Francis Drake playing bowls on Plymouth Hoe. In that same year a young Wykehamist, most reprehensibly, incised his name and description on one of the columns of the Cathedral, near the present south door of the nave where it can still be clearly seen.

JHON (sic) HASSALL
CHILDE OF WIN
CHESTER COLLEDG
1588

John Hassall was born about 1573, just after the death of Thomas Dackomb, the elderly minor canon around whose life we wrote the history of the Reformation in Winchester. Hassall came up to Winchester in 1587, the year of the execution of Mary Queen of Scots, and in the following year bequeathed his name to posterity in the way described.

The Cathedral which he entered and defaced in 1588 had many features which we see to-day, but there were differences. In 1588, there was no central south door to the nave. Two doors were used, one at the east end of the nave and one at the west end. As he stood perpetrating his misdemeanour he could see inscriptions in the floor which to-day have been rubbed out of existence by a myriad feet or lost beneath a sea of chairs. He could also see what we see as we stand where he stood: Wykeham's Chantry to the west and Edington's to the east. By his time the masses for the souls of these munificent benefactors had ceased. The inscriptions on the floor struck a chord which he was already beginning to comprehend, being an intelligent scholar trying to understand the Elizabethan Settlement, as his learned but adult successors have since described the times through which he was growing up, and fitting himself for a career in the Church that was to prove more exalted than that of Thomas Dackomb. A scholar of the College with the prospect of a place at New College, Oxford and a fellowship which he secured should achieve at least modest distinction. He did. For he became in due course Canon of Lichfield and finally Dean of Norwich. In 1588 the inscriptions that particularly caught his attention were (translated from the Latin):

> Robert Horne, an eminent
> Doctor in Divinity, at one time
> An exile for the cause of Christ,
> Afterward Bishop of Winchester.
> He died piously in the Lord
> June 1, 1580
> In the 19th year of his Episcopate.[2]

This, he said to himself, was the bishop who denuded the Cathedral of so much of its adornment.

Near by was another inscription that spoke not of destruction but of continuity:

> William Kingsmill, Prior ultimus
> Decanus primus Ecclesiae
> Obiit 1548.

Kingsmill was the last prior and the first dean. Edington, Wykeham, Horne, and Kingsmill — between them they summed up the puzzling religious expression which he called the Church of England.

The Dean and Canons

Among the canons of the Cathedral was John Harmer, also headmaster of the College and destined to become the Regius Professor Greek at Oxford. Perhaps he took Hassall into the Cathedral Library where he would see (as we may still see) a copy of Foxe's *Actes and Monuments,* the badge of true Protestants and enjoined by Horne as an essential part of the Cathedral Library.[3] He could also see the gift of John Warner (Dean of Winchester from 1559 to 1565) to the Library of Ruellius *De Natura*

Graffito on Nave Column near the South Door

Stirpiun which still carries on the title page the fact that Warner bought the volume and presented it to the Library in 1566. It was a book on herbs and was among the books then available which had enabled him to become first Regius Professor of Medicine at Oxford (1546 — 1554). The book had already been in the library for twenty-two years when Hassall saw it. The Headmaster had already translated Calvin and was working on Beza and Chrysostom.

The Dean in John's time was Laurence Humphrey, also President of Magdalen College Oxford. His sympathies were with the Puritans. He already had a number of books to his credit, the burden of which was to disprove the claims of Rome. He wrote the first biography of Bishop Jewel famous for writing that *Apology* (1562) which is still regarded as the first classical exposition of the position of the Church of England. The irony is that when Humphrey sought preferment in Jewel's diocese of Salisbury, the Bishops made it clear that he regarded him as a trouble maker and did not wish him to serve under him.

Bishop Cooper, 1584 — 1594

Somewhat more remote from Hassall was the Bishop, who was also the Visitor of the College. He was Thomas Cooper, who early caught the the attention of Queen Elizabeth because of his great erudition. In 1565 he had published *Thesaurus Linguae Romanae* a dictionary in Latin and English which the Queen esteemed so highly that she undertook to give him the best preferment at her disposal. And so in 1584 she raised him to the see of Winchester. Cooper was aware of Edington's dictum that Winchester may not enjoy the highest rack (or rank) but it did enjoy the best manger. Cooper wryly commented on his translation that the manger had been cleared of much of the provender.[4] The Bishop, as Hassall was increasingly to be aware, was the centre of a considerable controversy and which gave rise to a pamphlet warfare embodied in the *Marprelate Tracts*. The Bishop's response to these tracts was a formidable volume called: *Admonition to the People of England wherein are answered not only the slanderous untruths reproachfully uttered by Martin the Libeller (i.e. mar-prelate) but also other crimes by some of the brood objected generally against all bishops and the chief of the clergy purposely to deface and discredit the present state of the Church'* (1589). The agonies leading to the Elizabethan settlement were being shared in Winchester and the Winchester scholar was more and more aware of them. The Bishop had already been massively supported by one of his canons, John Bridges, with his 1,400 pages of *'A Defence of the Government established in the Church of Englande for Ecclesiasticall Matters . . ."*

The Recusants

The Church in general and Winchester in particular typified the Church of the day, walking an uneasy path between puritans and recusants, as Roman Catholics were then called if they refused to attend the services of the Church of England. The position of the recusants made difficulties not only for the Church of England but also for the Government. In 1570 when it was finally clear that Elizabeth was not going to follow her sister Mary, and embrace the Roman faith, she was excommunicated by the Pope[5]. Her subjects were absolved from loyalty to her and indeed opposition to her became meritorious. The Government was forced to react and declare that those who held such views were rebels and traitors to their country. Before Hassall left Winchester such recusants were publicly executed in the city. One such, Ralph Miller (1591), asked the Judge to take pity on his wife and children. The Judge replied: 'Go to Church Fool, and look to thy children thyself .[6] At this stage in the country's development everyone, puritan, recusant, or anglican believed that there was an essential tie between a county's religion and its government. Toleration and ecumenism were still far in the future. The struggle continued to rage and, in simple terms, led to the Civil War when the waxing claims of Anglicanism were finally overthrown. In Winchester the continuing hostility to Rome is recorded in the history of the Cathedral when the Dean and Chapter ordered the public burning (1617) of a Roman Catholic book entitled *Spiritual Lyme and Sand.* None of the canons would attend the occasion and the Precentor and Chapter Clerk were forced to undertake this ceremonial act.[7]

Bishop Bilson and the Coronation of James I

In 1593, Hassall left Winchester for New College, Oxford. This did not sever his links with Winchester because the Bishop of Winchester then, as now, was Visitor of New College. In those days such an office was far more than a sinecure and the bishop's participation in the affairs of the college, in appointments and any controversial matter, was real and decisive. While Hassall was enjoying his fellowship, there was a new bishop, Thomas Bilson. Bilson preached the sermon at the Coronation of James I in 1603 and saw the Court come down to Winchester later that year for fear of the plague in London. He was a firm believer in the divine right of kings as the choice of his coronation text indicates: 'The Powers that be are ordained of God.' The anointing of the Sovereign, he pointed out, had its origin in Holy Scripture, and the 'Romish error' that sovereigns had no right to have a say in the worship of their people cannot be sustained by the Scriptures. As a courtier he pays a gracious tribute to Queen Elizabeth and also to the new King: "since it pleased God, not long since, to take from us to his heavenly rest, a Prince, that with great moderation and wisdom swayed the sceptre . . . now God had been pleased to place on the throne as the rightful heir a King most worthy to succeed her, nothing inferior to her, in knowledge, prudence, magnanimity, bounty, mildness or disposition . . ."[8]

The Hampton Court Conference, and the Authorised Version

Bilson's eulogy of the King was more than fulsome flattery. The King really did believe he had a leading part to play in the life of the Church. One of the first steps he took was to call a Conference at Hampton Court to endeavour to secure "one doctrine and discipline, one religion in substance and ceremony." The best known consequence of the Conference was the initiation of steps which led to the translation of the Bible, commonly called the Authorized Version.[9] This translation involved a number of Cathedral

Clergy including Dean Abbot and Canon Harmer,[10] both eminent Greek scholars who helped to translate in particular the four Gospels. The Bishop, Bilson, was appointed to be one of the final revisers of the translations[11] of the six committees which sat — two each in Oxford, Cambridge and Westminster. This is a contribution of the Cathedral which has enriched the English speaking world for over three centuries. We shall never know just how much we owe to men like Abbot, Harmer and Bilson.

Between 1600 and the outbreak of the Civil War, Winchester had five bishops but only two deans. A few words are necessary about the first of these whilst a more extended reference is essential when we come to consider the second of them. John Young.

Dean Abbot, 1600 — 1609

Dean Abbot came to Winchester in 1600 and rose to be what a recent biographer described as *The Unwanted Archbishop.*[12] Despite his appointment by James I, the King had earlier been somewhat angry with the Dean. He had summoned Convocation to assist him in formulating a view about the right of a sovereign and his subjects to rebel against a *de facto* government held to heretical or tyrannical. The Dean displeased his monarch and drew the following reply:-

Good Dr. Abbot,

. . . . my reason for calling you together in Convocation was to give your judgement how far a Christian and Protestant King may concur to assist his neighbours, to shake off their obedience to their once sovereign, upon the account of oppression, tyranny or what else you may like to name it. If the King of Spain should return to claim his old pontifical rights to my kingdon, you leave me to ask others to fight for it . . . you tell us upon the matter in hand, his authority is God's authority if he prevail . . . . Meddle no more on it.

I commit you to God's protection, good Doctor Abbot and rest your good friend.

James R.

A Visitation, 1607 — 8

So far we have been writing of the more eminent men associated with the Cathedral but much routine work continued and the disciplinary powers of the Church still remained and were exercised at the north west corner of the Cathedral, where the Consistory Court presided over by the Bishop's Chancellor exercised judicial authority over certain types of offences. In

1607-8 Archbishop Bancroft held a visitation in the Consistory Court though the officer exercising the Archbishop's authority was Dr. Thomas Ridley, Chancellor to the Bishop of Winchester. In ten months the Chancellor reviewed over 600 cases. The offences were mainly sexual offences, failing to receive Holy Communion or to attend Church, failure to pay Church dues or to observe the Sabbath. One case was held at the Font of the Cathedral. When men and women were tried for not receiving Holy Communion they were often recusants or Roman Catholics who refused to accept the Anglican service.

Bishop Montagu, 1616 — 1618

In 1616 Bilson died and was succeeded by Bishop Montagu. If anything, he had a closer connection with his sovereign than Bilson. He was summoned to edit and publish the King's writings. Within three years two editions appeared: in 1616 and 1619. They reflect very much James' own notion of himself as a theologian with meditations on the Book of *Revelation* and upon the Lord's Prayer, (a work, which, incidentally, was translated into French). His collected works contain also his famous work on Tobacco, a work on Demonology and one on the Divine Right of Kings.

Dean Young, 1616

One of the most serious gaps in the records of the Cathedral is the absence of any *Chapter Book* covering the years 1600 to 1622. As a result there is difficulty in trying to reconstruct the history of the period. It covers the time when George Abbot was dean (1600 to 1609). The fact that he rose to become Archbishop of Canterbury suggests a man of influence and ability. And yet his biogapher can tell us only that George Abbot, Dean of Winchester, received the appointment for £600. In 1609 he was succeeded by Thomas Morton, who rose to become Bishop of Durham. Of him too there is little information save that he was Dean from 1609 — 1616.

Official documentation is still rare in 1616 when John Young became Dean. Fortunately in 1918 the Diary of John Young, Dean of Winchester 1616 to 1645 was discovered by Canon Madge in a chest of miscellaneous manuscripts. Ten years later Florence Goodman published extracts from the *Diary*[14] and so helped fill the total gap that had hitherto existed in the history of the Cathedral. The earliest entries in his *Diary* reveal how, very correctly, he called for the 'inventorie' of such things as are in the church.' Equally correctly he wrote to his Bishop. Thereafter the *Diary* continues until he was finally driven out of the Cathedral by the Commonwealth forces in 1645. Many of the details concern items of property and local personalities. The admission of a 'pettie canon' or 'singing man' is mentioned. Among early references, the most important is the installation, by proxy, of Bishop Andrewes which Young records as follows:

Bishop Andrewes, 1619 — 1626

3 Augusti 1618: Haveing received the King's Congé d'élire (i.e. the Royal licence to elect a bishop) upon the death of Bishop Montagu, for Bishop Andrewes, warning was given to Mr. Chanter (i.e. the Precentor) and John Bond to warn the company by setting up *in poenam contumaciae* (lest they incur a penalty for being contumacious) upon their stalls. First we went to morning prayer, and after the first lesson, from the Quire to the Chapter House, and caused the named to be called; then told the excuse of our meeting; then caused the King's letter to be read, and every ones voice read *Ego N* (i.e. name) *eligo N. in Epscopum Winton* (I....elect....to be Bishop of Winchester) and I (i.e. the Dean) *eligo et electum pronuntio* (I elect and declare elected) ... then those instruments to the King, to the Archbishop (i.e. Archbishop Abbot, one of Young's predecessors), and the Bishop (i.e. Andrewes), the certificate of the election sealed, and a proxie of number 4 to deliver it.

Until the *Diary* became available there was no known personal account of the election of the Bishop. The formal record is in *Ledger Book X*f.65r-v.

It is significant that Canon Welsby's life of Bishop Andrewes, the fullest yet written, refers only three times, and then in footnotes, to Dean Young. The first reference confuses the Dean with a bishop of the same name of the sixteenth century; another mentions a scandalous attempt at simony which does the Dean no credit. A certain Mr. Alexander Cook writing to Archbishop Usher of Armagh on November 30th, 1626, says (arising out of the death of Lancelot Andrewes) "Here is £1500 offered (as it's said) for the Bishoprick of Winchester, by the Dean of Winchester: And some say it is worth it, for he may make of the Leases, at his first entrance £10,000."[16]

The Dean's Son

One of the personal sorrows of the Dean's life was the loss of his young son, aged about eight. Only towards the end of the 19th century did the child's copy book come to light. It consists of sixteen pages of a small boy's first attempts to learn writing. It brings home a human touch, so easy to miss in the story of a great cathedral.

Bishop Neile, 1628 — 1632

In the event it was not John Young but Richard Neile, already Bishop of Durham, who was moved to Winchester. The Dean refers fully to the election in Chapter but has no reference to the enthronement of the Bishop.[16] It followed the custom of pre-Reformation and post-Reformation bishops. One of the prebendaries, in this instance Dr. Darrell, stood proxy for the bishop and was enthroned in his stead. The Archdeacon of Canterbury whose duty it is to enthrone bishops in Winchester was also represented by another of the prebendaries, the Vice-Dean, Dr. Kercher. These representative figures went through the ceremony of vesting at St. Mary Kalendar, processing to the Cathedral, being met by the Dean and Chapter and then taking the appropriate oaths on enthronement. So Dr. Neile became the legally enthroned Bishop of Winchester on February 25th, 1627/8.[17]

Bishop Curle, 1632 — 1647

Four years later the enthronement of Bishop Curle seemed to mark a new era of reform and activity within the life of the Cathedral. No doubt this was due to the waxing influence of Laud, already influential as Bishop of London but soon to reach the height of his power when translated to Canterbury in 1633. With the Laudian influence, backed by the King and receiving sympathetic reception from both Bishop and Dean, the Cathedral saw a period of intense activity until all was shattered by the outbreak of Civil War. A single saying of Curle sums up his viewpoint admirably: A puritan, he said, was "such a one as loves God with all his soul and hates his neighbour with all his heart." These words alone indicate just where his sympathies lay in days of bitter controversy.

Immediately in 1633 the Dean ordered an inventory of Church Ornaments. Laud was keen that the ceremonies and the services of the Church should be performed with due dignity and splendour. It is no accident that the first item recorded in the inventory is: "a rich canopy embroidered with pearl, to be carried over the King when his Majesty cometh to the Cathedral Church." This item is followed by a number of other palls of cloth of gold, all very splendid. There is a list of pulpit cloths, communion carpets of Turkey work and two white copes. There is a long list of cushions in red or crimson velvet, one in silver tissue and twelve square cushions in Turkey work. At that time the Cathedral possessed a good deal of communion silver dating from the early seventeenth century, including a silver basin given by the Dean. There is a certain amount of altar linen and a number of chairs including one of 'blew velvet in ye Lady Chapel.' This

Sacra Supellex
Ecclia Cathedralis
Winton

Novembris 29° 1633 perlustrata.
per Tho. Goad Sᵃᵉ Theologiæ pʳofessorᵉ
nuper Thesaurarium ejusdem Eccliæ,
ac comissa supinspectioni Gulielmi
Lewys Sᵃᵉ Theol. pʳofessoris Thesau-
rarij pʳximè succedentis. ex mandato
Johis Young Sᵃᵉ Theol. pʳofessoris Decani,
& Capitl.

Inprimis in the Chist wheri yᵉ Seale lyeth
a riich Canopy embrodered wᵗʰ perle, to be
caryed over the King when his Maᵗⁱᵉ cometh
to the Cathedrall Church.

Item a pall of cloth of gold vpon dark purple
vellatt wᵗʰ a Crosse stripe of brighter gold vpon
crimson velvet.

Another pall paned downward 3 of gold, and
4 of Crimson velvet wᵗʰ flower de Luces and
IHC being the greek Characters of Jesus

Part of Dean Young's Inventory

would seem to have been the one associated with Mary Tudor. Looking at the inventory to-day we see the sad note added by the faithful John Chase, Young's Chapter Clerk, which records that particular items were stolen during the days of the Civil War.

A visible sign of Curle's influence can still be seen at the south west corner of the Cathedral which indicates that the practice of using the Cathedral as a thoroughfare was to cease. The Latin words may be translated:-

←——— That way   comest to pray

thou who

This   way ———→

art pursuing thy walk.

Another Latin inscription in the narrow passage between the Cathedral and No. 11 The Close, called Curle's passage, emphasises the same point and may be translated:

Private property has yielded to public utility
Proceed now by the way that is opened to thee.

That way is consecrated to the choir
This way leads to the market.

Laud's Visitation, 1634.[18]

The Archbishop soon organised the visitation of all cathedrals, including Winchester. The Winchester visitation took place in 1634. Numerous questions were asked to ensure the discipline of the Cathedral body: "whether the boys be suffered to play in the cathedral church-yard, whereby church windows are sometimes broken." Prebendaries, singing-men and porters all fell under his scrutiny. Square caps had to be worn in church and thanks must be given to Almighty God for the saints. The care of the buildings was of particular concern and particular anxiety was expressed lest the church became a thoroughfare. An account was required of the Cathedral's estates.

As a result of the preliminary visitation precise injunctions were issued to the Dean and Chapter. Four copes, and a copy of the statutes, must be provided. The cathedral graveyard must be fittingly maintained; reverent behaviour was required during the saying of the services; and genuflections must be made on entering the Quire. There was to be no walking about during divine service and a virger must be in attendance during divine service, to ensure the observance of the new rules.

Tower Vaulting, 1633-4

The fabric of the Cathedral itself saw a number of major changes calculated to enhance the splendour and ornamentation of the building. Most noteworthy was the building of the tower vaulting. The Dean's diary reads as follows:

3 December 1633

We debated the business about the arching of the tower. We feared Dr. Goad's way because if any piece of timber or bell should jut against it. And then for the scaffolding: that way it must be from the ground, but the other a hanging scaffold will serve; and the other way will be stronger, steapper (sic), less timber, done easier, but that more beautiful. So I appointed 20s. to be given to the workmen, and that they should come back in the end of Jan: and the articles to be drawn betwixt us...if the one way, they are to have £70, the other £120, and we to find all materials and be at the charge of cutting of (coats) of armes.

16 Jan. 1634 (new style):

We drew and sealed the articles for arching the tower. The roof has numerous 'armes'. It also includes representations of Charles I and his Queen, Henrietta Maria. In the centre of the roof is a circular band or *corona* (through which bells may be raised or lowered when need arises) round which is written a verse of scripture: *sInt DoMUs hUIUs pII reges nUtrItII, regInae nUtrICes pIae. The words are based on the Latin text of Isaiah 49.23: And Kings shall be thy nursing fathers and their queens thy nursing mothers.* The capital letters in the Latin text are known as a chronogram because when placed in the correct order i.e. MDCVVVVVIIIIIIIII they give the date of the completion of the work, 1634.

The corbels at each corner once carried wooden busts of James I and Charles I. These were removed early in the nineteenth century but are still preserved in the South Triforium.

Bishop Curle, 1632-1647

The Bells, 1632 — 1642

Two manuscripts dated 1632 and 1642[19] reveal the full range of the bells at this time.

Campanae Ecclesiae Cathedralis Sanctae Trinitatis
Winton 14 Maii 1642
1. Prima campana sclt Sancte Johes ora pro nobis.
2. In multis annis resonet campana Johannis.
3. Sum rota pulsata mundi Maria vocata.
4. Missi de celis habeo nomen Gabrielis.
5. Eccle Gabrielis fiat hec campana fidelis.
6. Trinitatis sacrae fiat hec campana beata.
7. Ista dei laudes resonet campana perennes.

The great bell is mentioned in the will of Richard Bud, 1630. He left £40 to the Dean and Chapter if they would have the great bell of the Cathedral tolled for condemned criminals before their execution, and also cause a prayer to be read on their behalf. A bidding, followed by silent prayer, was still used even in the present century until the death penalty was abolished.[20]

The cost of the new frame was £40 and seems to have been set in hand in 1631 before the tower vaulting was ready.

Lt. Nowell Hammond visits the Cathedral August 4th, 1634.[21]

From the same period comes the first recorded description of the Cathedral by a visitor. Mr. Hammond, on leave from his regiment in Norwich (where Hassall had been dean since 1628) made a tour of western counties which included Winchester. With the eyes of a perceptive layman he left a full description of the "brave old Mother Cathedral," 200 paces long and the roof stately, fair, and rich on which "a great summe of money" had been very lately bestowed. This must refer to the Tower Vaulting in its pristine colours. He details the carvings over the quire stalls. (See pp. 50-52)

He did not think much of the Organs (sic) but speaks highly of Thomas Holmes, the organist (one of the rarest this land affords) and the quiristers "skilful, and the voices good, when they sing sweet and heavenly anthems." He devotes passing references to the chantries, the mortuary chests, Queen Mary's chair in the Lady Chapel and the Portland statue[22] recently put into position in the Guardian Angels Chapel. He also refers to the canopy and cushions of the 1633 inventory.

It can be seen, therefore, that the result of the Laudian reform, in fact, reached the ordinary churchman, nor did the impetus exhaust itself after the first proposals and the initial reactions.

A more famous visitor to the Cathedral was John Evelyn on September 6th 1642 when he mentioned particularly the 'Saxon Kings' Monuments' which he considered 'a worthy antiquity'.

The Inigo Jones Screen

In his *Diary* Young devotes several pages to the visit of the Sir Nathaniel Brent, Laud's Vicar-General, beginning on June 16th, 1635. The Dean's account is of the ceremonial and the music of the occasion and of the Vicar-General's insistence on greater reverence in the Cathedral. The Vicar-General sat covered while the members of the Dean and Chapter stood bareheaded, so great was the awe inspired by Laud's representative. The Dean offered fitting hospitality to so great a personage. Although Young does not mention this, it would appear that out of this visit came the move to erect the "New Front for the Quire". A recently discovered letter of Dean Young indicates that the King himself had recently visited the Cathedral, and had been unimpressed by the placing of the Chapter House, apparently within the *pulpitum* which the new Screen was designed to replace. As a result the Dean had consulted the workmen and found that there was no practical problem in the removing the old *pulpitum* and erecting an appropriate

The Inigo Jones screen — a part of the engraving from Gale's History of Winchester Cathedral.

structure "standing upon marble pillars." An item in the financial account fot 1638 for £234.4.0 indicates that the work had then begun for the money was "Laid out for part of ye charge which the Church hath been at this year in pulling down the old Chapter House and erecting the new building before the Quire." So began Inigo Jones' screen. The whole work has been exhaustively documented by Mr. J. M. G. Blakiston in the *Winchester Cathedral Record* in the years 1976, 1977 and 1978.

Statues of James I and CharlesI

A separate contract was then drawn up for the erection of two royal statues.

June 17 1638

I, Hubert Le Sueur, Sculptor have bargained with the King's Majesty of Great Britain to case in brass two statues of 5 feet 8 inches high: one that represented our late Sovereign Lord King James and the other our Sovereign Lord Charles for the sum of £340 of good and lawful money of England to be paid in this manner viz. £170 before-hand and £170 after the work shall be finished and delivered to the Surveyor of his Majesty's works in the March ensuing. And the said Hubert Le Sueur is to receive the aforesaid sums without paying any fees for the receipt thereof

Hubert Le Sueur

I was present and witness in this bargain.

Inigo Jones

The Chapter in 1640 paid £18 to the King's workmen for setting up the statues.[22] Inigo Jones' Screen continued until the nineteenth century. It is depicted for example by Ackermann in 1816. To-day the centre part of the screen is in Cambridge while a few fragments are in the North Triforium. There have been proposals to restore it to the Cathedral or to some position in the Close but cost and the possible unsuitability of the stone in an outdoor situation have so far ruled against the proposition. A further problem exists in that the Screen is only intended to be viewed from one side.

Charles I   *James I*

The Mayor and Corporation

Laud's Reforms did not everywhere meet with approval. Turning to the affairs of the Cathedral it was a small point of procedural etiquette between Dean and Chapter and Mayor and Corporation which proved the flash point and led to conflict between the two bodies. What caused particular trouble was the right of the Mayor and Corporation to carry their Mace before them into the Cathedral. At first the Dean and Chapter refused. The Mayor and Corporation appealed. The Dean and Chapter were upheld. The Mayor and Corporation continued their protest and at last, in 1641, after four years' dispute the Mayor and Corporation prevailed. The Mace would be (and still is) carried when the Mayor and Corporation come to Cathedral. *(W.C.D. Vol. 2. p.1. and 18).*

The Parochial Clergy

The spirit of reform did not limit itself to the details of ornament or ceremonial. In 1637 the King sharply reminded the Dean and Chapter that as patrons of a number of livings they had a duty to make adequate financial provision for the incumbents:-

> CHARLES R
> Whereas formerly due care hath not been taken by you or by your predecessors to provide sufficient maintenance for the Vicars and Curates which officiate in the parochial churches appropriated to the Dean and Chapter of that Church, Our will is that forthwith provision be made for the augmentation of all such vicarages and cure . . .

It is probable that the direction was prompted as a result of Laud's enquiry or possibly following a visit to the Cathedral by Charles and his Queen. Glass with the royal arms of King and Queen are part of the Long Gallery in the Deanery and may well commemorate the visit.

Cathedral Statutes, 1638[24]

Until Laud's time the Cathedral had followed the statutes decreed by Henry VIII. Charles I and Laud had different views about the Church. For the Cathedral that meant a new series of statutes which were finally produced in 1638 after due consultation with the Chapter. The new statutes covered 38 sections. In the main the statutes define the positions and privileges of the members of the foundation: the Dean, the Canons, Precentor, Sacrist, Subsacrists (to-day Virgers). The King's signature (Charles R) is at the top of the first folio while Laud's signature (W. Cant.) is at the foot of every folio. The Dean and Chapter were required to send a copy of the Statutes to the House of Commons. (W.C.D. Vol. 2. p.27).

Cathedral Music

The waxing influence of William Laud reflected itself, amongst other ways, in the increased attention to the ceremonial and hence the music of cathedral services. Winchester did not escape this influence. Dean Young's *Diary* (1616 — 1645) has many incidental references to the appointment of "pettie" canons, singing men (one a counter tenor): On Jan. 26th, 1622 he writes: "George Bath admitted Master of Queresters and organist." We find two musical graffiti: one of George Bath on the north wall of the Quire: and one Thomas Holmes (Organist 1631-1638) on one of the columns in the Nave.

On occasion the Dean comments on the 'good voice' of a lay clerk. When Curle was elected bishop in 1632, *Te Deum* was sung.

These reforms were summed up musically in the Statutes of 1638 which stipulated that there should be "six Choristers, boys of tender years, of resonant voices . . . . ten lay clerks . . . . (and) one who is skilled in singing and playing upon the organ, who shall apply himself zealously to playing at the right time and to singing of Divine Offices, and shall take pains to teach and train the Choristers". This musical foundation was to be under the direction of the Precentor whose duty it is "decently to conduct those who chant in the Church." Scales of pay were

Master of the Choristers	£5. 2.0.
Lay Clerks	£2.19.2.
Choristers	£0. 0.0.

Already the organ had been removed from the centre of the old Choir Screen (due no doubt to the requirements of the new Inigo Jones Screen) and placed on the north side of the Choir.

Adrian Batten

In Elizabethan times the basic provisions of Merbecke and Sternhold and Hopkins possibly met contemporary needs. Men like Bishop Horne and Dean Humphrey (1580 — 1589) were concerned more with theological controversy rather than with musical performance. There is no indication what influence, if any, Thomas Tallis (1510 — 1585) or William Byrd (1538 — 1623) or Thomas Weelkes, organist of Winchester College, had upon the music of the Cathedral.

The change came in the following century and is epitomised for Winchester in the career and compositions of Adrian Batten who, contrary to all the canons of right conduct in church, incised his name upon the east wall of Gardiner's Chantry.

Born in Winchester about 1590 Batten was a chorister of the Cathedral and proceeded first to Westminster (1614) and finally to St. Paul's (1624). As a composer he wrote at least seven services and some fifty anthems. While at St. Paul's the policy of Laud (then Bishop of London) gave him the opportunity to write music for the choral celebration of Holy Communion which had fallen into disuse during Elizabeth's reign. He was one of the first musicians to introduce bar lines. His music is still re-printed and finds an appropriate place within the repertoire of the present Winchester Choir.

Adrian Batten's name on Gardiner's Chantry.

Manuscripts and Archives

In his *Diary* for June 28th, 1622 the Dean refers to his instructions to set 'our records in order' in the muniment room. This was probably the Exhibition Room of the present Library. It is noteworthy that in 1621/1622 three important books and manuscripts were started: a new Ledger Book begun in 1621, a large imperial folio containing much of the business of the Chapter as they handled their property and also recording the enthronements and installations of bishops, deans and canons; a new Chapter Book in 1622, there being no such book to cover the years 1600 to 1622; and last of all, there emerged more than three centuries later a single folio in the handwriting of the King's Librarian, Patrick Young, the Dean's brother, a list of the manuscripts then held in the Cathedral Library. As this list is nowhere available it is here transcribed with help from Mr. Barr, Librarian of York Minster and of York University.

The last item on the list stated to be in the Library of Winchester College in 1622 is now, by courtesy of the Warden and Fellows of the College, returned to the Cathedral Library though both foundations have instant and ready access to either or both volumes.

M.S.S. in (Bibliotheca *or* Cathedrali)
Wintoniensi:

1 Biblia latina 2 bus vol   Large and faire fol.
2 Augustinus in Joh: fol.bon.
3 Martini Poloni chronicon et Hist: Britonum Galf. Monum: fol.
4 Vnum ex quatuor Zachariæ Chrysopol: et Hieronymus de membris
    d(omi)ni.   fol.
5 Annales Nicolai Triuetti   fol.
6 Concordantiæ Bibliorum   fol.
7 Alcueni epistolæ   4to
8 Nicolai vita per Joh: diaconum et Alphegi vita per Osbernum   4to
9 Cassiodorus in psalmos   fol.
10 Hieronymus in Isaiam libris 18   fol.
11 Lexicon anglico latinum vna cum tractatibus quibusdam dere
    grammatica   fol.
12 Bedæ historia ecclesiastica   fol.
13 Eiusdem martyrologium, Hieronym(us) de vita Pauli, Antiqu.,
    Antoni(us), Hilarionis, vita Patrum
14 Eiusdem translatio de græco exhortationum ad monachos (?)   fol.
15 Godrici heremitæ vita per Galfridum monachum   8uo
16 Reuelationes Elizabethæ, vita s(anc)ti Edwardi Regis, vita s(anc)ti
    Thomas Cantuariensis . . . sacrosanctum . . . requiter impugnat
    hostis antiquus et cæt.   fol.
17 De Mirabilibus mundi Joh: de Mandeuill   4to
18 Tabula antiqua et ampla de antiquitate et fundatione eccl(es)iæ
    Wintoniensis parieti affixa
19 Chartularium antiquum Regum et Pontificum de terris et fundis
    eccl(es)iæ Wintoniensis   fol.
    In Bibliotheca collegij Winton:
20 Paschasius Radvertus (monoachorum peripsoma *interlined*) in Threnos
    Jeremiæ ad senem Odilmannum Seuerum   fol. bon.

Mercifully these manuscripts mainly survived the Commonwealth for in

List of Cathedral MSS. c.1622

1697 a list of the majority of them was published in Oxford and are now
in the Cathedral Library.

The Puritans

By narrowly concentrating on the history of the Cathedral, royalist in sentiment and loyal to the ecclesiastical movement inaugurated by Laud, it is easy to lose a sense of perspective. Godfrey Davies in his volume on *The Early Stuarts* provides the perspective we need. He writes ". . . by 1640 the puritans were wholly estranged from the church.[25] We have seen that at Hampton Court they received no concessions. The position was further exacerbated by the attempt to thrust the Anglican Liturgy upon Scotland in 1637. Add to these the fear of Rome and the fervent appeals to stand for the faith of the Marian martyrs and the explosion against crown and mitre was unavoidable. The pent up frustrations of the puritans swept into the Cathedral on December 12 1642. *Mercurius Rusticus* tells us that on a horrendous day in December, 1642 Parliamentary soldiers entered the Church . . . . . "burnt the Books of Common Prayer and all the singing books belonging to the Quire. They threw down the Organs . . ."[26] The organist of those days was Christopher Gibbons, father of the more celebrated Orlando Gibbons. Cathedral music was henceforth forbidden.

The life of the Cathedral was thus gravely threatened and it was not long before, by process of law, it was utterly abolished in 1645. The seemingly irresistible progress of Laud and his King was suddenly arrested. After a period of confusion, and a battle at Cheriton,[27] it was clear that the old ways had ended. John Young and members of the foundation were scattered, just as John Hassall and his colleagues in Norwich were scattered. Only a minority of them saw the Restoration of 1660. By a co-incidence both Hassall and Young died in 1654 while living in obscurity in a country parish within the dioceses of which their cathedrals had been the mother churches. Both died as among those who were defeated (to use Rose Macaulay's phrase). The outlook for the cathedrals of Norwich and Winchester and indeed for the Church of England as a whole was extremely dark.

NOTES

1 T. F. Kirby. *Winchester Scholars.* London, 1888. p. 153. John Hassatt (sic)

1 A. Wood. *Fasti Oxonienses.* Oxford, 1691.

2 S. Gale. *The History and Antiquities of . . . Holy Trinity in Winton,* 1715. p.37.

3 W. H. Frere. *Visitation Articles, 1559 — 1575.* London, 1910. p. 321.

4 *D.N.B.* s.s. Cooper T.

5 J. R Tanner. *Tudor Constitutional Documents, 1485 — 1603.* C.U.P. 1922. p. 143.

6 G. Anstruther. *The Seminary Priests. 1558 — 1603. p.103.*

7 F. R. Goodman. *The Diary of John Young.* London, 1928. p.58.f.

8 *Bilson* op cit. p.

9 J. R. Tanner *Constitutional Documents of James I.* C.U.P., 1930.p.63.

10 A. W. Pollard, *Records of the English Bible.* London, 1974. p.52.f.

11 *ibid.* p.58.

12 P. A. Welsby. *George Abbot, the Unwanted Archbishop,* 1562 — 1633. London, 1962. The King's letter is printed in D. Wilkins' *Concilia Magnae Britanniae,* 1737. Vol.IV, p.405.

13 A. J. Willis. A Hampshire Miscellany. *A Metropolitical Visitation of the Archdeaconry of Winchester, 1607 — 1608.* Privately printed, 1973.

14 F. R. Goodman *op cit.*

15 P. A. Welsby. *Lancelot Andrewes, 1555 — 1626.* London, 1958. p.61., p.107., p.261. In his *Diary* (31 Oct. 1623) Young admits offering money to secure a bishopric.

16 F. R. Goodman *op cit.* p.81.

17 *L.B.* XIII. ff.7v 8.

18 *The Works of William Laud.* Oxford, 1853. Vol. V. p.464.

19 *C.C.P.* 1632 and 1642.

20 F. R. Goodman *op cit.* p.91.

21 *Camden Miscellany Vol. XVI.* 1936. R. N. Quirk. *W.C.R.* 1953. pp.9 — 15.

22 *Treasurer's Book* 1640 fol. 8

23 W. R. W. Stephens and F. T. Madge. *W.C.D.,* 1636 — 1683. xxxiii.f.

24 A. W. Goodman and W. H. Hutton. *The Statutes Governing the Cathedral Church of Winchester, given by King Charles 1.* C.P., 1925.

25 G. Davies. *The Early Stuarts.* C.P., 1949. p.77.

26 *Mercurius Rusticus, 1685.* pp.144.ff. (The pagination in this book is erratic).

27 J. Adair. *Cheriton.* London, 1973.

FURTHER READING

Baigent Papers V. p.218. Will of Preb. Wm. Haward. 1581 — 1623.

C. A. 1553 — 1600 and 1622 — 1645. (C.A. 1600 — 1622. Missing) MSS.

C.C.P. 15　　— 1599; 1600 — 1645. MSS.

D.N.B. s.v.

Batten A. chorister	Humphrey L. dean
Bilson T. bishop	Jackson T. preb.
Cooper T. bishop	Laney B. preb.
Curle W. bishop	Lewis W. preb.
Duncon E. preb.	Meetkerke E, preb.
Gawen T. preb.	Montagu James. bishop
Goad T. preb.	Morton T. dean
Harmer J. preb.	Neile R. bishop
Harris J. preb.	Oliver J. preb.
Holmes T. organist	Warner J. preb. and dean.

L.B. 8 books from 1561 __ 1645. MSS.

Treasurer's Books: 1618, 1627, 1629, 1640. MSS.

Winchester Cathedral Register of, baptisms, marriages, and funerals begins in 1599.

Winchester Cathedral. Dugdale's Monasticon, 1655

Chapter VIII

Destruction and Restoration

The Civil War: 1642 — 1649

From the point of view of members of the Church of England in general and of the clergy and people associated with Winchester Cathedral in particular, the period of the Civil War and the Commonwealth from 1642 to 1660 was disastrous. The Dean and Chapter was, by law, 'utterly abolished'. The building itself suffered grievous harm, *Mercurius Rusticus* has already been quoted. A further excerpt underlines the grievous damage done:

> "on Tuesday the 12 of December, 1642. about twelve of the Clock . . . (the Rebels) sate down before the City of Winchester . . . and entered the City that afternoon between two and three: being Masters of the City, they instantly fall upon the Close . . . they seize the Prebends Horses, and demand their Persons with many threatning words: That night, they break into some of the Prebends Houses; . . . on Thursday morning between nine, and ten of the Clock . . . they violently break open the Cathedral Church, and . . . pollute his Temple ... they enter the Church with Colours flying, their drums beating, their Matches fired . . . until they came to the Altar . . . and burnt the Books of Common Prayer, and all the Singing Books belonging to the Quire . . ."

And so the narrative continues detailing the sacrilegious acts committed at that time.

It would not be wholly fair, however, to imply that the black picture of *Mercurius Rusticus* was the whole picture. Among Cromwell's generals was Nicholas Fiennes, a member of the Wykeham family. Tradition has it that he stood at the entrance to Wykeham's Chantry and firmly forbade any of his troops to enter or despoil it.[2] So was preserved one of the Cathedral's important monuments at a time when it might so easily have been gravely damaged.

Colonel Boles

It is not surprising to find that the Cathedral body favoured the royalist cause. No more heroic champion of that cause was there than Colonel Richard Boles who met his death in Alton Church in 1643 in a valiant but unavailing attempt to repel the Parliamentarians. The last desperate struggle took place in the Church itself where the marks of the conflict still remain. Boles was killed and in 1689 a memorial brass was placed in the Cathedral in his memory. It recalls the words of Charles I when he heard of the Colonel's death:

> Bring me my mourning scarf, I have lost
> One of the best Commanders in the Kingdom.

The brass is on the column just west of Morley's tomb and is the earliest surviving brass in the Cathedral.

In 1645 the Dean and Prebendaries were deprived of their houses and of their financial support from Cathedral properties. Some tried to remain in obscurity and to avoid confrontation, while others fled abroad. Even so those who remained in England were summoned before the Parliamentary Commissioners in 1647.

Then in 1649 there was a Parliamentary Survey of the Houses in the Close, as well as of the lands formerly belonging to the Dean and Chapter. Houses and lands were sold to supporters of the new regime. Copies of these surveys still remain.

Books and Archives and John Chase

Nor did Library and the Archives of the Cathedral escape the attention of the authorities of the Commonwealth. In 1645, the books were placed in the care of John Woodman, who lived in one of the Close Houses. Woodman neglected his duty. The books were held to be of value to the ministers of the City and so an instruction was issued on April 30th., 1647 that, in accordance with long standing practice chains should be affixed to them so that they could be available to such as wished to use them. They were valued at £200 and a catalogue, now lost, was made. The books were later taken to London but, after several requests, were brought back to Winchester College, in all about 170 volumes and fifteen manuscripts. This list still

One of the Close houses of the 17th century; now the Pilgrims' School.

survives and the books and manuscripts themselves, with few exceptions, are now back in the Cathedral Library. Most of them can be readily detected by the number on the fore-edge of the book which corresponds to the number in the list made during the Commonwealth.[3]

The fate of the archives was different. Some were wantonly destroyed or scattered. Soldiers on the rampage paid scant respect to music and service books. They reckoned without the faithful servant of the Dean and Chapter, John Chase, who had been appointed in 1620 by Dean Young. He made every effort to rescue and to list and preserve every possible document which had any reference to the history of the monastery or the Cathedral. Sometimes a document was rescued from the gutter in the street; sometimes from a shopkeeper about to wrap her sales in a monastic charter. Despite set backs, Chase persisted in his collection and cataloguing so that if there is one man more than any other to whom students of the Cathedral are indebted for the preservation of any record prior to 1660, that man is John Chase.

One section of the archives which does not seem to have been threatened is that part which referred to property. As a consequence the so called *Ledger Books* or *Books of the Common Seal* which tell among other things of the properties belonging to the Dean and Chapter are all safe. These were needed for legal purposes by Commonwealth Lawyers when they settled claims and values of church property which had been forcibly alienated from its previous owners.

The Winton Domesday

Did the Dean and Prebendaries try to save any books or manuscripts belonging to the Cathedral? Like many in similar position down the ages we may conjecture that they did so hoping, with the return of better times, to restore what they tried to save. One such case is Dean Young himself who took possession of the *Winton Domesday* (recently re-edited and annotated).[4] The book is not only famous for what it tells us of Winchester about the end of the eleventh century but also for its binding. The manuscript remained in the Young family until 1773 when it was sold for six guineas. In 1790, it was bought by the Society of Antiquaries who have continued to be its owners from that day to this. The book is a basic document for the study of Mediaeval Winchester.

The emergence of Antiquarian Scholarship

The anxiety of John Young and John Chase to preserve the records of the past was not just limited to Winchester. Possibly because of the threat to the past, men turned themselves to the scholarly preservation of past records. The story in general is well described by D. C. Douglas in his scholarly survey of *English Scholars, 1660 — 1730* (London, 1951). Among these scholars was William Dugdale who published *Monasticon Anglicanum* in 1655. It was he who gave us the first impression we have of the exterior of the building. He also provided a good deal of the monastic documentation (pp.31 — 38).

Douglas also has a chapter on the precocious scholarship of Henry Wharton who published two folios, *Anglia Sacra* (1691). These were editions of mainly ecclesiastical records and include in their number Thomas Rudborne's texts of two works by one of Winchester's most erudite monks. These annals of the Cathedral cover the period from the time of the mythical Brutus (supposed to have given his name to Britain) to Henry VI[5]. The shorter version was translated into English by James Stevenson in the 19th century.

It was as though when the cathedral was threatened, scholars and citizens (as we shall soon see) rallied to the support of that which they treasured.

The Commonwealth, 1649 — 1660

During the years of the Commonwealth the Cathedral was used, though the precise extent of that use is hard to ascertain. The most remarkable fact is that despite considerable damage it was preserved. We owe this to the general feelings of the citizens of Winchester who gave expression to their opinion through the Recorder, Cornelius Hooker. The document containing the petition was only discovered in 1879 and was, even then, very frail and fragile. It has, however, been carefully preserved. The latter half of the petition reads:-

We therefore, out of zeal for the propagation of the Gospel and not out of any superstitious conceit of holines in the walls do humbly desire that that goodly Fabric may continue and be preserved as a place meet and decent for the public worship of the only true God and not be made a heap of stones and rubbish, like that which is commonly called the Temple of Dagon near adjoining to it.

The petition is dated 1652.

Not only was the building preserved but it did receive some small repairs, details of which have also been recorded. "It being generally known that Trinity Church . . . be a very imminent and useful place for preaching and hearing God's word yett it doth dayly decay for want of reparations. We whose names are subscribed . . . . willingly contribute . . . money . . .[6]

The actual use of the building is more difficult to describe. There is no record of any baptism or wedding. There is a record, however (not complete), of twenty burials which took place in the Cathedral. An observant visitor can still detect an occasional gravestone with a date in the 1650s. recording a burial during the time of the Commonwealth. There is no record of any regular services but we do know that three (or possibly four) ministers were appointed to preach: Theophilus Gale, said to have been 'an incomparable preacher'; Humphrey Ellis, and, possibly Faithful Teate.[7] There is also still in print an *Assize Sermon* preached in Winchester by a certain Edward Buckler on July 22nd, 1658. He was one of Oliver Cromwell's chaplains and preached before him four times a year. Buckler was Minister of Calbourne in the Isle of Wight. The title of his sermon is *Salus Populi* or A Nation's Happiness. It would be a reasonable inference from this known occasion to infer that the traditional Assize Sermons, although with a different form of service, continued during the period of the Commonwealth. It is improbable that any other building could have been used for such an occasion, there being, prior to the Commonwealth, no non-episcopal churches available.

The Restoration of Cathedral Life

On May 29th 1660, King Charles II returned triumphantly to London. He returned to his own. And, it went without saying, the Church likewise returned to its own. It is true that while abroad in Breda, the King had issued a statement that he would deal sympathetically with tender consciences on his return. Attempts were made between Episcopalians and Presbyterians to reach some form of accommodation. Some leading Presbyterians, for example Richard Baxter, were offered bishoprics. Negotiations were held between representatives of the two main theological parties. In the end agreement was impossible, though a few concessions were made in the Book of Common Prayer, but all to no avail.

Prebendary Stanley

While these negotiations were afoot in which George Morley, soon to become Bishop of Winchester, played a prominent part, the Cathedral life slowly resumed.

The first recorded service took place on August 19th 1660, when Prebendary Stanley was the preacher, taking as his text the words: "Who shall give salvation unto Israel?" In the course of his address we can catch the excitement of the day:

> "This is one of Christ's miracles . . . that though we were unworthyly cast out, yet we are met again . . . whether it be the Quire or the Body of the Church, it matters not; but here we are by God's mercy, and the ship itself is, we hope secured; though much torn and ransacked, as you see . . . after a long captivity, you see it hath pleased God to bring us hither again."

On the following January 30th, the anniversary of the death of Charles I, Prebendary Stanley again occupied the pulpit and preached on the text *Lamentations* c. 4. v.2.:-

> "The breath of our nostrils, the Anointed of the Lord, was taken in their nets, of whom we said, Under his shadow we shall live among the heathen."

This gave him plenty of opportunity to extol the virtues of the martyred King whom he clearly held to be near divine: "How glorious was he in his Meekness, in his Patience, in his Magnanimity, in his Charity, in his Contempt of the world, and all the Glory of it . . . as was said of the Proto-

Martyr St Stephen, so it might be said of the Royal Martyr too, All that sat on the Council saw his face as it had been the face of an Angel."

His final surviving sermon, preached not long before his death, was an Assize Sunday, 1661 when he found the appropriate text: "I will restore thy judges as at the first, and thy counsellors as at the beginning: Afterwards thou shalt be called, the City of Righteousness, the faithful city" *(Isaiah* c.1. v. 26.).[8]

That he held his duty as a preacher in high esteem was recorded on his tombstone (he died in 1662) which was placed near the pulpit in the nave. In his day the pulpit was near the column by the present south door. Not far from him was buried his brother, a medical doctor, whose gift to the Library still survives. It is a handsome folio Bible dated 1638. On the front cover is a diamond shaped brass plate inscribed:-

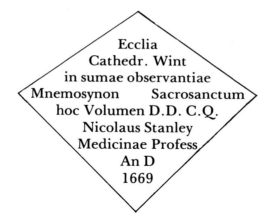

Ecclia
Cathedr. Wint
in sumae observantiae
Mnemosynon   Sacrosanctum
hoc Volumen D.D. C.Q.
Nicolaus Stanley
Medicinae Profess
An D
1669

The book has two clasps. The uppermost clasp bears four Greek words: Who is worthy to open. *(Revelation* 5.v.2.).

The Completion of the Cathedral Chapter

On September 10th, 1660 the Crown appointed a successor to the late Dean Young — Alexander Hyde, so that with the surviving prebendaries a *quorum* was possible to resume the business of the Cathedral. The first and most pressing business was the election of a new bishop, Bishop Curle having died during the Commonwealth.

The Crown nominated Brian Duppa, tutor to Charles II and to whom Charles I had committed the spiritual upbringing of the young prince. He must, directed the King, pay no attention to the Queen in spiritual and ecclesiastical affairs for she was a Roman Catholic. In all such matters he must look to Dr. Duppa. Duppa had lived quietly at Richmond during the Commonwealth and was already over seventy on the King's return. The King soon raised him to Winchester and, following legal precedent, the Dean and Chapter had to 'elect' him. This they did.

Naturally others who had served the King during his exile, clergy and laymen, looked to him to restore their decayed fortunes and to give them some preferment or appointment or to show then some act of charity in the case of those in urgent need. In the case of the canons, one of the first to be appointed was Thomas Gumble, who had served as a chaplain in the Life Guards (his grave is still visible recording this fact) under General Monck. Gumble was appointed canon in 1661. In due course (1671), he wrote the *Life of General Monck*.[9] a work regarded as of sufficient importance to be translated into French. A highly academic clergyman was Robert Sharrock (first appointed in 1665) an expert in Canon Law who re-issued Lyndwood's *Provinciale*, the edition which is still basic for students in this field of study. By way of contrast he also wrote a small work on vegetables.[10] Steadily the full complement of twelve was reached.[11]

Thomas Ken: 1669 — 1684

The most famous of all the Restoration canons who served the Chapter at Winchester is undoubtedly Thomas Ken, first appointed in 1669. He is one who is known throughout the English Speaking world for two of his hymns:-[12]

> Awake, my soul, and with the sun
> Thy daily stage of duty run

and

> Glory to thee, my God, this night
> For all the blessings of the light.

The Hymns were originally written for Winchester College but have won their way into most collections of hymns of whatever denomination. Ken is perhaps even better known for his refusal to give Nell Gwynne lodging on an occasion when Charles II visited Winchester and wished to find accommodation for his mistress. Despite the rebuff that the King received, he was magnanimous enough to recognise the quality of Ken and to prefer

Your very umble, & faithfull servant —
Tho: Ken.
Wing: Coll:
Dec. 4th 1667

him to the Bishopric of Bath and Wells. Among the more personal reminders of Ken is his walking stick which has a whistle in the handle with a high pitched note capable of calling his dog to his side when out walking.

Another glimpse into the character of Ken comes in the inscription which he was fond of inscribing into his books, including the New Testament which he had constantly by him. It is a verse from *Jeremiah* 35.5: Seekest thou great things for thyself? seek them not. Being a scholar he inscribed the verse in Latin as given overleaf.

Thomas Ken's favourite motto: "Seekest thou great things for thyself? Seek
them not."

Ken's house was situated in what is now the Deanery garden where there
is a tablet indicating the fact. A drawing of the house just before it was
demolished in the 1850s shows a house which could well have been little
changed from the time of Ken's own residence.[13] Mary Woodforde in 1685
described the house as "very pleasant . . . far better than ever I would hope
for."

Evelyn in his Diary tells of an occasion when Ken, by now Bishop of
Bath and Wells, returned to the Deanery for a visit by James II. The subject
of their conversation was miracles. Evelyn writes (16 Sept. 1685):

" . . . . his Majestie farther said, that he was so extreamely difficult
of Miracles, for fear of being imposed on, that if he should chance to see
one himselfe, without some other witnesse, he should apprehend it some
delusion of his senses: . . . . . To all which the Bishop added a greate
Miracle happening in the City of Winchester to his certaine knowledge,
of a poore miserably sick & decrepit Child, (as I remember long kept
unbaptized) who immediately on his Baptisme, recover'd . . . ."[14]

The boy to whom the Bishop refers is a certain Matthew Cante who
lived in the parish of St. John's, Winchester where Ken ministered for a
time.[15]

Dr. Ken's house in the Close at Winchester.

Restoration of the High Altar

One of the first needs in the Cathedral, when returned to the Dean and Chapter, was a new High Altar. Services that were held during the Commonwealth had no such need. But with the restored use of the *Book of Common Prayer,* the Altar was first on the list of requisites. A particular interest attaches to this piece of restoration for it is the only part of which a very rough plan which has survived. The manuscript is much worn and when found was almost in three pieces. Because of its unusual nature it is reproduced and a transcription added (by the kindness of Mrs. D. Coldicot) on the opposite page.

What the final result of the restoration was like we know from an engraving in Francis Sandford's *Genealogical History of the Kings of England* p. 22. published in 1677.

Three hundred years later the Bible and the Prayer Book visible in the engraving still stand behind the altar. Rufus' tomb was removed in 1868; the commandments have been removed and the other ornamentation round the altar changed during the nineteenth century. Sandford is of further interest because he includes engravings of the burial place of Richard, son of William the Conqueror in the south presbytery wall; and of Cardinal Beaufort's chantry.

Other Restorations

A few glimpses into the gradual restoration of the Cathedral may be given as representing the enormous undertaking. Amongst the very earliest acts was an order to restore the Communion Plate to the Cathedral which had fallen into the hands of a certain Jack Dash during the years of the Commonwealth *(W.C.D.* 2.103). This was essential if the Holy Communion was to be celebrated at Christmas 1660 in accordance with the notions of the time. In the following year the loyalty of churchmen to the Crown tried to make good the sacrilege inflicted on the relics of ancient princes and prelates. The translation of the Latin on one of the Mortuary Chests built in 1661 to encase the earlier survivals may be translated as follows:

> In this chest, A.D. 1661, were promiscuously laid together the bones of princes and prelates which had been scattered about by sacrilegious barbarism in the year 1642.

Repairs to the Deanery and other houses were set in hand in 1662 (*W.C.D.* 2.135f.). Then, and this is hardly surprising, despite the valiant stand of Nicholas Fiennes the chantry of William of Wykeham was in need

Transcription

The meshuer of ye Altter

The plaine where ye Commandements are writ is 8 Foot & 4 inches deepe & a 11 Foot wide

The hanging betwixt the bottome of the Commandements & the Altter table
. . . . .Foot wide and 6 Foot deepe at
. . . . the only of ye table: ye bot . . . . me of both end
For 2 Foot 7 inches is . . . . . inches
wide for there is no aney hanger behind
the table. The hanging is cut in this manner

Diagram

The Altter table is 7 Foot
Long: 3 Foot broad & 3 Foot 4 inches high

of restoration and this was undertaken by the College in 1664 at a cost of £11.7s. The work was undertaken by William Bird (or Byrd) of Oxford (See T. F. Kirby. *Annals of Winchester College,* p.353). By 1666 the Sacrist was able to draw up an inventory which indicates that the furnishings of the Cathedral began to look more like our expectations. Two references are of particular interest. One refers to a Purple Prayer Book which seems to have differentiated it from the Prayer Book over the altar bound in crimson which was a gift of Charles II. The purple suggests that it was either given by or intended for the Bishop. In addition there is a reference to 12 large Turkey cushions for the Chapter House. These were for the prebendaries whose successors, though diminished in number, can now have the cushions both in the Chapter Room and in the Sanctuary. The Elbow Chair (presumably for the Dean) and the 12 chairs of Russian leather no longer survive. (*W.C.D.* 2. 120.)

Convocation and Parliament

The new Dean and Prebendaries could have been excused if they had said that they had enough to do caring for their Cathedral, the Close and Choir and immediate problems without sharing in the wider councils of the Church. On the contrary, with Bishop Morley setting an example, they took their full part in the Convocations or Parliament of the Church. The Bishop was not only a member of the Upper House of Convocation but, even more important, he was a member of the Upper House of Parliament at a time when the House of Lords wielded considerable power. The votes of the bishops could sway or topple governments. The Dean and Canons had no such position. The Dean, however, was *ex-officio* a member of Convocation and the Chapter had one representative or proctor, Nicholas Preston. Bishop, Dean, and Canon played their part in the new Prayer Book of 1662 with its additional services: *The Form of Prayer for the Thirtieth of January* (i.e. the martyrdom of Charles I); *The Form of Prayer for the Twenty Ninth of May* (i.e. the return of Charles II); and the *Ministration of Baptism to such as are of Riper Years,* a service intended for those who had not been baptised during the years of the Commonwealth and also for the natives of the colonies in North America and for 'others converted to the faith.'

Opposite: The restoration of the High Altar as depicted by the engraving in the Genealogical History of the Kings of England, published in 1677.

The High Altar, 1677

For political reasons the life of the newly restored Convocation was short lived, so that it soon became impossible for either Dean or Proctor to take part in any of the central councils of the Church.[16] The position of the Bishop was different. Although he could play no part in a non-existent Convocation, he was able to, and did, in fact, play a very full part in Parliament, not missing a meeting of the Upper House until infirmity prevented him. He observed that his purpose in that House was "the securing of the legally established government of the Church . . . and the State".[17]

Bishop Duppa

The Bishops of Winchester although closely associated with their Cathedral play little part in the day to day running of it. They act as Visitors and exercise certain episcopal duties in them, particularly ordination. The Restoration bishops were no exception. They were not enthroned in their Cathedral, save by proxy, and ordinations were rare. In fact, only two ordinations in the Cathedral can be traced between 1660 and 1684, the year of Morley's death. The Cathedral, therefore, was left very much to itself. At the same time Winchester was fortunate at this juncture in its history in having in quick succession two bishops who were very interested in it: Brian Duppa from 1660 to 1662[18] and George Morley from 1662 — 1684.

Duppa is best remembered in the Cathedral for his return of the statues of James I and Charles I which were removed during the Civil War and which finally lay buried in the Isle of Wight. The full story of the statues is revealed in a letter in 1660 from the Bishop to members of the Dean and Chapter. The only factual point which needs adding is that the Bishop paid £100 from his own purse so that the statues could be restored, not to their position at the west end of the Cathedral, but to their original places in the Inigo Jones Screen at the entrance to the Quire which had survived the Commonwealth. When the Inigo Jones Screen was removed in the 19th century the statues were placed in the new stone screen of Garbett. When that in turn was replaced by the present wooden screen of Sir Gilbert Scott, the statues were moved to their present position at the west end of the Cathedral: James I is the one nearer the north west door; Charles I is on the south side. For many years a sermon was preached on the anniversary of the death of Charles, January 30th., and a wreath placed upon the statue. The special service for that day remained in the Book of Common Prayer until 1859. An annual procession was still made to the statue in Dean Hutton's time (1919 — 1930) on January 30th and a wreath placed upon it.

Bishop Morley

Morley's association with the Cathedral and with Winchester was greater because of the longer period which he had in which to show that interest, even so he did not come to Winchester to be enthroned. Prebendary Bradshaw was his proxy for the occasion. As Visitor it was his duty either of his volition or because requested by the Archbishop to ensure that the services of the Cathedral conformed to the highest standards. The Cathedral was immediately visited by Archbishop Juxon in 1662. [19] In 1670, Archbishop Sheldon reminded Morley that the cathedrals were to set the standard for the parish churches 'in the solemnity and decent manner of reading the Liturgy and administering the Holy Sacraments . . . The Holy Communion ought to be celebrated by one of themselves at least every Sunday and Holy day in the year'. The Archbishop's instruction was duly heeded and the Chapter Book reveals that action was taken for the 'better and more orderly celebration of divine services and sacraments.' Failure in this matter rendered the offending canon liable to the considerable fine of forty shillings.

The Library

There are, however, three visible reminders of Morley's influence on the Cathedral and on Winchester which are still much alive nearly three hundred years after his death: the Cathedral Library, the Morley College, and Wolvesey Palace. A scholar himself, he realised that the Cathedral Library was almost wholly destroyed and that the clergy themselves in the parishes did not have the resources to accumulate libraries of any substance. Nor were there any libraries to which they might resort (once they had left Oxford or Cambridge). At an early stage, therefore, he let the Dean and Chapter know that it was his purpose to leave them his library in his will[20]. Meanwhile, the Library was given a new floor and books, manuscripts, and archives which survived the Commonwealth were returned from Winchester College. In 1672 he drew up a provisional manuscript catalogue of his books and ten years later a definitive catalogue written in a handsome vellum volume.[21] It contained some two thousand titles, more in Latin than in English; about two thirds from countries in the rest of Europe and on every subject which interested a seventeenth century scholar: theology, of course, but also history, politics, travel, the emergent sciences, geography and literature.

Morley died in 1684 and two years later the transfer of his Library with the purchase of the globes which he requested in his will was complete. Shelving, possibly dating from c 1620 and coming from Farnham Castle, was used and a library of over two thousand volumes came into existence. A few years later Bernard's catalogue of manuscripts was published revealing that the Cathedral manuscripts were now only seventeen in number.[22]

Morley College, 1672

A new work of charity became visible in The Close with the erection of the Morley College for the widows of clergy from the dioceses of Winchester and Worcester (where Morley had previously served) and from the Manor of Taunton Dean (from which the Bishop derived some of his revenues). The Dean and Chapter were trustees for the College and contributed the sum of £161 annually (which they still contribute) to the running of the College. As years passed many of the canons and others left legacies to increase the funds.

The College was rebuilt in the 19th century and again completely restored in 1976 so that it is still fulfilling the purpose for which it was established. To-day help is given to eight clergy widows. Financial responsibility for the College has been greatly broadened.

THE COLLEGE FOR MINISTERS WIDOWS

This College was erected by Bishop Morley Aᵒ. 1672 for the Maintenance of ten Ministers Widows.

Wolvesey

Characteristic of the man was the fact that the last thing Morley did was to build a Palace at Winchester for himself. He never enjoyed it himself but caused a most gracious house to be built, possibly by Sir Christopher Wren.[23]

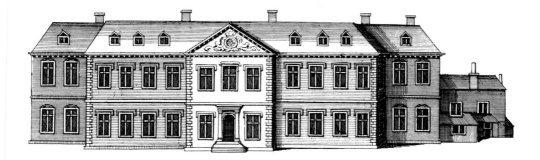

THE BISHOP'S PALACE.

This palace was begun by Bishop Morley who died October the 29th Anno 1684, but was finished by Sr Jonathan Trelawney.

The Bishop's Palace to-day.

Cathedral Music and Musicians

In 1660 the musical tradition fostered by Laud had been broken for some fifteen years. The very skills of cathedral music were in danger of being forgotten. What was true generally, was true of Winchester in particular. Two precious musical links with the past survived: William Taylour, the Precentor, and Christopher Gibbons, the Master of the Choristers. At the time of the abolition of the Dean and Chapter, Gibbons had joined the Royalist cause. In 1660, he took up residence in Cheyney Court and for the 'tyme being' was allowed "to keep his song schoole there". He did not stay long, being promoted organist of the Chapel Royal, Westminster Abbey and Organist to Charles II in 1661.

To guide the few remaining musicians and especially their pupils there was published in 1661 and again, in revised form in 1664, *A Short Direction for the Performance of Cathedrall* (sic) *Service, publish't for the information of such Persons as are ignorant of it, and shall be call'd to officiate in Cathedral and Collegiate Churches, where it hath formerly been in use.* The author was Edward Lowe, professor of music in Oxford. A copy of these guide-lines is still in the Cathedral Library, indicating the awareness that existed of the need to learn again the essentials of the tradition of Cathedral music. The art of imparting this information fell to Christopher Gibbons' successor, John Silver.[24] He had a more immediate problem. He needed an organ. Organ builders were few and far between and the Dean and Chapter had to give it its due place in their priorities among the needs of the Cathedral itself, its primary essentials for worship, the restoration of the cathedral staff and their necessary accommodation. All of which meant that the organ had to wait till July, 1665 before it could be rebuilt. Of the four organ builders[25] in the country they chose Thamar of Peterborough and signed a contract with him. To add to the problem the Chapter had to migrate to Alresford to avoid the plague. The ensuring fumigation of the music cost 2s 6d. At last by Christmas 1665 "the chanting service" was resumed. The new organ was erected on the north side of the Quire and was due to be completed by St. Michael and All Angels' Day (September 29), 1666. In the event, the account was not finally settled until 21st. November, 1670. The life of the organ proved to be short. The organist at this time was Randal Jewett. He was succeeded by John Reading (author of *Dulce Domum*) in 1675. Both are mentioned in the *D.N.B.* A strange reference (*W.C.D.* 2.177) is a letter from a certain Thomas Webb, who writes to the Dean to say that he has 'faithfully performed my owne duty'. Was he a *locum tenens?*

A

REVIEW

Of fome Short

DIRECTIONS

For performance of

Cathedrall Service.

Publifhed for the Information
of fuch, as may be called to Officiate in Cathedral or Collegiate-
Churches ; or Religioufly defire to
bear a part in that Service.

The Second Edition.

With many ufefull Additions relating to the
Common Prayer-Book, as it is now eftablifhed.

By *E. L.*

OXFORD
Printed, by *W. Hall,* for *Richard Davis,*
(A. Dom.) M.DC.LXIV.
1664

A Choristers' Contract, 1690.

Reading was succeeded by Daniel Roseingrave (1681 — 1692). As it has never been printed before we add an excerpt from a chorister's contract dated April 28th, 1690: [26]

. . . . The condition of this obligation is such that whereas John Bryon son of John Bryon deceased is admitted a chorister of the Cathedral Church aforesaid . . . . . the said John Bryon shall from time to time and at all times hereafter be constantly at Morning and Evening Prayer at the said Church and shall daily be at the Singing School of Mr. Daniel Roseingrave, master of the choristers of the said church at such hours and times as he shall appoint and not depart thence without the leave of his singing master and shall from time to time observe the directions and instructions . . . . . until he shall be by the Dean and Chapter therefrom acquitted and discharged.

Renatus Harris (1693)

The shortage of organ builders led to the importing of continental builders such as the famed "Father" Smith (Bernhardt Schmidt) and the French René (or Renatus) Harris. The latter was called in to rebuild the organ in 1693. This work, reported the Dean and Chapter on November 25, 1700, was "soe much out of tune that the services and anthems cannot be played thereon." Nevertheless one of the Harrises continued to tune the organ until 1743 when Mr. Bridge was given the contract.

The Bells

Though organists and campanologists find it hard to co-exist in, the pursuit of their arts, this is an appropriate place to refer to the restoration of the Cathedral bells which had no doubt remained silent during a more puritanical regime. In 1674 a contract was agreed by the Dean and Chapter and Henry Knight, bell-founder of Reading. The final account shows that two bells, the Treble and the Second bell were re-cast. The cost was 14 shillings per hundred weight. The local carrier, Henry Spearing, took the old bells to Reading and brought back the new ones. For his trouble he received £3.11.0, with £1.15.4 for "Four dayes and three nights expenses for two men and two horses." (*C.C.P.* March 10th., 1674).

Other Lay Members of the Foundation

Among the virgers we must pay particular attention to John Baskerville whose burial took place in the north transept. This stone and that of his wife and young child can still be seen. Baskerville was clearly a very competent person. He was respectful to the Dean and Canons, at the same time managing their affairs. One quotation from his letter to the Dean, staying in London in 1675, indicates what manner of man he was:

Winton Jan: 15: 75

Reverend Sr.

God be praised, all freinds at Winton are in good health . . . . . (then follows a list of practical details which he has attended to for the Dean) . . . . . . I propounded a wall to be built a distance from ye Deanry house and 2 or 3 buttrises which Dr. Beeston approves very well of: . . . . . there was a Chapter called for as soone as your Worship went from Winton . . . . . Humbly craving your Worship's Pardon for them who be

Your Worship's obedient Servants

John Baskerville.

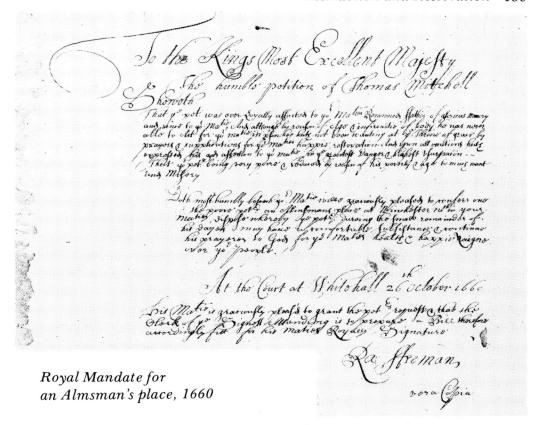

*Royal Mandate for
an Almsman's place, 1660*

Almsmen or Bedesmen

The Cathedral Statutes requiring the Dean and Chapter to look after 12 poor men were soon re-invoked. On October 26th., 1660 the King commanded a place for a certain Thomas Mitchell due to his 'infirmitie of body'. On April 27th 1661 a further place was commanded for John Heath.

An almsman's place was awarded at the direction of the King. Each document tells of the service given by the proposed almsman or bedesman and often describes his wounds. There must have been some harrowing sights around the Cathedral. We quote one: The King addresses the Dean and Chapter:-

Trusty and Well Beloved Wee greet you well. Letting you weet that Wee minding the releife of Our poore Subject John Hewett who served Us on Board our Ship the Expedition . . . . . was blowne up by Powder which occasioned the loss of the sight of both his Eyes

The King then requests an almsman's place for John Hewett.

At any one time we have to imagine twelve such men, almost always old soldiers or sailors pensioned in this way and living round the Cathedral. The cost of 12 almsmen was £80 a year.[28]

Izaak Walton

Most famous of all the laymen who lived in the Close is Morley's own steward or *oeconomus* Izaak Walton, who lived with Morley first in Worcester, then in Farnham Castle and finally in one of the Houses of the Close. It was at Winchester that he wrote his will.[29]

> AUGUST the ninth One thousand six hundred eighty three
> IN THE NAME OF GOD AMEN.
>   I Izaak Walton of the Close Winchester being this present day in the ninetyeth yeare of my age and in perfect memory . . . .

Then follow his legacies to his son, another Izaak Walton, to his son in law Dr. Hawkins (in whose house he lived in The Close), to his birthplace, Stafford, and finally to other beneficiaries. Mourning rings he left to a number of his friends including Thomas Ken. After his death the inventory prepared for probate lists many items of his in Winchester: books, a cabinet and concludes with:-

> ITEM Fishing Tackle and other Lumber, 10s.

To such a modest end came the fishing rods of the Complete Angler.

Walton knew Morley before Cromwell came to power. When Morley returned to England in 1660 he soon got in touch with him and appointed him his Steward at Worcester where Morley was Bishop. When he came to Winchester (the bishop's residence was at Farnham Castle), Walton came with him, still as Steward (oeconomus). In due course his family became related to the Ken family by marriage and Walton spent some time not only at Farnham but also in the Close. During Morley's time he completed a quintet of lives of churchmen which are among the jewels of English prose. The first one had been produced in 1640, the Life of John Donne. After the return of the Church in 1660 he wrote, under the protection of Morley, the lives of Hooker, Herbert, Sir Henry Wotton (Walton's close friend and fellow angler, famous for the adage that an ambassador's duty was to lie abroad for the benefit of his country) and finally in 1678, the Life of Bishop Sanderson. It was Sanderson who wrote the famous Preface to the Book of Common Prayer which begins: "It hath been the wisdom of the Church of England, ever since the first compiling of her Publick Liturgy, to keep the mean between the two extremes . . . . ."

Lovers of beautiful prose will wish to read the whole passage.

The memory of Walton still lingers persistently in the Cathedral, his tomb being visited by many thousands every year.

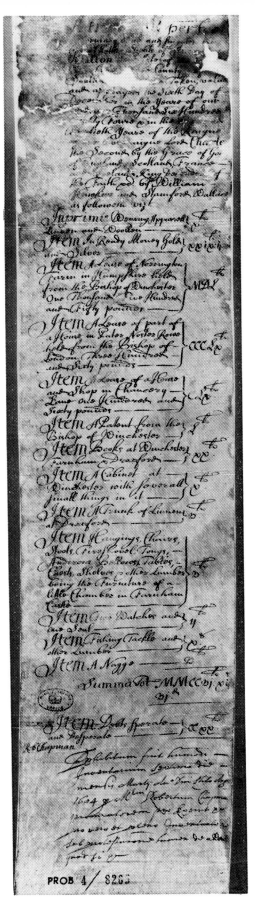

Part of Probate inventory

of Izaak Walton.

Cathedral Finances

To meet the annual stipends of the Dean (£200) and of the canons (£31.11.4) money was necessary as it was for the other servants of the Cathedral: musicians, works staff, virgers. In addition, much work had to be undertaken in repairing the Cathedral; and re-building or repairing extensively the houses in the Close. By degrees the Cathedral recovered its lands and properties which had been sold to others when Cromwell came to power. They now had to be returned to their original owners, i.e. to the Dean and Chapter. This was inevitably a painful process for the dispossessed. Charles asked that the process be made as considerate as possible and so far as ministers of religion were concerned they had until August 24th, 1662 to decide whether or not they could accept the use and teaching of the Book of Common Prayer.

So painfully, the lands which had previously belonged to the Dean and Chapter in 1642 were returned to their original owners, and the rents arising out of these lands made it possible to pay stipends and salaries and to begin repairs on Cathedral and Close. Some idea of the extent of the income can be gathered from the fact that in the ten years 1660 to 1670 the Dean and Chapter spent £59,485.

One amusing item of expense was found in the Cathedral Clock listing some repairs in 1673:-

	£	s	d
To work done repairing St. Joseph			8
Cleaning . . . . . the Holy Spirit			6
Repairing the Virgin Mary before and behind and making a new child		4	8
Screwing a nose on the devil, putting a horn on his head and glewing a piece on his tail		5	6

In October, 1660, only four of the 13 houses in The Close were standing. Cloisters and Library were ruined and there was no place where a meeting could be held. Those in Dome (Latin: *domus,* house) Alley were first built and others followed later. One house (No. 1) has the date of the foundation stone still visible: Aug ye 22. 1699. The rebuilding of The Close took at least forty years. It is possible to see in the *Wainscott Book* every detail of the cost of this rebuilding as it spread over the years and as finance became available. The last house (No. 11) to be completed was built early in the next century.

Izaak Walton

Reverend Landlords and their Tenants

The sources for these necessary funds to restore the Cathedral and the houses of The Close continued to be what they had always been: the estates scattered over Wessex from Hampshire to the Bristol Channel. Their mode of administration continued to be substantially what it had always been despite changes on the estates themselves. For example there were now no more serfs working on the land. The administration was recorded no longer on rolls but in books. A popular and informative account of the period so far as it affected the estates of Winchester Cathedral is given in Florence Goodman's, *Reverend Landlords and their Tenants*.[30] The book quotes extensively from surviving correspondence of the period.

The principal manors and rectories held by the Dean and Chapter were:

Manors	*Rectories*
HAMPSHIRE	Aldbourne
Barton	Alton Parva
Bransbury	Barton Stacy
Chilbolton	Binstead and Kingsley
Crondal	Blandford
Exton	Bulkington
Hinton Ampner	Candover, Preston
Littleton	Christchurch
Manydown	Collingbourne
Moor Court	Crewkerne
Shipton Bellinger	Durrington
Silkstead	East Challow
Thurmonds	Gresford
Upsomborne	Hursley
Whitchurch	Keevil
Wonston [Wonsington]	Langhorne
	Letcombe Regis
SOMERSET	Litttleton
Bleadon	Nutley
	Piddletrenthide
WILTSHIRE	Quidhampton
Aldbourne	Romsey
Alton Parva	Titchfield
{ Beechingstoke, Botwell,	Wanborough
and Longstreet	
Elstub and Everly hundred	
Ham	
Hinton Parva	
Westwood	
Wroughton	

It is little different from the list of monastic manors before the Reformation.

Instead of prior and monks it was now the Dean and canons who went on progress with their officials to their estates to collect their rents and to keep an eye on the behaviour of their tenants. A typical progress in August, 1682 is representative of annual progresses:

Progress, August, 1682

14th *Bransbury* court and dinner. *Chilbolton*, night.
15th *Chilbolton* court, dinner, and night.
16th *Shipton* court and dinner, *Longstreet* night.
17th *Wroughton* court and dinner and night.
18th *Wroughton* dinner. *Hiniton* night.
19th *Hiniton* dinner and night.
20th *Wanborough* dinner and night (Sunday).
21st *Ham* court and dinner and night. Monday.
22nd*Whitchurch* borough court and dinner and night.
23rd *Whitchurch* manor court dinner and night.
24th *Wonsington* court and dinner and home at night
25th *Barton* Court and dinner, home at night.
26thand 27th. *Winchester* (Sat. and Sun.)
28th *Manydowne* At night.
29th *Manydowne* court and dinner and night. Tuesday.
30th *Crondal* court dinner and night.
31st *Crondal* court dinner and night.

Then the total of income from the manors was transferred to the Treasurer who, from 1691, also had a book in which to keep the Cathedral accounts for each particular year.

Charles II and James II

One final feature is worth noting. During this period there emerged the last indication that Winchester might become once again a royal city, a kind of English Versailles. Charles II was very fond of Winchester. It took him away from London, offered him the kind of recreation he liked and was strategically placed between Portsmouth, so important because of the Royal Navy, and London, the seat of government and decision.

In 1683 Charles II issued what today might be called a compulsory purchase order which forbade the Dean and Chapter to sell any land or property which lay in the route of the proposed mall which he had in mind from the main entrance of the Palace to the great West Door of the Cathedral.[31] The only relics of the proposal are the four massive columns in the centre of the barracks now occupied by the Royal Green Jackets. As for Nell Gwynne, when accommodation was sought for her, Thomas Ken, most saintly of canons, refused to give 'poor Nellie lodging'. Nevertheless in 1684 the King appreciated Ken's strong character and not only offered him the bishopric of Bath and Wells, but when he lay dying he asked that Ken might visit him on his death-bed.

Charles was present at a service in the Cathedral on September 9th, 1683. Then we have records of royal occasions within the Deanery. The Long Gallery is traditionally the place said to have been added to the Deanery to provide an area where Charles, and later James II, and his guests could move about freely. The diarist John Evelyn tells of his own visit to the Cathedral and the Deanery in 1685. He had visited the Cathedral over forty years earlier and records his impressions of 16th September, 1685:-

> "I went to see the Cathedral, a revered pile, & in good repaire: There is still the Coffins of the 6 Saxon Kings, whose bones had been scattered by the sacrilegious Rebells of 1641 (sic), in expectation (I suppose) of finding some valuable Reliques: and afterwards gather'd up again & put in new chests, which stand above the stalls of the Quire: Here lies the body of their Founder, . . . & several other Bishops &c."

Evelyn later left the Deanery and saw the progress being made on the New Palace which Charles II had begun "and brought almost to the covering . . . . a stately fabrique of three sides, & a corridor, all built of brique, and Cornished, windoes, Columns at the break & Entrance, of freestone: intended for a hunting House, when his Majestie came to these parts."

Thus by the end of the century the Church in Winchester was visibly restored. The Bishop had his new palace; Dean and Prebendaries had their houses; the Cathedral itself was repaired and adorned and the necessary manpower to maintain the music and work of the Cathedral along with its estates had once again been recruited. The destruction wrought in 1642 and subsequent years was more or less made good. Inevitably there were losses that could never be replaced. But only the eye of faith and certainly not the calculations of worldly wisdom in 1654 when Dean Young died, would, have thought that within less than a decade the Church would return and that within a further generation it could boast some of the most eminent churchmen who have brought lustre to the history of the Cathedral. Morley, Ken, Walton and Evelyn are indeed names of which to be proud.

NOTES

1 *Mercurius Rusticus*, 1685.p.145.
2 *W.C.R.*, 1955.pp.6 — 8' *Wykeham's Chantry and Nathaniel Fiennes.*
3 *W.C.D.* 2. pp. 71 — 74.
4 M. Biddle. *Winchester in the Early Middle Ages.* Oxford, 1976. p.2.
5 *Historia Maior* is in H. Wharton *Anglia Sacra.* 2 Vols. 1691. Vol. 1. pp.179 — 286.
6 *W.C.D.* 2. p.98.
7 A. G. Matthews. *Calamy Revised.* Oxford, 1934. s.v. Gale T., Ellis H., Teate F.
8 E. Stanley. *Three Sermons, Preached in Winchester Cathedral, 1660 — 1661.* London, 1662.
9 T. Gumble. *The Life of General Monck,* 1671. M. Ashley, the latest biographer of General
Monck (1977). refers frequently to Gumble. He admits that Gumble's work made his own
undertaking 'much more comfortable'.
10 R. Sharrock. *Provinciale,* 1679. *History of the Propagation of Vegetables* 1660.
11 Ses Le Neve *Fasti, 1541 — 1857.* Ed by Joyce Horn. *London, 1974.*
12. T. Ken. *A Manual of Prayers for the Use of the Scholars of Winchester College.* 1674.
13 E. Marshall *Winchester Meads.* London, 1902. p.136.
14 E. S. de Beer. *Diary of John Evelyn.* 6 Vols. Oxford, 1955. Vol. IV. pp.468 — 472.
15 E. H. Plumptre. *The Life of Thomas Ken.* 2 Vols. London, 1889. Vol. 1.p.92.
16 E. Cardwell. *Synodalia.* 2 Vols. Oxford, 1842. Vol. 2. pp. 692.ff.
17 H.M.C. *Leeds Papers* p.14.
18 *Correspondence of Bishop Duppa and Sir Justinian Isham, 1650 — 1660.*
Northamptonshire Record Society, 1951.
19 *W.C.D.* 2.106.
20 *W.C.D.* 2. p.141. (October 3rd., 1667).
21 *Catalogue of Bishop Morley's Library Winchester Cathedral, 1682.* Ms.
22 E. Bernard. *Catalogi Librorum Manuscriptorum Ecclesiae Cathedralis S. Swithuni apud Winton.*
Oxford, 1697.
23 C. Wren. *Parentalia.* 1750. p.326.
24 John Silver also incised his name on one of the columns of the nave.
25 J. S. Bumpus. *A History of English Cathedral Music, 1549 — 1889.* 2 Vols. London, n.d. p.113.
26 Winchester Cathedral Ms.
27 Winchester Cathedral Ms.
28 Documents signed by the Sovereign requesting an almsman's place are numerous in the Cathedral
Archive from the reign of Charles I to that of George III.
29 P.R.O. Prob. 11/375.
30 F. R. Goodman. *Reverend Landlords and their Tenants.* Winchester, 1930.
31 A full account of the proposed royal palace at Winchester can be found in the seventh
volume of the Wren Society, Oxford, 1930. pp.11 — 72 and pp. 231 — 233.

FURTHER READING

F. Bussby. *Izaak Walton and Winchester.* Winchester, 1975.
C.A. 1660 — 1696 & 1696 — 1739
C.C.P. 1645 — 1661; 1662 — 1664
C.S.P.D. 28th Feb. 1661. Christopher Gibbons
F. Costa L'Oeuvre D'Izaak Walton. Toulouse, 1973.

D.N.B.   s.v. Fiennes N. M.P.   Markland A. preb.
    Gawen T. preb.   Meggot R. dean
    Gibbons C. organist   Reading J. organist
    Gumble T. preb.   Roseingrave D. organist
    Hyde A. dean   Sharrock R. preb.
    Jewett R. organist   Ward Seth preb.
    Levinz B. preb.   Woodforde S. preb.

Fiennes C. *The Journeys of Celia Fiennes.* Ed. C. Morris. London, 1947. p. 47.
Kennett W. *Register* 1660 — 1662. Numerous references.
L.B. Vols. XIV — XXII: 1660 — 1707. MSS.
R.B. Receiver's Books.
T.B. Treasurer's Books.
F.Turner. *A Sermon Preached before the King in the Cathedral Church of Winchester* . . . .
Septemb. 9. 1683. London, 1683. After the frustration of a conspiracy against the King.
D. H. Woodforde. *Woodforde Diaries and Papers.* London, 1932. (1684 . . .).

The Quire in the 18th century

Chapter IX

The Life of a Prebendary

"The life of a prebendary" wrote Edmund Pyle,[1] prebendary of Winchester from 1756 to 1776 "is a pretty easy way of dawdling away one's time; praying, walking, visiting; and as little study as your heart would wish." Speaking of a colleague, Arthur Ashley Sykes (1740 — 1756), a prolific author, he writes "Old Sykes is here, brewing a pamphlet to prove historically that the Resurrection (of the body) was never any part of any Christian creed, for the first three hundred and fifty years".[2]

In a rapid survey of the eighteenth century these quotations (and the first has been used on a number of occasions) could easily leave the impression that the whole church during the eighteenth century was lethargic, cynical and decadent. In the case of Winchester we might add, for bad measure, the case of Prebendary Alsop (1715-26) who, in 1717, was sued for breach of promise and obliged to flee the country after paying £2,000 damages.[3]

A somewhat farcical incident is recorded in 1722 when a visiting clergyman inveighed against all those who enjoyed better preferment than he did. The Dean and prebendaries sent the virger to tell him to come down from the pupit. He refused to do so and was only finally silenced when the organist began to play.

Another prebendary who might be quoted as an easy going clergyman is John Hoadly (1737 — 1760), son of Bishop Hoadly, friend of Hogarth and author the the play *The Suspicious Husband,* first published in 1747 which offered a vehicle for the acting skill of the celebrated David Garrick. He could write to Hogarth to say that he visited his parish at Old Alresford occasionally as the shepherd should be seen among his flock even if only to fleece them. At the same time he could succeed Alured Clarke as Chairman of the newly created Hospital in Winchester and leave a generous bequest to the Morley College.

The Cathedral Fabric

The above, like any quotations and illustrations, need to be kept in perspective. In addition, no century should be judged by standards of a later century. It has to be remembered that in 1660 the Cathedral had been much damaged and its life wholly disrupted. A major effort ensued in which fabric and life were restored. It would be natural, therefore, to find a slackening of effort after the intense activity of a generation or more. This is exactly what we find. The Treasurers' books, faithfully kept over the years, give detailed accounts year by year of money spent on every aspect of cathedral life.

Although the cathedral had no need of major reconstruction, a number of additions were made to the fabric during this period. Those which have since disappeared are Bishop Trelawney's throne (1706) built in classical style to match the Inigo Jones screen; the classical urns placed in the niches of the reredos where formerly had stood the figures of the saints (1700). On the other hand, certain works still remain to adorn and serve the cathedral: the handsome candelabra donated by Dean Cheyney in 1756; the iron screen donated by Prebendary Eyre (1701 — 1722) in front of what is now the Venerable Chapel; and the massive wooden frame for the holding of the bells in the tower which was so well constructed as still to be serviceable despite the great weight of bells rung week by week. Nevertheless these works were comparatively minor as the sums expended on the fabric and recorded in the Treasurers' books. Taking the middle of the period, say 1735 to 1740, the following sums were expended:-

1735	£288	1738	£222
1736	£195	1739	£ 55
1737	£ 74	1740	£193

There is not a great difference in any of the years from 1700 to 1775.

Bishop Hoadly, 1734 — 1761

For a large part of this period, the Bishop of Winchester was Benjamin Hoadly whose writings gave a name to a whole period of theological thought and controversy. Before coming to Winchester, he had been Bishop of Bangor from 1715 to 1721. His writings[4] and the writings of his theological opponents came to be known as the Bangorian Controversy. It raged round the thesis that the Gospels afford no warrant for any visible church authority. His monument in the cathedral placed Magna Carta in juxtaposition with the

The Rt. Rev. Benjamin Hoadly.

Gospels. Such a view suited entirely the statesmen of the day and it was to them that Hoadly looked for promotion. From Bangor he went to Hereford, from there to Salisbury whence in 1734 he wrote the following letter to the Prime Minister Sir Robert Walpole, craving promotion to the see of Winchester (*The Gentleman's Magazine,* 1811. Vol. III p.236.).

Aug. 8th., 1734.

Sir,

Hearing from all hands the desperate condition in which the Bishop of Winchester is (if not already dead) I flatter myself you will not take it amiss that I express to you . . . my entire dependence upon those kind words you have often said to me upon this subject . . . Sir, it would be the highest indignity towards you if I did not, upon this occasion repose myself without uneasiness or doubt upon you . . . I am sure, for myself I shall study, through my life, to shew myself in an uncommon manner and upon all possible occasions, Sir, your most faithful and obedient servant

BENJ. SARUM

The letter achieved its desired result. Hoadly was translated to Winchester. Not that, so far as we can tell, he ever visited the city or the cathedral. Nevertheless, he did influence it because it was he who appointed the canons who in turn were men sympathetic to Hoadly. As though to underline his view point he published, about the time of his translation, a new edition of his work *A Plain Account of the Nature and End of the Sacrament of the Lord's Supper*. His minimising theology was again apparent. Moreover, it drew a response from William Law, the celebrated nonjuror, a man of great spirituality who was serving at this time in the household of the famous Edward Gibbon, historian of the *Decline and Fall of the Roman Empire*.

Looking at the Bishop's monument in the Cathedral where he and his wife are buried, Milner declared that 'both living and dying he had undermined the church of which he was a prelate'.[5] This phrase gave rise to a controversy in which John Sturges (1759 — 1807) took the author to task, resulting in a famous series of letters by Milner (a Roman Catholic bishop) entitled *Letters to a Prebendary* which were several times reprinted even as far away as Cork (1802).

As with prebendaries, so with deans, it is possible by a selective use of quotations to imply that they lived a life of aristocratic ease unworthy of their office. Pyle,[6] in the year he described his own new life, describes an event at the Deanery: "The Dean of Winchester has a fine and large garden which is a place of resort on summer evenings for all the persons of fashion in the city." He then goes on to describe a ball given by the Dean for the benefit of the Hessian officers then in the city. He comments: " . . . all the gentry and quality were put together there; and for three hours twenty five couples danced on the lawn". He sums up the evening by referring less favourably to the dancing "of the English gentlemen ... (which) was what one may call 'romps run mad'."

Pyle's comments about himself and his Dean do not give a rounded picture of the time. It is necessary to look in some detail at these men. During this period there were seven deans: John Wickhart; William Trimnell; Charles Naylor; Zachary Pearce; Thomas Cheyney; Jonathan Shipley and Newton Ogle. Only two of them have been deemed sufficiently distinguished to merit a place in the *Dictionary of National Biography:* Zachary Pearce and Jonathan Shipley. The others, like most servants of the Cathedral, served it according to their lights. Little is known of Wickart, though he seems to have served William III overseas from time to time as chaplain, interpreter or secretary. Trimnell is recorded on his monument in the Cathedral as having "adorned his office as dean, being busy in fair and prudent administration; regular in preaching and at the services; and generous to the poor." This is no bad epitaph for any man. Naylor only lived to be forty-seven when he was buried beside his 'indivisible friend' Bishop Willis in the south aisle of the nave.

Zachary Pearce, however, was a considerable scholar and rose to be Bishop of Rochester. He earned Samuel Johnson's gratitude for sending him some twenty etymologies for his *Dictionary* when no one else gave him any help.[7] In return, Johnson added forty paragraphs to Pearce's autobiography and commented on his edition of Longinus *On the Sublime* (still in the Cathedral Library) that it was characterised by 'vigour and caution'.[9] Even a modern scholar declares that he has been helped by Pearce's translation, it being the best that there is (A. O. Prickard).[10] Pearce edited Longinus and Cicero and published commentaries on the Gospels and other books of the New Testament. After his death four volumes of his sermons appeared 1768. To his old cathedral he presented fifty volumes for the Library. His own works are still preserved there.

G. H. Blore has published a short account of Cheyney's life: *Thomas Cheyney, Wykehamist, Dean of Winchester, 1748 to 1760* (1950). Cheyney was educated at both foundations of William of Wykeham and spent all his life on his foundations apart from four years as dean of Lincoln. He returned to Winchester as dean in 1748. To-day we remember him because of the candelabra[11] and because of his charity to a French galley slave.

Jean Serres

In the Epiphany Chapel there is a monument to Jean Serres, who died in 1754 at the age of 85.[1] Behind the memorial is an interesting story. Serres was condemned to the galleys in the days of Louis XIV of France. He served for twenty-seven years. In 1713, as a result of the Peace of Utrecht, a number of galley slaves were freed. Among them was Jean Serres. He came finally to live at Winchester. The story of Jean and his two brothers who shared the same fate for their faith is told in *Les Trois Frères Serres* written by Gaston Tournier and published in Cevennes in 1937. Strange, writes Tournier, that three French Protestants should be better remembered in Winchester than anywhere else. Serres gave the Dean his French New Testament and his certificate of liberation. His letter to the Dean may be translated as follows:-

Dear Sir,

Here is the New Testament annotated by Monsieur Martin ... which he presented to me when I was a slave on the galleys in France for the sake of the Word of God, because of the great persecution of Louis XIV .... The divine book remained with me for many years in my chains, but the word of truth which it contained was not bound and helped me to overcome the lie and error of the papists which furiously assailed me. When God had finally broken my heavy chain, I carried it with me as proof of the miracle of his Providence who had preserved me among the thousand great dangers which surrounded me ...

Winchester. 1st August, 1740.

The date of the letter suggests that Cheyney came to know Serres while he was still at the College and before he became Dean.

On July 20th, 1888, the Huguenot Society of London as a body visited the Cathedral. There was a special service and Dean Kitchin gave an address, the text of which is preserved in the Huguenot archives.

Jonathan Shipley, 1760 — 1769

Perhaps the most distinguished of eighteenth century Deans was Jonathan Shipley, first a prebendary (1743 — 1760) and later Dean (1760 — 1769). Shipley's fame rests mainly on his political views. While Balguy, a fellow member of Chapter, preached on the disloyalty of American subjects rebelling against their King with their "inroads of infidelity and atheism," Shipley was increasingly friendly towards Benjamin Franklin and entertained

Dean Shipley

him at Twyford. His views, originally royalist, changed and his sympathies lay with the American colonies. He said: "I look upon North America as the only great nursery of freemen left on the face of the earth." These radical views did not prevent Shipley's elevation to the bench of bishops and he subsequently voiced his views in the House of Lords. Franklin said of him, on his death, had the "counsels of his sermon and speech been attended to, how much bloodshed might have been prevented . . . and disgrace to the nation avoided." Shipley was, in fact, a radical statesman. Three of his speeches in the House of Lords are included in the two volume edition of his sermons published after he left Winchester, in 1792.

Prebendary William Lowth, 1696 — 1732

Coming to the prebendaries of the Cathedral, we start with William Lowth. A pupil of Merchant Taylors, he learned Hebrew at school and, judging from a Syriac New Testament in the Cathedral Library he seems to have shewn interest in Syriac too during his later school days. From there he went to Oxford and distinguished himself as a good Hebrew scholar. On coming to Winchester a series of works on the Old Testament flowed from his pen. Johnson commented on them, in characteristic style: "To be sure, Sir, I would have you read the Bible with a commentary; and I would recommend Lowth and Patrick on the Old Testament".[13] In his later years Lowth co-operated with Bishop Patrick in a number of combined editions of Old Testament commentaries.

Beginning in 1714, he wrote commentaries on *Isaiah, Jeremiah, Ezekiel, Daniel and the Twelve Prophets* which appeared at regular intervals. His pastoral concern is revealed in a book which was several times reprinted: *Directions for the Profitable Study of Holy Scripture.* His commentaries were reprinted on a number of occasions in omnibus editions, sometimes along with the commentaries of Bishop Patrick and thus forming part of a complete commentary on the Bible. An interesting development was the issue in weekly parts of his commentaries towards the end of the eighteenth century.

Lowth was also Rector of Buriton where his epitaph reveals the true pastor that he was:

> "Near the outside of this wall lyeth the body of William Lowth, late Rector of this Church, who died May ye 17th 1732. And being dead desires to speak to his beloved parishioners, and sweetly to exhort them constantly to attend public worship of God, frequently to receive the Holy Communion and diligently to observe the good instruction given in this place, to breed up their children in the fear of God and to follow peace with all men and holiness, without which no man shall see God.
>
> "God give us all a happy meeting at the resurrection of the just."

William Lowth is a worthy representative of that large body of Anglican clergy who, through the years, have combined scholarship with pastoral zeal to a quite remarkable degree making them, among their contemporaries the *stupor mundi,* the amazement of the world.

DIRECTIONS

W^m FOR THE *Sanford*

Profitable Reading

OF THE

HOLY SCRIPTURES.

TOGETHER

With some OBSERVATIONS for the
Confirming their Divine Authority, and
Illustrating the Difficulties thereof.

By *WILLIAM LOWTH*, B.D.

Prebendary of WINCHESTER.

The THIRD EDITION.

LONDON:

Printed by J. BETTENHAM, for JONAH
BOWYER, at the *Rose* in Pater-noster Row:
and STEPHEN AUSTEN, at the *Angel* in
St. Paul's Church-Yard. 1726.

Archdeacon Robert Lowth, 1750 — 1756

William Lowth had an even more distinguished son, Robert, who was
born in The Close in 1710. After being Professor of Poetry at Oxford, he
became Archdeacon of Winchester in 1753 when he published one of the
epoch-making works of Biblical scholarship, the findings of which are still
accepted by Old Testament scholars throughout the world. He had given a
course of lectures at Oxford entitled: *De Sacra Poesi Hebraeorum* (The
sacred poetry of the Hebrews).[14] The work, a series of lectures in Latin, has
as its main theme the thesis that Hebrew poetry consists in various types of
parallelism. Two examples will give the reader an idea of his work. There is

a synonymous parallelism in which two members of a verse say more or less the same thing:-

> When Israel came out of Egypt
> And the house of Jacob from among the strange people.
>
> Psalm 114 v.1.

Then there is antithetic parallelism in which the second line is opposed in idea to the first:-

> Faithful are the wounds of a friend,
> But the kisses of an enemy are profuse.
>
> Proverbs 28 v.6.

This main thesis was elaborated by the author but its main lines have never been seriously challenged. Johnson's assessment of Robert Lowth was that "all Scotland could not muster learning enough for Lowth's prelections" (on Sacred Poetry).[15] The work attracted European attention. Professor Michaelis of Göttingen published Lowth's work in two volumes in Göttingen adding his own notes, in 1770.[16]

Edmund Gibson
Archdeacon of Surrey, 1710 — 1716

In a quite different field, another member of the Cathedral foundation was Edmund Gibson. In those days Surrey was in the diocese of Winchester and when Gibson was created archdeacon his installation is recorded in the Ledger Books of the Cathedral (xxiii.f.31). During his years of office he wrote a short book for the benefit of the parochial clergy, churchwardens and sidesmen informing them of the law of their church. This was the area of knowledge in which he became (and still remains) famous. The short lectures were followed three years later (1713) with a large two volume work entitled: *Codex Iuris Ecclesiastici Anglicani.*[17] It was published in enlarged form in 1761. Its subject is a detailed explanation of church law going back to its very beginnings and is still a rich source book for those concerned with the subject.

From the archdeaconry of Surrey he went to the bishopric, first, of Lincoln in 1716; and later, in 1723 of London. In 1734 he had the opportunity to return to Winchester but refused the offer, thus making way for Hoadly. Two centuries later Gibson's first major biography appeared in 1926. It was also the first major work on Church History by Norman Sykes who later became Dean of Winchester from 1958 to 1961.

King George College of Divines

This formidable learning on the Cathedral Chapter no doubt played a part in the suggestion among Archbishop Wake's papers[18] (Wake died in 1737) that there should be in Winchester a King George College of Divines in the King's House. The purpose of the proposed college was "To breed up fitting clergymen to the glory of God; the service of the Church of England as by law established; the peace, security of the realm and the safety honour and welfare of His Majesty."

The students were to be called Fellows because they were to be graduates in equal numbers from Oxford and Cambridge. Each was to have an award of £30 per annum to cover incidental expenses. All college expenses were to be met. Five professors of Divinity were to be elected to instruct fellows in:-

1.   Hebrew and Chaldee of the Old Testament; the Greek of the New; with the Greek Version of the Old.
2.   A Catechetical Course of Divinity to make them perfect in the whole body of it.
3.   Polemical divinity, especially with relation to the controversy of the Church of England with the Dissenters

Unfortunately the project came to nothing.

The King's House c.1750 (Victoria County History)

The Cathedral Library

After so many scholarly references this is perhaps the place in which to refer to the Cathedral Library. New catalogues of the Library were made, one for the Dean (*In usum Decani,* 1717) and one for more general use. Inscriptions in a number of books indicate that presentation copies were often received and the Chapter Records indicate that there was a steady augmentation of the holdings in the Library. The type of book added is noteworthy. The new interests in science and history are well represented. Indeed, an American scholar has made a detailed study of *Reading Vogues at English Cathedral Libraries of the Eighteenth Century.* The study, published in New York in 1964 by Dr. Paul Kaufman, is based on *The Borrower's Book* begun in 1728. It has the following note on the inside of the front cover: "Rev,end Sr. You are desired, when you have occasion to borrow any book out of this place, to set down ye name of the book, together with your own name & the day of the month, in this book."

The first book to be borrowed was *William of Malmesbury* and the first borrower Prebendary Lowth. Among the routine inspirations of the Dean and Chapter was the purchase of first editions as published and which have since become valuable. Between 1760 and 1775, a separate *Library Account* was kept but more usually the place is given each year, within the general accounts of the Treasurer, to Library income and expenditure. In the terms of the day it is called *Cista Bibliothecae* (The Library Chest).

There were no manuscript additions during this period but books by Winchester authors are well represented. Bishop Hoadly's works are present in three handsome imperial folios which were edited by and presented by his son John, himself a prebendary. He prefaces the work with a biography of his Father. The Bishop presented four volumes of Wilkins' *Concilia.* The works of Lowth, father and son, are well represented, so are Gibson, Pearce, and Shipley. The *Liber Donorum* (the Book of Gifts) lists the donations made each year. Even the apparently cynical Pyle left twenty volumes of pamphlets which are of great value to historians of the period. The wife of one of the Cathedral's most distinguished librarians, a scholar in her own right, Florence Goodman, has already made them the subject of a study entitled *Pretenders from the Pulpit* (Cambridge, 1933). An unusual gift to the Library was a fine collection of Roman coins by Prebendary Eyre (1730) which unfortunately were sold to the University of Leeds in 1954. The catalogue of the coins, made by Nott was written in 1837 "as far as his health enabled him to do so". In 1736 a catalogue of deeds and documents then in the possession of the Dean and Chapter, was written.

Joseph Bingham

The Library was designed primarily for the prebendaries. It was also intended for the diocesan clergy. One who early took advantage of this provision was Joseph Bingham, Rector of Headbourne Worthy. Bingham had been a Fellow of University College, Oxford and had been sent down to the country because some of his teachings were thought to be dangerous. Being 'sent down' was a serious sentence to a scholar. Outside Oxford and Cambridge there were no libraries. Even the British Museum had not been founded. Of course, bishops and noblemen and scholarly men like John Evelyn had their personal libraries. For the exiled Rector of Headbourne Worthy, however, it was but a short ride or walk to avail himself of the provision made by Bishop Morley. This he quickly did and for sixteen years he was concerned in producing a succession of volumes: in 1706, *The French Church's Apology for the Church of England;* between 1708 and 1722 he produced ten volumes of his *Antiquities of the Christian Church;* and between 1713 and 1714 he wrote *A Scholastical History of Lay Baptism.* The *Antiquities* quickly made a reputation in Europe and were translated from English into Latin in the University of Halle (1724-1731). In the preface to this work, both in English and Latin, there is this tribute to the Morley Library:-

> "The chief assistance I have hitherto had, is from the noble benefaction of one, who being dead, yet speaketh: I mean the renowned Bishop Morley, whose memory will for ever remain fresh in the hearts of the learned and the good; who, among many other eminent works of charity and generosity . . . . . bequeathed a very valuable collection of books to the Church of Winchester, for the Advancement of learning among parochial clergy. "

Within a generation, therefore, the Morley Library was known to scholars all over Europe. Bingham's *Antiquities* is still an authoritative work consulted by historians concerned with ecclesiastical precedents and recognised by historians as full and authoritative on early Christian practice and beliefs.

Further evidence of the stature of the work and that of Gale and Gibson in European eyes can be seen in the *Acta Eruditorum* which were published annually in Leipzig from 1682 to the middle of the eighteenth century. As each volume appeared it contained a series of (Latin) reviews which was circulated to scholars of all subjects throughout the whole of Europe. The reviews can still be examined in the Cathedral Library [19]

The Cathedral Library

Books about the Cathedral

Another facet of the advancement of learning in this period is the emergence of books *about* the Cathedral. In earlier times books had been written in Winchester on general history in which Winchester figures prominently from the days of the Anglo-Saxon Chronicle onwards. But we have to wait until the eighteenth century before we have a book exclusively about the Cathedral. The first such guide book was started by Henry Clarendon and completed and published by Stephen Gale in 1715. It appeared in a second edition in 1723. It is valuable for two main reasons. It

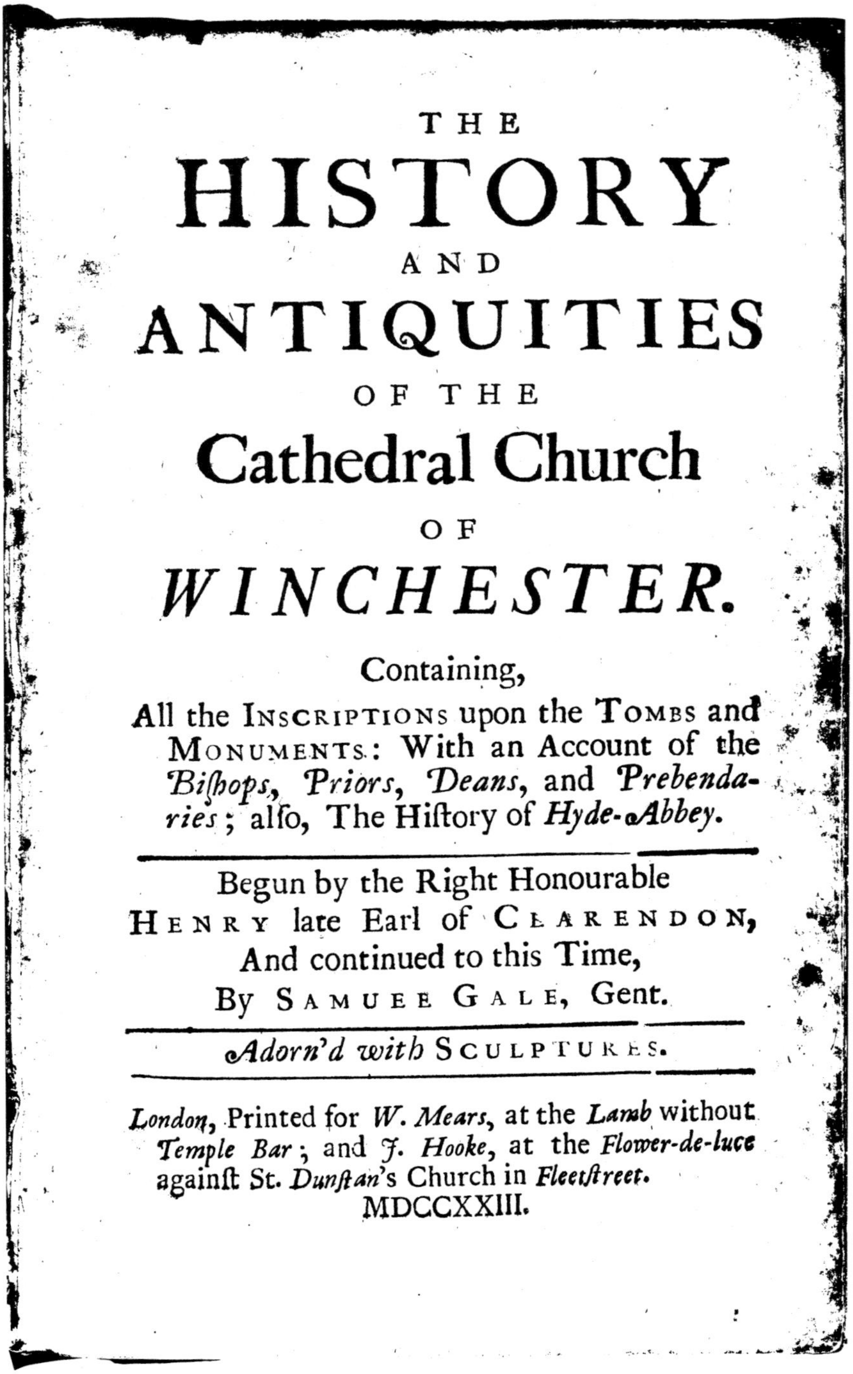

THE
HISTORY
AND
ANTIQUITIES
OF THE
Cathedral Church
OF
WINCHESTER.

Containing,

All the INSCRIPTIONS upon the TOMBS and
MONUMENTS: With an Account of the
Bishops, *Priors*, *Deans*, and *Prebenda-*
ries; alfo, The Hiftory of *Hyde-Abbey*.

Begun by the Right Honourable
HENRY late Earl of CLARENDON,
And continued to this Time,
By SAMUEL GALE, Gent.

Adorn'd with SCULPTURES.

London, Printed for *W. Mears*, at the *Lamb* without
Temple Bar; and *J. Hooke*, at the *Flower-de-luce*
againft St. *Dunftan*'s Church in *Fleetstreet*.
MDCCXXIII.

The first printed guide to the Cathedral. Second edition (1723) described the building as it was two and a half centuries ago. Its engravings provide a picture of features which have disappeared: the Inigo Jones screen, the accoutrements of the figure of Sir John Cloberry, the busts over the Earl of Portland in the Guardian Angels chapel, the wording of inscriptions now so worn as to be difficult or impossible to read. Gale, we may note, is also reviewed in the *Acta Eruditorum* (1716 Supplement pp. 392-395).

This was followed in 1773 by a guide to Winchester as a whole published in two volumes of which volume one is almost wholly devoted to the Cathedral.[20] The name of the author is not given but is generally thought to be Richard Wavell, a member of a Hampshire family which has produced devoted clergy and distinguished soldiers.

The County Hospital, 1736

The Prior and monks gave land in the 13th century on which the present St. Thomas Hospital, London, is built.[21] The custom of alms and charity was an integral part of monastic life. At the Reformation, the Statutes given by Henry VIII and revised by Charles I[22] continued that emphasis. Besides countless acts of casual charity, the Dean and Chapter maintained over twenty men and women in need of home and money in 1736. The twelve almsmen were a feature of Cathedral life right up to the reign of George III. A royal mandate, signed by the king himself, was necessary to make provision for one of the crown's loyal subjects who had been wounded or maimed in the service of his country. There were 12 almsmen at any one time. In addition, since Bishop Morley's day, the Dean and Chapter had made provision for the widows of clergymen. Such provision by one body was a great contribution to the welfare of the community.

In 1715, Robert Nelson had written an *'Address to Persons of Quality and Establishment'* suggesting that wealthy people both on humanitarian and religious grounds should finance a whole range of philanthropic endeavour, including hospitals. The idea was first taken up by one of the prebendaries of Winchester, Alured Clarke, in *A Sermon preached in the Cathedral Church of Winchester before the Governors of the County-Hospital for Sick and Lame, &c. at the Opening of the said Hospital on St. Luke's Day, October, 1736.*[23] This is the origin of the present Hampshire County Hospital. At first the hospital was in the city proper but in the time of Florence Nightingale it was removed to what was deemed a more healthy site, a mile or so up a hill outside the city. This is England's oldest provincial hospital. This proud achievement was repeated by Clarke when, in due time, he was preferred to the Deanery of Exeter where he set up another such hospital. The movement suggested by Nelson and inaugurated by Clarke resulted in the establishment of 135 hospitals by the end of the century. Clarke's portrait is still in the Board Room of the Hospital and the link between Hospital and Cathedral is still maintained after over two hundred and forty years through the chaplaincy service and by an annual St. Luke's Day service. At the end of the original sermon there are diet sheets for various types of patients and for many years the Cathedral had special forms which were given to patients which certified that the Cathedral would be responsible for any financial expense involved for the patient. Clarke's achievement was epoch making and reveals the Cathedral's charitable concern during the eighteenth century. Clarke was succeeded by another of the prebendaries, John Hoadly, son of the bishop of that name, as chairman of the hospital.

Cathedral Music

After the faltering resumption in 1660 of Cathedral music, the early eighteenth century, so far as Winchester was concerned, failed to achieve any particular distinction. Nevertheless some mention must be made if we are to attempt a balanced view of the activities of the cathedral.

Vaughan Richardson, 1692-1729

The organist at the beginning of the century was Vaughan Richardson. He composed a certain amount of church music and was associated with the Festival of St. Cecilia celebrations in Winchester early in the century. His choir seems to have been small: nine lay clerks and four to six choristers.

John Bishop, 1729-1737

On Vaughan Richardson's death in 1729, the Dean and Chapter were undecided between the claims of John Bishop and James Kent. Bishop, though organist at the College, had also been a lay clerk at the Cathedral since 1696 and had the sympathy of the Dean and Chapter even though Kent was deemed the better player. In the end, the age of Bishop and his amiable disposition prevailed so that he succeeded to the vacant post. He held it for eight years and was succeeded by his defeated rival, James Kent.

Such reputation as Bishop has is associated with Winchester College. For Bishop, like so many Cathedral organists, was organist to both societies (See Bumpus. *English Cathedral Music* Vol.1.pp.230-232). The ordinary reader can easily meet Bishop's Music in *Hymns Ancient and Modern Revised:*

1.	Now that the daylight fills the sky.
503.	The eternal gifts of Christ the King.
650.	From all that dwell below the skies.

All three hymns are set to Bishop's tune *Illsley.*

James Kent, 1737-1773

Defeated in his application in 1729, Kent was successful eight years later on the death of Bishop. In the intervening years, he had occupied the post of organist at Trinity College, Cambridge. Kent was thus returning to the place of his birth and continuing a family connection with the Cathedral that went back as far as 1663 when Samuel Kent was a bellringer. In 1672, an earlier James Kent had been a chorister to be followed in the same role by the present James Kent between 1711 and 1714. Early in the nineteenth century, says Bumpus, the anthems and services of Kent were immensely popular throughout the country. Only near the end of his life could he be persuaded to publish his anthems in 1773. Further editions were published with additional services, by Joseph Corfe and Vincent Novello. His own presentation copy is still in the Cathedral library.

Warden Huntingford of the College (which shared Kent's services with the Cathedral) writes of him: "He was conscientiously diligent, not only in punctual attendance at times of Choral Prayers, but also in the more laborious and indispensable requisite parts of an organist's duty, the teaching of the boys. His manner of playing was neither indecorously rapid, nor heavily slow; but such as became the sanctity of the Church and the solemnity of the Service. He was reputed to be one of the best players of Dr. Croft's music in the kingdom." This last judgement perhaps explains the ample archive of Dr. Croft's organ music still surviving in the Cathedral. Samuel Arnold in his Collection published (Vol. 1., 1790) a further anthem of Kent's *Hearken unto my voice.* This is generally regarded as the best of Kent's anthems and was selected as one of the four anthems for the coronation of George IV in 1820 when it was orchestrated by Thomas Attwood. It was also sung at the wedding of Queen Victoria on February 10th, 1840 in the Chapel Royal.

Charles Dibdin

During Kent's tenure of office Winchester had its most celebrated choir boy, Charles Dibdin of Southampton. Besides being a chorister at the Cathedral, he began a musical career in the city which led him to London and to becoming a celebrated impressario. He is best remembered to-day for his Sea Shanties, the best known of which is *Tom Bowling:-*

> Here, a sheer hulk, lies poor Tom Bowling,
> The darling of our crew;
> No more he'll hear the tempest howling,
> For death has broached him too.

Each of the three verses ends with the line:- For Tom is gone aloft.

There is a lengthy article on Dibdin in the *Dictionary of National Biography* and a separately published biography of him with a collection his verse, by Thomas Dibdin, illustrated by the celebrated George Cruikshank and published in 1841.

The Organ

Near the end of Kent's time the organ again received attention. In 1768 a contract was signed between the Dean and Chapter and the firm of Charles Groom of Salisbury, for the construction within the existing case of a "useful and substantial Choir Organ." Groom agreed, in addition, to put in order the Great Organ. The cost was £166 and the work took nine months to complete *(Ledger Book* xxx f.155.).

Weddings in the Cathedral

A piece of legislation which affected the Cathedral was Lord Hardwicke's Marriage Bill of 1753 which aimed at stamping out irregular marriages, the most notorious of which were known as Fleet marriages. He therefore enacted that henceforth no wedding should take place until banns had been called three times in the respective parish churches. The Bill was passed and from 1754 to 1869 no wedding took place within the Cathedral.

John Wesley, 1771

John Wesley[24] too has left a comment on the Cathedral. On October 3, 1771 on seeing the tomb of Cardinal Beaufort he wrote: "the sight of the bad cardinal . . . . in a posture of prayer brought to my mind those fine lines of Shakespeare, which he puts into the mouth of King Henry VI:

> Lord Cardinal
> If thou hast any hope of Heaven's grace
> Give us a sign. He dies, and makes no sign.
> *2 Henry VI. Act iii. scene iii. 27*

The Sermon

The sermon played a prominent part. There were the usual sermons expounding the scriptures. Then there were the special sermons to mark royal anniversaries, Assize Sundays as for example when Thomas Fenton preached the Assize Sermon on March 6th, 1739 in the presence of the 'hanging' judge, Mr. Justice Page. Sermons were not only preached but printed and here too the prebendaries had their share of printed sermons. A few may be mentioned: prebendary Markland's sermons were published in 1729 in two volumes. After his death, Dean Pearce's sermons were collected into four volumes and published in 1778. The prebendaries also preached outside their cathedral when invited to preach before Parliament or University, as for example when Prebendary Eyre preached on the anniversary of the martyrdom of Charles I in 1708. Two years later, on the same anniversary, Prebendary West was the preacher. Prebendary Balguy preached before Cambridge University (1754).

Besides the customary sermons there were the more formal charges delivered in the Cathedral by those prebendaries who were also chancellor of the diocese or archdeacon. Such was Thomas Balguy[25] who gave his charges every three years from 1760 onwards on important topics of the day: The Character and Conduct of a Minister of the Gospel; Religious Liberty; The Sacraments. On July 4th 1776 the American colonies declared for independence. On 13th December a general fast was appointed and Balguy was the preacher. For him the Scripture proclaimed that through God 'kings reign, and princes decree justice.' Any revolt against the crown was infidelity and atheism and these mean tyranny. They cannot possibly be otherwise. So far as Balguy could see the American Revolution was wholly indefensible.

Cathedral Life

In evaluating the life of the Cathedral in the eighteenth century, we have to be careful not to think of it in terms of twentieth century restless and increasing busy-ness, nor in terms of turnover and tourism. Eighteenth century churchmen saw their cathedrals and churches as places for a reserved style of worship. John Wesley's "enthusiasm" was too horrid a thing for them to contemplate. The offices of morning and evening prayer predominated. The sacrament was celebrated rarely. Given these premises it is clear that Winchester followed the manner of the times. The *Attendance Registers* (from 1743 onwards to the present day) prove that the services were held in unbroken continuity, that Dean and prebendaries discharged their limited residence in accordance with the statutes.

A single manuscript dated 29th September, 1735 gives a summary of the residences of Dean and Prebendaries during a typical year (see opposite).

These eighteenth century clergy were mainly learned men. They were Europeans to a far greater degree than most of their successors, either clerical or lay. The prebendaries of Winchester (and it is Prebendary

Resident between mictm.ʃ 1734, Xmitnmʃ 1735

Days

Mr Dean	149
Mr Cook	115
Mr Sturges	172
D Clark	61
Mr Soley	81
Mr Woodroffe	218
Mr Morgan	91
D Hayley	29
Mr Eyre	218
Dr Noyes	107
Mr Bourne	119
Mr Inett	23
Mr Stephens	89

Calendar of Cathedral Papers, 1735.

Sturgess (1721-40) who left us *Acta Eruditorum)* were aware of the scholarship of Italy, France, Germany, Switzerland and the Low Countries just as scholars in those countries were aware of the work being done in Winchester by such men as Bingham or Gale or Gibson.

Had the deans and prebendaries of the eighteenth century been asked, as were their successors in the following century, what they believed to be their role in society, they would have been assailed by none of the doubts that have afflicted the twentieth century. They considered that it was their duty to maintain part of the established order of Church and State. This meant the daily maintenance of the services of the Cathedral, championing the cause of the establishment by sermons and by the printed word both against Dissent and Roman Catholicism. They were gentlemen and scholars living lives that accorded with such presuppositions. Among them were men of formidable scholarship. And finally they acknowledged the duty of charity to the poor in accordance with the dictates of their holy religion.

NOTES

1 A prebendary is a canon of a cathedral who has a *prebenda* or share in the funds of the cathedral to which he is attached.
2 A. Hartshorne. *Memoirs of a Royal Chaplain.* London, 1905. p.266.
3 *D.N.B.* s.v. Alsop A.
4 J. Hoadly. *The Works of Benjamin Hoadly.* 3 Vols. London, 1773.
5 J. Milner. *History . . . . . . of Winchester.* 2 Vols. Winchester, 1798. Vol. 2. p.33.
6 A. Hartshorne op. cit.
7 G. B. Hill and L. F. Powell, Boswell's Life of Johnson. 6 Vols. C.P. 1934. Vol. 1. p.292.
8 Z. Pearce. *Longinus* 3rd edn. London, 1743.
9 G. B. Hill and L. F. Powell op. cit. Vol. 3 p.489
10 Longinus. *On the Sublime.* C.P., 1949. p.xxi.
11 C. C. Oman. *English Brass Chandeliers.* The Royal Archaeological Society 1937. p. 275. Plate X: 'an excellent example of baroque art'.
12 The Monument was originally situated in the North Transept.
13 G. B. Hill and L. F. Powell *op. cit.* Vol. 3 p.58.
14 R. Lowth, *De Sacra Poesi Hebraeorum.* Oxford, 1753. An English translation of this work was published in London in 1847.
15 G. B. Hill and L. F. Powell Vol. 5.p.81.
16 J. D. Michaelis. *Robert Lowth de Sacra Poesi Hebraeorum.* Goettingae, 1770.
17 see *D.N.B.* s.v. Gibson E. "a magnificent monument of research . . . still the highest authority on church law". (Perry).
18 The Archives of Lambeth Palace.
19 *Acta Eruditorum,* Leipzig. See Index volumes published in 1714, 1723 and 1733. s.v. Bingham J., Gale S., and Gibson E.
20 *The History and Antiquities of Winchester.* 2 Vols. Winchester, 1773.
21 F. G. Parsons. *Chartulary of St. Thomas Hospital.* Privately printed.
22 Cathedral Statutes of 1638. Statute 27.
23 A. Clarke. *A Sermon preached in the Cathedral Church of Winchester before the Governors of the County Hospital.* London, 1737.
24 N. Curnock. *The Journal of John Wesley.* 8 Vols. London, 1938. Vol. 5.p.431.
25 T. Balguy. *Discourses on Various Subjects.* Winchester, 1785.

FURTHER READING

A.R. 1. 1743-1748.
C.A. 5,6. 1696-1776.
D.N.B.
Ayscough, F. preb.
Bingham J. rector
Clarke A. preb.
Hoadly B. bishop
Kent J. organist
Lowth W. preb.
Pyle T. preb.
Sykes A.A. preb.
Balguy T. preb.
Bishop J. organist
Dibdin C. chorister
Hoadly J. preb.
Lowth R. archdeacon
Pearce Z. dean
Shipley J. preb. and dean

Defoe D. *A Tour through the Whole Island of Great Britain.* London, 1974. Winchester. Vol. 1. pp.181-187.
Goodman F. R. *Pretenders from the Pulpit.* Sermons etc., from Tracts Scarce and Curious in Winchester Chapter library Illumined by the Tale of the last Stewarts. Cambridge, 1933.
L.B. Vols. XXII — XXXI. 1697-1785.
Nichols *Literary Anecdotes* Vol. 3. pp.107-111 Pearce).
Receiver's books.
Treasurer's books 1-4. 1691-1776. Mss.
Vice-Dean's book. MS. 1730 . . .
Wainscott Book MS. Close Houses throughout this period.

The Quire, c.1809

Chapter X

Revival   and   Reform

Newton Ogle was appointed Dean of Winchester in 1775. One event makes his tenure of office a turning point in the history of the Cathedral. His appointment co-incides with a new resolution on the part of the Dean and Chapter to ensure that the fabric of the Cathedral should be regularly and professionally inspected. After the great effort of reconstruction between 1660 and 1700, the first three quarters of the eighteenth century slipped away in leisured ease and scholarly calm. The first sign that a proper concern for the actual building and its surroundings emerged a few years earlier when the Dean and Chapter put out in 1763 an *Advertisement,*[1] which aimed at improving the surroundings of the Cathedral. The churchyard was used as a convenient place for the inhabitants of the city to display their washing and to spring clean their belongings. Shops and stalls were erected and workmen followed their trades.

Twelve years later the Dean and Chapter turned to the more important part of their responsibility, the actual building itself. In 1775 and following years, they appointed James Essex, James Wyatt (sometimes known as 'The Destroyer'), William Porden, a pupil of Wyatt, the celebrated John Nash, and Edward Blore to inspect and advise. Their reports still survive and agree on the weakness of the building especially in the area of the south transept. Rather later, in 1809, the Dean and Chapter appointed their own architect, William Garbett and he too dutifully made an annual survey. The result of this vast amount of expertise was to confuse. Set out in chronological order it is as follows and runs to scores of pages:

1775:	Report by James Essex
1782:	Report by James Essex
1809:	Appointment and report by William Garbett, the Cathedral Architect
1810 — 1815:	Garbett's annual reports.
1813:	Porden's report
1820:	Blore's report
1820/1:	Correspondence and conflicting reports of Garbett and John Nash.
1834:	The justification of Garbett's work. [2]

By this time not only was the south transept the subject of anxiety but also what one report of Nash calls the 'falling piers', those adjacent to Edington's Chantry on the south side of the Nave. Much to Garbett's disappointment the advice tendered by Nash was accepted and his own rejected.. This decision caused division in the Chapter, an appeal to the Visitor, and pain to the architect. Years later his son felt obliged to write a lengthy justification of all that his Father had done (1834).

Thus the step taken in 1775 led to fifty years of feverish building, repair, and alteration and reached its financial peak between 1820 and 1822 when over £7,500 were spent. By then Ogle and indeed his successor had come and gone and Cathedral affairs were largely in the hands of the dynamic Prebendary Nott; Dean Rennell seemingly agreeable.

Edward Blore, architect

Of course, what was done did not please everybody. A detailed critique of what was being undertaken was written by Blore in 1820. It consisted of a lengthy report of twenty-two foolscap pages. It mixed approval and disapproval. Beginning with the outside of the building, he disappproved of the closing of the two doors at the east and west ends of the southern nave aisle and the consequent replacement by a single door in the centre even though it copied the original style. He objected to alterations in certain windows, especially in the north transept. The screen which replaced the Inigo Jones Screen he considered 'a great improvement'. At this stage it was proposed to place a new organ over the quire screen. To this Blore objected. It would look 'mean' and he drew attention to the fact that at Westminster Abbey the organ had recently been removed from the quire screen. The new bishop's throne (by Garbett) he considered a 'wanton and unnecessary mutilation'. Turning his attention to the great screen he considered the removal of the 'clumsy canopy' over the high altar as a judicious alteration. The ceilings placed by Prebendary Nott in the transepts and which screen the original beams, he thought to be a 'gross violation of good taste and propriety'. He thought that the paintings in the Holy Sepulchre Chapel were too decayed to be capable of restoration. Work in the retrochoir is commended though the moving of certain tombs is objectionable. The cleaning of the roof paintings in the Guardian Angels' Chapel wins his approval. The arrangements in the Lady Chapel, he understands, are of a temporary nature only, while the major repairs to the Cathedral are in progress. Alterations to the Langton Chantry he holds to be 'bad taste'. The Crypt, he informs us, is used as a thoroughfare. After so much condemnation he adds that there are many changes, unspecified, which are 'justly entitled to applause' though his final judgement is one of regret at the changes as a whole. Persistence in the plans must bring 'obloquy' on 'the Gentlemen in whose care this magnificent fabric rests'.[3]

Turner and Constable

In 1795 the young Turner, long before he had been recognised as one of the nation's finest painters, made a delightful sketch of the west end of the Cathedral. The foreground shows the dilapidated state of the churchyard with gravestones all awry.

An unexpected contemporary comment on the architectural work of the period is preserved in a letter of Archdeacon Fisher of Salisbury written to the painter John Constable on October 24th, 1821:

> My dear Constable,
> . . . . . . I think the earlier you come the better. I project, if the weather be fine, to go and see Winchester Cathedral. The roof has been near falling in, owing to the constant cutting away of the great supporting pillars (of folly and bad taste) . . . . . .[4]

Perhaps it was on this visit in the autumn of 1821 that Constable painted his little known work of Winchester Cathedral.

The Churchyard

Slowly the *Advertisement* of 1763 had its effect. A popular misconception is that the Churchyard served as a graveyard for the Cathedral. Until this date those closely associated with the Cathedral could be buried within its walls. The Churchyard acted as a public cemetery for the military and for the citizenry of Winchester. It continued as such for a further century and even the forceful Dean Kitchin had to meet with opposition to his attempt finally to clear the outer churchyard as we now expect to find it. Old prints give clear indication of tomb stones leaning at every possible angle, long grass, uneven surfaces and grazing sheep. The Dean and Chapter had to protest that too many soldiers (who came from away) were being buried in the churchyard and making it difficult to find space to bury local citizens. They did, however, leave (and indeed encourage) one stone to be left — that of a Hampshire Grenadier who died in 1764. His epitaph reads:

> Here sleeps in peace a Hampshire Grenadier
> Who caught his death by drinking cold small beer;
> Soldier, be wise from his untimely fall
> And when your hot, drink strong, or not at all.

The inscription needed renewal in 1802 when two more lines were added:

> An honest soldier never is forgot
> Whether he die by musket or by pot.

The memorial is not to everyone's taste. The Regiment still maintains the stone and, when necessary, sees that the lettering is made legible.

Among the citizens of Winchester in the Churchyard was the landlady of Jane Austen.

Dean Holmes, 1804-1805

All was not fabric and churchyard even though these were the most obvious aspects of the Cathedral. Ogle died in 1804 and was succeeded by the scholarly Robert Holmes. A scholar of Winchester College, he proceeded to New College, Oxford where he quickly settled to what was to be his life work — an examination and publication of the Greek manuscripts of the Old Testament.

Winchester 13th *October*, 1763.

ADVERTISEMENT.

THE *DEAN* and *CHAPTER*, having taken the *Church-Yard* into their own Hands, *give Notice*, That they will not *suffer* any Linen, or Wearing Apparel to be hung on Lines, or laid on the Ground, or on the Rails, or any Gravestone or Tomb, in that Part of it that lies West of St. *Maurice* Church Porch: Nor any Linen, *&c.* to be hung in the *great Walk*, between the *Widows* College and the *Wheat-Sheaf*:--- Nor any Bed Cloths, Coverlids, Blankets, Bolsters, Pillows, Feather-Beds, Mattrasses, or Carpets, to be aired or beaten in any Part of the *Church-Yard*;--- Nor any Brewers Grains, or Soap-Ashes, or Wood to be laid; nor any Saw-Pit made, nor any Fire for melting Pitch or Tar, or other Purpose;--- Nor any GOODS exposed to Sale; nor Stall set up, nor Carpenters Work-Bench in any Part of the said *Church-Yard*:

And, that whoever shall after this *Publick Notice*, do any of the Things forbidden above will be prosecuted.

WINCHESTER: Printed by M. AYRES.

There still survives the letter in which he asked the permission of the Archbishop of Canterbury to be away from Winchester to complete his great work of collating manuscripts at Oxford. Holmes began his work in 1788 and the Dean and Chapter, along with other bodies, subscribed annually towards the cost of the necessary research.[5] Something of the scale of his researches may be gathered from the fact that there are 164 volumes of manuscript collations in the Bodleian Library which Holmes wrote in preparation for his massive work.[6] A scholar describes Holmes' endeavors as 'an almost unequalled monument of industry and learning, and will perhaps never be superseded as a storehouse of materials'.[7] Although succeeding years have brought other insights and information for such study the magnitude of the original work is still valuable. A collection of his essays was published posthumously in 1806 by the Oxford Press: *Treatises on Religious and Scriptural subjects.*

Dean Rennell, 1805-1840

Holmes lived too short a time to make much impression upon the Cathedral. In any case his *forte* was in the world of scholarship. With the appointment of Thomas Rennell as Dean and perhaps even more with the appointment of the energetic Prebendary Nott in 1810, the Cathedral began to see a period of great activity. William Pitt the Younger held that Rennell was the "Demosthenes of the pulpit." He had already been put to the test in the Cathedral on the Sunday after the death of Marie Antoinette. He took as his text: *Wherefore thus saith the Lord, Woe to the bloody city.* (Ezekiel 24.6).

For Rennell the rule of Kings was a divine ordinance and he judged the days in which he lived as the worst since the destruction of Jerusalem in 70 A.D. Rennell was aware that the French Revolution in its early stage had admirers in England (including the poet Wordsworth). To them he uttered this warning: "Be warned then in time, my brethren and fellow subjects . . . . let us pray that God will grant victory to those arms which have no other object in this necessary and defensive war, than to restore peace and order in France, and to secure and perpetuate the blessings and comforts of civil society to every nation in Europe."[8]

A note added by Rennell to his published sermons affords an interesting side-light on the effect of the French Revolution upon Winchester. He tells how he had received personal accounts from French ecclesiastics who had taken refuge in the King's House at Winchester. The contacts had convinced him of the superiority of the good nature in the spirit of true Protestantism, and in the principles of its most evangelical church which had opened its arms when charity and benevolence were required. The Cathedral played its part in making financial provision for refugees from the Revolution.[9]

A lengthy manuscript letter written in 1810 by the Dean to a certain M.G. is revealing both about the Dean himself and about the recipient. The first thing he must do is 'to consider the proofs of the existence of an All wise and powerful Creator of the Universe. He then goes on to commend to this correspondent Ray's *Wisdom of God in Creation* (1691). With such help he is sure that the divine revelation in the Gospel of Christ will lay claim to his acceptance. Other necessary reading is Bacon, Newton, Locke, Boyle, Clarendon and Addison; all of them, he points out, being laymen and, therefore, unbiassed in their profession and defence of Christianity. Not that he belittles the clerical authors; Taylor, Barrow, Tillotson, Bentley, Clarke, Butler, Sherlock and South, all of them noteworthy for their transcendental exertions. He reminds his reader of the pain, misery and mortality that are inseparable from our human condition, not to mention the hazards of the field of battle and the devastation of war which the Europe of 1810 knew only too well. None of us, he concludes, can stand for a moment in God's eye without a mediator. In fine, Christ in both his characters, human and Divine, is alone adequate and exclusively able to make this satisfaction on the Cross. There is no other name by which salvation can be obtained.[9]

The only clue to M.G. is that he was a man of honourable profession and long and meritorious service. Whoever he was the Dean honoured him by treating seriously the implied request for proof of the Christian faith.

"Blood and Brains"

Pitt may have thought Rennell's sermons (which accorded so well with British foreign policy) the words of a Demosthenes. On the other hand when they came to be printed the waspish Sydney Smith in the celebrated *Edinburgh Review* commented: "We confess ourselves long since wearied with this kind of discourse . . . . bespattered with blood and brains . . . . . It is not possible to ensure the draggling and daubing of such a ponderous limner as Dr. Rennell, after the ethereal touches of Mr. Burke." Somewhat contemptuously Smith adds that if only the Dean could correct his shortcomings he could become 'a star of the third or fourth magnitude in the English Church'. Rennell's long tenure of office came to an end in 1840.[11]

Prebendary Nott, 1810-1841

Nott came to Winchester about the age of forty-three. He had already had a distinguished career: Fellow of All Souls (1788), and Bampton Lecturer (1802). The subject of his lectures, *Religious Enthusiasm* (dedicated to George III) reveal the man's mind. He was a sober member of the Established Church, and highly distrusted all those who, like Methodists, claimed (in Horace Walpole's words) to be the peculiar favourites of the divine being. It is important not to give the usual twentieth century definition to a word which for two centuries had the sort of meaning indicated by Walpole. Fifty years before Nott's lectures Bishop Butler had described Wesley's enthusiasm as a "very horrid thing." Nott concurred with this view and expressed the hope "that these sermons may contribute, in some degree, towards the repressing of that restless spirit of Enthusiasm, the fatal tendency of which has always been to unsettle the religious opinions of mankind, and to destroy the peace of the Church."

His wide scholarship covered a two volume edition of *The Works of Henry Howard,* Earl of Surrey and *Sir Thomas Wyatt the Elder* (1815) and two Italian publications, *Fortunatus Siculus ossia L'avventuroso Ciciliano* published in Florence in 1832, the year after he had published in London *The Book of Common Prayer* in Italian, a book which he had translated while recovering from his accident. A manuscript sermon of Nott survives which he preached on the death in child birth of Princess Charlotte Augusta, who died in 1817 at the age of 21. Nott had been one of her tutors.[1][2]

Nott is best remembered, however, for his practical impact upon the Cathedral. He was keenly interested in its fabric and his curiosity and concern persuaded him to ascend ladders to see for himself. On one occasion on January 6th, 1816 he fell some twenty-four feet and suffered injuries from which he never really recovered. Nevertheless, his interest continued. Along with his Dean he pursued the maintenance of the fabric (witness the succession of distinguished architects) and its adornment within. Four features may specially be mentioned: the ceilings of the north and south transepts; the restoration of the quire bosses; a new quire screen; and the opening of Fox's tomb.

When Nott came to Winchester the whole of the nave, quire and tower, all originally with an open timber roof, had been given an inside roof by Wykeham, Fox and Curle. There remained the transepts which still presented the Norman appearance of their first building, as surviving engravings show. The timbered roofs were still visible and no monuments were visible save wall tablets. Nott designed the ceilings still visible in each transept. He also caused the quire bosses to be cleaned and restored.

Prebendary Nott

The Quire Screen

Another undertaking, surprising to later generations, was the removal of the Inigo Jones screen at the entrance to the quire. It was replaced by what contemporaries described as "a new stone screen . . . . of the best Portland stone, and a very pleasing imitation of the style which prevailed in the 14th and 15th centuries . . . . . . it constitutes a medium between the western portal, and the highly ornamented screen which terminated the presbytery. The design for it was imagined by a prebendary (G. F. Nott) of the cathedral, revised by Mr. Garbett....Handsome oak doors, corresponding in decoration with the style of the screen, have been substituted for those which were 'more fitting a tavern than a cathedral', bearing upon the inner side the date of the erection, and upon the other the following brief exhortation

vigilate et orate
(Watch and pray. St. Mark 13, 33)

In due course this screen was replaced by the present wooden screen in 1873 and the old doors used for the present south door of the Cathedral.

The screen is the work of Sir George Gilbert Scott.

Fox's Chantry, 1820

On Saturday, January 22nd, 1820 Garbett the architect reported that men were at work on the steps leading to Fox's Chantry. A stone was removed which led to the fall of rubbish upon the coffin below, which in turn broke the lid of the coffin. The broken lid was carefully removed and the figure of a man in full episcopal robes became visible with a wooden crosier lying at his left side. Upon the hands were episcopal gloves, apparently leather; on the feet were sandals. In the sepulchre was a series of fragments of purbeck marble with faint signs of painting. A leaden box had a piece of vellum with the inscription (translated): 'The fifth day of October 1528, there died and was buried Richard Bishop of this Church. He ruled over the Church for twenty seven years.'

The crosier and the fragments of purbeck marble were removed and the rest carefully returned to its place. The only missing items which led to the suspicion that the tomb had been opened at some unknown date was the absence of the Bishop's ring. A careful search was made but no ring was found. A new stone was placed over the sepulchre on January 28th. and Prebendary Nott and his fellow prebendaries were present to see all was done respectfully. Concluding his report to the President of Corpus Christi College, Oxford, he writes: "It may be satisfactory to yourself and the College to be informed that . . . there was an air of peace and repose in the whole, which, it was soothing to the mind to contemplate. It assimilated itself to the firm belief we are permitted through God's mercies in Christ, to encourage, that the Good are blessed, and that their works follow them; that they are more than at rest, and that they are in joy and felicity, as soon as they cease from their labours. The sacred calm that seemed to hover round the remains of your Venerable Founder, operated on me powerfully to subdue that dread of death, which sometimes we indulge . . . I did not quit the spot till all was secured: and when the Stone closed upon the Good Bishop's Tomb, not to be removed I hope, till the last day, I fervently ejaculated within myself 'O may my latter end be like his'."[13]

Part of the wooden Crosier found in the tomb of Bishop Fox, Jan. 22nd, 1820

Nott's Final Legacy

Nott accummulated a vast personal collection of books (and also a collection of coins) — over 12,000 volumes. Indeed it took 13 days for the books to be sold at an auction, at which the Dean and Chapter spent £100. The only regret is that it was impossible to buy the whole collection which would have made the Cathedral Library extremely distinguished.

Then because he was executor for his Uncle, Samuel Nott, a physician, there came into his hands and finally to the Cathedral several volumes of the physician's diary and log book as he travelled throughout Europe and as far east as Madras and Canton.

On the east wall of the north transept is a long inscription near his burial place. Part of it reads:

> In 1816 while personally superintending the very
> Extensive Repairs and Restoration of the Cathedral
> Undertaken in great measure at his Suggestion
> He met with a severe and almost fatal accident
> Which, from that time disabled him from
> Active exertions, whether of body or mind
> Being obliged in consequence to spend some years
> In Italy in pursuit of health, He employed himself
> During that time in a new and valuable
> Translation of the Book of Common Prayer
> Into the Italian Language.
>   . . . the bulk
> Of his property he appropriated to the benefit
> Of the matrons of Bishop Morley's College.

Society of Antiquaries

This period was characterised by a vigorous production of books about the Cathedral. It opened with two specialised studies of parts of the Cathedral. Both were published by the *Society of Antiquaries*. The first appeared in 1784 and was devoted to the Lady Chapel and in particular to its wall paintings. This is the earliest artistic attempt to reveal that the wall paintings actually looked like. The second appeared in 1789 and was devoted to some of the chantries and to the mortuary chests.

Milner's History

Just before the century ended Joseph Milner, a Roman Catholic priest in Winchester produced the first authoritative work on the history and description of the Cathedral up to date. It is entitled: *History, Civil and Ecclesiastical, and Survey of the Antiquities of Winchester in two volumes, 1798-1801.* This was followed by a second enlarged edition in 1809 and by a third large edition with supplement and memoir in 1839. The bibliographer Lowndes describes the work as 'among the few standard works of English topography.' Milner was the first to penetrate the riddle of the significance of the figures on the Font associated with Henry of Blois. Some writers had thought the bishop was Birinus; some a saint; but Milner realised it was the story of St. Nicholas. Along with these major editions there was a continuing demand for smaller abbreviated editions.

The work provoked controversy. Prebendary John Sturges (1759-1807) saw traces of Roman Catholic prejudice in the book and wrote to that effect. Milner felt bound to reply and in a courteous book entitled *Letters to a Prebendary*, first published in 1800 and thereafter re-published on several occasions and at least once in Ireland (Cork, 1802), defended himself against charges of prejudice. The controversy only finally died away with the last edition of *Letters* in 1843.

Other works proved less controversial and consisted mainly of plates showing different features of the building, just as Milner had included a large number of plates. These volumes were J. H. Storer's *The History and Antiquities of the Cathedral Church of Winchester* (1813); J. Britton's *The History and Antiquities of the Cathedral Church of Winchester* (1817)[14] and Winkles' *A Descriptive Account of Winchester Cathedral* (1839). The most sumptuous of these is Britton's but all are valuable because they indicate the changes going on at this period, for example in the south wall of the nave adjoining The Close and in the transepts, before and after the insertion of the ceilings placed there at the instigation of Prebendary Nott. A number of minor features of individual memorials can also be seen.

This historical and archaeological interest in the Cathedral may be held to have been summed up in two conferences held at Winchester in 1845: *The Second Annual Congress of the British Archaeological Association* (1845); and *The Annual Meeting of the Archaeological Institute* a month later. Although the scope of both gatherings was wider than the Cathedral, both reports have details of the Cathedral. In particular, the second report contains what is still the classic architectural history of the Cathedral contributed by Professor Willis. The former gathering has contributions on the paintings in the Holy Sepulchre Chapel and the Lady Chapel. In view of the dramatic changes in the wall paintings of the Holy Sepulchre, this paper of J. G. Waller is of particular interest.

The atmosphere of the time and the interest generated by the subject can be seen in a drawing in the *Illustrated London News* which shows Professor Willis lecturing a highly fashionable audience. On the wall behind the lecturer is a presentation of the Cathedral (no doubt to illustrate his own lecture), suggesting the western towers which disappeared before Edington began his rebuilding. To round off the spate of enthusiasm of the period there was also O. B. Carter's *Ancient Painted Glass of Winchester Cathedral* (1845). Its particular value is that it indicates what the glass over the reredos was like before the changes which were later to be made and before St. Bartholomew, who held the centre light, was disposed of to the Victoria and Albert Museum.

Frederick Iremonger, 1818-1820

Another prebendary who deserves to be singled out is Frederick Iremonger, a pioneer of education. In 1813, he wrote *Suggestions to the Promoters of Schools on Dr. Bell's System.*

In 1820 at the early age of 39, Iremonger was taken ill and died within three days. The shock was felt throughout the Diocese, particuarly among the children. *The Hampshire Chronicle* of May 22nd observed: "Wherever there was poverty, affliction, or disease, there was Frederick Iremonger." Schoolchildren accompanied his coffin beyond the confines of the city as it was taken to the family home at Wherwell for interment. In due course, a meeting was held which resolved to erect a monument, to him and his work, within the cathedral. Subscriptions poured in from all over Hampshire, the first being one of £2 from the children of Upton Grey. The required sum of £500 was raised in a few weeks, the fund was closed, and the celebrated sculptor Sir Francis Chantrey was commissioned to prepare a design. The result can still be seen in the fine monument in the north transept.

Cathedral Music

The fame of James Kent the organist, came late in his life and even posthumously. He had died in 1776 and was succeeded by Peter Fussell. He in turn was helped by George Chard from 1791 and succeeded by him in 1802. Chard held the office for the next 47 years. He is probably the only cathedral organist to become Mayor of Winchester (in 1833) and seems to have found his activities outside the Cathedral more congenial than those within. The Dean and Chapter on one occasion at least begged him to instruct the choristers "to make the reponses etc in a decent, uniform manner and not at the highest pitch of their voices as at present, which resembles a street cry rather than a religious rite". Long before he became Mayor he only attended the singing room fourteen times in a whole year (1817-18).

Professor R. Willis lecturing in 1845 on The Architectural History of
Winchester Cathedral

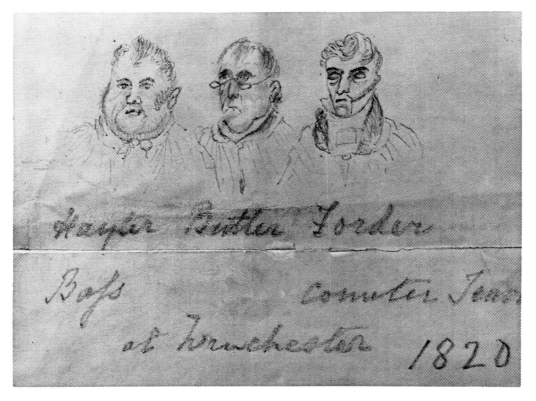

Hayter, Butler and Forder. Three Lay vicars, 1820.

Whatever the failings of the organist the lay vicars are in evidence. There is an attractive pencil drawing of three of them in 1820.(as above).

More significant is the *Collection of Anthems, Psalms and Hymns as Sung by the Choirs of the Cathedral and the College, Winchester* which was published by another lay vicar, William Garratt, in 1827.

Little either of the music of Fussell or Chard still remains in the Cathedral musical archive and none in the repertoire. Through the courtesy of the Dean and Canons of Windsor transcripts of Fussell's *Evening Service in A* and Chard's *Kyrie Eleison* have recently been added to the collection. Mr. Kenneth Mummery has also kindly presented to the Archives Chard's manuscript *Hearken Unto my Voice*.

Lay Vicars and Choir Boys

For a short period in 1809-1810 and again between 1819-1822 an attempt was made to keep disciplined control of the choristers. Two books remain indicating the behaviour and progress of the lay vicars as well as of the boys during this short time. In the former book mention is made most

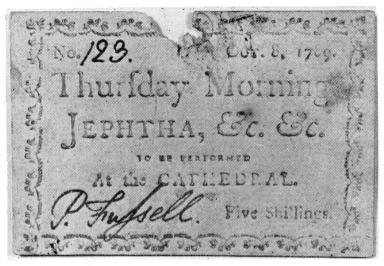

Admission ticket to Handel's Jephtha signed by the organist Peter Fussell.

often of fines inflicted for absence from services and rewards are also given for services attended. From time to time the name of the Bass Hayter appears as a regular attender at service.[15] The later book is devoted to the choristers and has much of the atmosphere of old school reports which speak of boys' conduct as being good on the whole. There were, however, recalcitrant boys who appear from time to time just to prove that choir boys are human e.g. 'gross misconduct on the part of Dyer'. Apparently he had obtained leave of absence under false pretences (Sep. 30th, 1820). Dyer appears several times as the villain of the Choir.[16]

Organ Problems

The *Attendance Registers* indicate that the quorum was regularly maintained for the daily services though the absence of an organ for several years must have been a strong discouragement. Twice during this period there was extensive work to the instrument. In 1799 it was completely rebuilt by Avery as a modest three manual instrument. This lasted a short time. Another instrument was soon needed and was built by Blyth of Islington. This step was marked by the lamentable removal of the old renaissance organ case erected in Thamar's time on the advice of the architect Edward Blore. This too was a three manual instrument.[17]

In all, the period was an undistinguished one from a musical point of view urgently needing the reforming drive brought by Samuel Sebastian Wesley in 1849.

The Cathedral Library

In years immediately before and after 1800 the Cathedral Library played a not undistinguished part in the scholarship of the day. In the field of Anglo-Saxon scholarship the two volume dictionary of Anglo-Saxon by Lye and Manning was added in 1776. In 1805 Turner's three volume *History of the Anglo-Saxons* was added and in 1839 the six volumes of Kemble's *Codex Diplomaticus Aevi Saxonici*. These last volumes are still in frequent use because they contain the texts referring to the donation of many of the manors given to the Monastery of St. Swithun and the Bishop of Winchester. Following logically on these volumes is the printed edition of *Domesday Book*. This book, originally kept in the treasury of the Cathedral was printed, for the first time, by the Government in 1773, although the printing was not finally completed until 1816. These volumes are still in the Library and have a special interest because of the inscription on the fly-leaf.

"John Sturges LL.D. Prebendary of the Cathedral Church of Winchester presents to the Library of that Church his copy of *Domesday* which belonged to his very eminent and most kind friend, the Rt. Hon. Charles Wolfram Cornwall, later speaker of the House of Commons, 1784."

In 1800 the Government asked the Dean and Chapter to make a return of its charters, registers, and manuscript books. The Chapter Clerk duly completed the return. This was one of the steps taken at the time to help construct a national register of all such important documents. In return, the Record Commissioners sent copies of their publications, free of cost, to the Dean and Chapter. The works then published are of great historic value.

On a fly-leaf at the beginning of these volumes is the following inscription:

This Book
is to be
Perpetually Preserved
In and for
the use of
The Cathedral Church
of
Winchester

It comes as a surprise to read such words. It has to be remembered that until the 19th century there were few libraries which an individual could visit and in which he could study. It is heartening to know that the charge to keep such books 'perpetually' has been honoured.

To round off this period of scholarly additions the Dean and Chapter added the revised edition of Dugdale's *Monasticon* with its new plates in eight volumes in 1846.

Jane Austen

Besides attention to the main structure during this period, there was enrichment of the interior by the addition of memorials famous because of the people they commemorate and frequently because of their particular inherent beauty. The most famous of all reminds us of Jane Austen. She only lived for about two months in Winchester at the close of her short life between May and July, 1817. That short association has linked her name with Winchester throughout the world. Born in Steventon Rectory within the diocese in 1775, she knew a great deal about the Cathedral through her Father, who from time to time visited the Cathedral for the 'charges' to which he listened and which were delivered by the scholarly archdeacon Balguy. Later in her life Jane Austen moved to Chawton, not a dozen miles from Winchester, and then in a desperate bid to find a doctor who could help her she moved to Winchester one wet day in May, 1817. Her hope was that Mr. Lyford would be able to remedy her complaint. She took up lodgings in College Street, just south of the Cathedral in a house still marked with a plaque to indicate her residence there at one time. On May 17th, 1817 she wrote:-

> . . . Mr. Lyford says he will cure me, and if he fails I shall . . write a memorial and lay it before the Dean and Chapter, and have no doubt of redress from that Pious, Learned and Disinterested Body".

Jane's health did not improve. However, she was sufficiently alert to write some doggerel to commemorate St Swithun's Day in that year:-

VENTA
Written at Winchester on Tuesday the 15th July 1817

When Winchester races first took their beginning
It is said the good people forgot their old Saint
Not applying at all for the leave of St Swithun.

A few days later she died. Her sister, Cassandra under the first shock of bereavement, wrote:-

> "her dear remains are to be deposited in the Cathedral . . . . It is a satisfaction to me that they are to lie in a building she admired so much . . . her precious soul I presume to hope reposes in a far superior Mansion."

At 9 o'clock on Wednesday morning, July 24th, 1817, the Precentor, Rev. Thomas Watkins, took the service and laid her to rest in the north aisle of the nave of the Cathedral. A short account written by her brother Henry survives:- " . . .She was buried on the 24th July 1817 in the Cathedral Church of Winchester which, in the whole catalogue of its mighty dead, does not contain the ashes of a brighter genius or a sincerer Christian."

The words on her gravestone, which speak of her as a Christian believer simply and not as a great writer:-

In Memory of
JANE AUSTEN
youngest daughter of the late
Rev'd George Austen
formerly Rector of Steventon in this County
she departed this life on the 18th of July 1817,
aged 41, after a long illness supported with
the patience and hopes of a Christian.

The benevolence of her heart,
the sweetness of her temper, and
the extraordinary endowments of her mind
obtained the regard of all who knew her, and
the warmest love of her intimate connections.

Their grief is in proportion to their affection
they know their loss to be irreparable
but in their deepest affliction they are consoled
by a firm though humble hope that her charity
devotion, faith and purity, have rendered
her soul acceptable in the sight of her

REDEEMER

Surprisingly the entry in the Cathedral Burial Register contains an error. It reads:-

Name	Abode	When Buried	Age	By whom the Ceremony was Performed
Jane Austen	Winchester	July 16th	41	T. Watkins

Jane Austen. Silhouette done by herself

During this period the Cathedral had other famous visitors. In 1778, George III and Queen Caroline visited the Cathedral, staying the night at Mr. Penton's house in Southgate Street. Three years later John Wesley came to the Cathedral to see West's painting behind the high Altar, *The Raising of Lazarus*. His *Journal* says:-

> I was disappointed. I observed that there was such a huddle of figures....I should not have guessed what they meant; the colours in general were far too glaring such as neither Christ nor His followers ever wore (9th. October 1781).

Wesley visited Winchester annually to encourage his supporters and in 1783 he visited the Cathedral again. This time he expresses appreciation of the kind hospitality afforded him by Prebendary William Lowth (1759-1795). Incidentally, Wesley opened the first preaching house in Winchester in November, 1785.

John Keats

John Keats visited the Cathedral in August, 1819. In several of his letters written from Winchester he refers to the 'beautiful Cathedral', the 'fine Cathedral'. On one occasion he writes of going 'into the Cathedral yard which is always interesting; then I pass under the trees along a paved path, pass the beautiful front of the Cathedral, turn to the left under a stone door way . . . then I am on the other side of the building, which leaving behind me I pass on through two college-like squares seemingly built for the dwelling place of Dean and Prebendaries, garnished with grass and shaded with trees.'

His re-action to the inside of the Cathedral is less complimentary. The singing, he commented, 'is bad'. To Fanny Brawne he wrote that he would be able to read her letters 'during the service up and down the aisle'. His literary work at Winchester amounted to about 1,500 lines of verse in which is included the poem *St Agnes' Eve*. In one letter to his sister he spoke of palatine Venice and abbotine Winchester and he began a poem which included the lines:-

Upon a sabbath day it fell;
Thrice holy was the sabbath bell
That called the folk to evening prayer.

William Cobbett

The celebrated William Cobbett visited the Cathedral in 1822, and heard 'a sort of jangling, made by a bell or two in the Cathedral.' On coming out of the Cathedral he was asked why it was that such places could not be built any more. "My dear," he said "That building was made when there were no poor wretches in England called *paupers;* when there were no poor-*rates;* when every labouring man was clothed in good woollen cloth; and when all had a plenty of meat and bread and beer." Such was his somewhat romantic view.

His description of the present is less flattering. Describing his visit for morning service on Sunday October 30th 1825 he writes:

"The 'service' was now begun. There is a *dean* and God knows how many prebends belonging to this immensely rich bishopric and chapter: and there were, at this "service" *two or three men and five or six boys* in white surplices, with a congregation of *fifteen women and four men!*"[18]

It so happens that we can partly check the truth or otherwise of Cobbett's words for the attendance Register for that day survives. It indicates that the Dean was present and three prebendaries and four lay vicars. it is not possible to say how many boys were present though the full complement of boys, assuming all were in good health, as the Chapter Act Book records in November of that same year, is six.

Bishop Sumner, 1828-1869

The nomination of Charles Sumner to the see of Winchester was, for the Cathedral, an epoch making event. To-day it seems natural that a bishop should be enthroned in person in his own cathedral. In Winchester this did not happen for centuries. It was Charles Sumner who for the first time in three hundred years came personally to be enthroned. His son, George Henry Sumner, wrote his Father's biography and gives an ecstatic account of the ceremony. On 18th January, 1828 he writes that the new Bishop came to Winchester for his enthronement: "The citizens were most cordial in their welcome . . . a short distance from the town some fifty tradesmen met him on horseback, and with a band of music at their head, preceded him into the city . . . the bells from the Cathedral and the various churches of the town struck up merry peals, and the whole scene was one of much enthusiasm." The enthronement was on the following day and is formally recorded in *Ledger Book 37 pp.114-116*. The biographer goes on to tell of the procession forming up at St. Lawrence Church and making its way to the Cathedral. The enthronement was performed, following ancient (and modern) practice, by the commissary or representative of the Archdeacon of Canterbury. Commenting on the appearance of the Bishop, a strikingly handsome man in his younger days, some one described him as the very embodiment of 'the beauty of holiness'. This proved to be the beginning of a reign of just over forty years.[19]

Yet in this long period his personal links with Winchester were few. It is true that in 1832, he spent a few weeks at Wolvesey in order that he might become better acquainted with the clergy and laity of his Cathedral City and its neighbourhood.[20]

Where he most influenced the Cathedral is in his own strongly held views which were opposed to the Tractarian Movement as he clearly indicated in his Charge of 1841. His views meant that Cathedral appointments tended to be of clergymen with more evangelical sympathies and in this way, he played a key part in affecting the tone of the Cathedral throughout the whole of his long episcopate.

Tractarians and Evangelicals

The fact that John Keble lived at Hursley (near Winchester) as Vicar from 1836 to 1866 and that Charlotte Yonge, long associated with the parish of Otterborne, early fell under his influence, makes it surprising that the Cathedral itself seems rarely to have been in touch with such distinguished church personalities. The Cathedral proved antipathetic to this expression of churchmanship and favoured more the evangelical tradition. The Bishop gave a lead in the matter and, with members of the Clapham sect as members of the diocese of Winchester, it is easier to find evangelical rather than Tractarian influence at work.

For a moment it looked as though an effort was being made to bring both these new developments in the life of the Church together. On September 27th, 1836 Canon Dealtry, formerly Vicar of Clapham, an evangelical and chancellor of the diocese, invited John Keble, recently instituted as Vicar of Hursley to preach the customary sermon at the Chancellor's Visitation of the clergy. Keble took as his theme *Primitive Tradition Recognised in Holy Scripture.*[21] This was a lengthy and scholarly discourse. He argued his case with an impressive list of Anglican Scholars from the 16th to the 19th century to support it. The sermon met with disfavour. The reason was that the prevailing view insisted upon the pre-eminence of Holy Scripture as containing all things necessary to salvation. To give a place to tradition was, in the opinion of many, to make way for dangerous innovations.

And so Keble was never again invited to preach in the Cathedral. Neither Dean nor Canon felt able to ask him to occupy the pulpit. All that Keble stood for was further imperilled by the publication about the same time of one of the *Tracts for the Times* which the Tractarians published to expound their beliefs. The one which caused the Cathedral offence was Tract 75: *On the Roman Breviary as Embodying the Substance of the Devotional Services of the Church Catholic.*[29] Its author was John Henry Newman who was steadily veering more and more towards the Roman Catholic Church into which he was received in 1845. What made this Tract particularly offensive to the Dean and Chapter was its inclusion of a series of devotions for Bishop Ken's Day, March 21st. It spoke of nocturns, antiphons and benedictions. This was a dangerous innovation and one which the Cathedral could not accept. Newman's *Tract 90* was shortly to follow and to draw the Bishop's express disapproval. And so the Cathedral missed the enrichment it might have received from a good man, John Keble. In his early ministry it was only the tradition of the evangelicals which had any chance of making headway in the Cathedral. Sumner's ideal was summed up in one of his earliest appointments, William Dealtry. The sort of standing held among evangelicals can be deduced from the fact that he was invited from Winchester to preach the Sermon at Holy Trinity, Cambridge on the Sunday, the day immediately after Charles Simeon's burial at King's College, Cambridge, Nov. 20, 1836. Dealtry was at the very centre of that influential evangelicalism of Clapham and Cambridge. A later Canon of Winchester, William Carus, wrote what is still the fullest biography of Simeon and includes in it lengthy excerpts from Dealtry's sermon. He took as his text 1 Sam. ii. 30 *Them that honour me, I will honour.* Dealtry said he had no right even to try and honour such a man as Charles Simeon. He knew that Simeon would re-echo the words of St. Paul — *not I, but the grace of God which was given me.*

We have moved a long way from the life of an eighteenth century prebendary, even from the earnest scholarship of an eighteenth century scholar. A new note had been struck. Dealtry lost no opportunity to continue to strike that note in his position in the Cathedral. For besides being a Canon, he was also Chancellor of the Diocese and so had the opportunity to make known his views among the clergy at their regular visitations. In 1831, he spoke to them about *The Church and Its Endowments.* He sided at a time when cathedral bodies were nervous about 'Reform', with those who look "ahead in the work of improvement . . . for the building of new churches . . .for adding to the value of poorer livings." Here was no defensive attitude. In 1834, he gave a further charge, this time on the relation between the established Church and Dissent. His main theme was the value to Dissent of an established Church which did so much in its nearly 11,000 parishes to remind people of their Christian faith. This was a benefit to all who called upon Christ. The high standard of education among the clergy had its impact too upon all Christian ministers. In support of the missionary work of the Church, he reminds the clergy of the American Indian Bible in the Cathedral Library and which was ordered to be printed and paid for by the Corporation in New England, for the propagation of the Gospel amongst the Indians in New England. He gives one or two examples of missionary giving from parish registers:

Durley Parish,
Towards the printing of the Bible at Lithuania. 1661 3s 0d.

Upham Parish
Collected for the persecuted in France, 1699. £5. 0. 0.

In Dealtry's last charge during this period, and published in 1838, he devoted himself to the *Obligations of the National Church*. This theme is summed up in a quotation from an American journal which is alleged to state: "since the reformation of 1649 there has been no example of so much combined and earnest zeal against her as these times are displaying." Despite this hostility he counters with facts based on Hampshire alone. There are 19,526 children in Church schools; in addition there are 29,940 Sunday school scholars. This is years before compulsory education. In the first ten years of his episcopate, he reports the bishop as saying that he had consecrated 56 churches within the diocese. During the same period nearly 300 more churches had been improved or enlarged.

Such was the new voice from the Cathedral. It was the voice of an evangelical clergyman from an evangelical parish. The appointment was of a new order. It prepared the way, necessarily lengthy, towards a more outward looking view of the ministry of a cathedral.

Dean Rennell 1805-1840

NOTES

1 G.3.2.
2 *W.C.C.* 1800-1865 (see Index).
3 J. Nash. *Correspondence re the Falling Piers.* Ms.
4 C. R. Leslie. *Memoirs of the Life of John Constable.* London, 1951. p.86.
5 *T.B.*
6 R. Holmes and Parsons. *Vetus Testamentum Graecum.*
7 H. B. Swete. *Introduction to the Old Testament in Greek.* C.U.P., 1914. p.187.
8 T. Rennell. *Discourses on Various Subjects.* London, 1801. pp.193-209.
9 G.3.1.
10 *Edinburgh Review,* 1802.
11 G. H. Blore. *Thomas Rennell.* Winchester, 1952.
12 G.5.3.
13 *Fox's Chantry* Ms.
14 The drawings in this volume are the work of Edward Blore.
15 *The Choir* Ms. 1809-1810.
16 *Choristers* Ms. 1819-1822.
17 G. St. M. Willoughby. *Organs of Winchester Cathedral, 950-1905.* Typed script, 1929.
18 W. Cobbett. *Rural Rides.* 2 Vols. in 1. London, 1973. Vol. 1 p.290.
19 G. H. Sumner. *The Life of Charles Richard Sumner.* London, 1876. p.136.f.
20 *ibid.* p.222.
21 J. Keble. *A Sermon Preached in the Cathedral Church of Winchester September 27, 1836.*
22 J. H. Newman. *Tracts for the Times.* No. 75. 4th edn. London, 1840.

FURTHER READING

A.R. Mss.   3 vols. 1776-1839.
F. Bussby   *Jane Austen in Winchester.* Winchester, 1973.
C.A. Mss.   1776-1803
            1803-1824 (Index: E. Foss)
            1824-1850 (Index: E. Foss)
Charter xvii. Ms.

H. Colvin   *A Biography Dictionary of British Architects,* 1660-1840, London, 1978. Prefaced by an authoritative essay on the emergence of the profession of architect. It contains mention of every architect in the text.

D.N.B.

Balguy T. preb.	Noel G. T. preb.
Chard G. W. organist	Nott G. F. preb.
Garnett W. preb.	Rennell T. dean.
Garnier T. preb. & dean.	Wilson W. preb.

W. Dealtry   *Visitation Charges,* Hampshire. (1831,4,5, 1843,6) see also *D.N.B.*
Fox's Chantry Ms.
L.B. Mss.   9 Vols. xxxi — xxxix. 1770-1840.
Records of the Cathedral Close, 1739-1966. Mss.
T.B.   Treasurer's Books. 5 Vols. 1776-1845.
G. Wilkinson   *Turner's early sketchbooks.* London, 1975.

The Great Screen.   (See Page 340)

Chapter XI

The Victorian Cathedral

In 1841, an era in the life of the Cathedral ended. Dean Rennell had died a year before and Prebendary Nott died in 1841. The reform of cathedrals was now on the Statute Book of England and its implications for Winchester inescapable.

The most obvious result was to be a reduction of manpower and money. It was not easy for those closely threatened to see the proposed redistribution of revenue as an act of greater justice to the Church at large, enabling churches and clergy to function where before there had not been the means for such a ministry, particularly in areas affected by the Industrial Revolution. By the end of the century the Visitor of the Cathedral (the Bishop of Winchester) could persuade the Chapter of those days that all had been done wisely and well.

In 1835 and 1836, legislation was proposed and passed under which commissioners were established to administer the revenues of cathedrals and bishoprics not only for the benefit of the cathedrals and the bishops (which meant a diminution in their income) but also for the benefit of the church at large, which meant a releasing of income for wider purposes. In 1836, cathedrals in general made their protest. Among the signatories was C.J. Hoare.[1] Then individual cathedrals sent their own protests. Winchester submitted its own. The Dean and canons maintained that it was vital for the Church to have what it was then fashionable to stigmatize as sinecures so that the theological learning of the Church could be preserved. They went on: "We do not make light of our daily service of prayer and praise... neither would we depreciate the value of our Sunday services . . . But we beg leave to state it as our entire conviction, that the utility of cathedral institutions is not to be measured by considerations of this nature alone."

Cathedrals were "retreats of learned leisure, where, free from the anxieties attendant upon a narrow income, and from the incessant cares which belong to the cure of souls, they could give themselves more entirely to the higher walks of literature and theology . . .". Thus spoke the Winchester Chapter. They instanced among their predecessors who had fulfilled just such a role men like Lowth and Balguy.[2] Modesty forbade them to mention any of their own number by name though they might reasonably have mentioned George Frederick Nott. The Minor Canons too forwarded their case and begged that their minimal stipends might be augmented by the holding of a benefice, attached to their minor canonry.[3]

Dean Garnier, 1840-1872

In 1840, Thomas Garnier, who had been a canon since 1831, was made Dean. His canonry was filled by one of the most energetic canons ever to serve the Cathedral, Samuel Wilberforce. The new Dean held the living of Bishopstoke and had a great reputation as a gardener.[1] He was a member of the Linnaean Society and in due course became its oldest fellow. Perhaps we may see something of his concern for gardens in the clearing and beautifying of The Close which took place during his long tenure of office. In 1840, there were more immediately pressing problems. For less than a year the old order continued. In the following year the process of Reform began with its inevitable logic. For twenty-five years the Dean and Chapter endured what must, for them, have been the despiriting process of seeing their numbers and their income steadily diminished. The office of Dean was to remain. The number of canons was to be cut from twelve to five. This concession was an acknowledgement of the great extent of the diocese, it being conceded that an extra canonry was necessary to finance the archdeaconry of Surrey. In legal terms all was done in accordance with Stat. 3 & 4, Vic. c. 113. In more immediately understood terms it meant that the first canonry to be suppressed was that previously held by Nott who died in 1841. Thereafter, as canonries fell vacant, they were suppressed one by one in 1844, 1846, 1847, 1854, 1859 and, by a final irony, that previously held by the protester C. J. Hoare, in 1865. The result was that by 1865 Dean Garnier no longer had twelve canons but only five and one of those was archdeacon of Surrey and heavily involved in work in the southern outskirts of London where the Diocese was actively at work in buildings, churches, vicarages, schools.[5] The six minor canons were reduced to four. Against such a background it is not surprising that there was uncertainty and discouragement.

It was about 1840 that the term 'prebendary' was finally abandoned and the use of the word 'canon' generally employed. This was due to the new legislation.

All this could account for a description of the Cathedral which Dean Kitchin reports he received from Sir Arthur Phelps in 1854: the Cathedral is "somewhat of a sad sight. You have Grecian monuments cutting into Gothic pillars; the doors shut for the greater part of the day; only a little bit of the building used; beadledom predominant; the chink of money here and there; . . . the singing indifferent; the sermons bad".[6] He went on to write that the Cathedral was too big for the religion it sheltered. It had become "a dried up thing that rattles in an empty place."

Samuel Wilberforce, 1840-1845

When Wilberforce took Garnier's canonry he was more concerned about his parish of Alverstoke and his Archdeaconry of Surrey than he was for his Canonry at Winchester. In addition, he had early attracted notice and had become Chaplain to the Prince - Consort. His own personal tragedy in losing his wife at this early stage in his career meant that he devoted himself all the more earnestly to his work to deaden the pain of his grief.[7] A detailed glimpse of Wilberforce in Winchester became possible with the discovery in 1955 of a large number of the letters of Wilberforce. These were edited by Dr. R. K. Pugh for the Buckinghamshire and Oxford Record Societies in 1970. Dr. Pugh includes 33 letters written from The Close, Winchester in less than thirteen months between February 1843 and February, 1844. The contents of these letters are concerned with the problems of Alverstoke and of his Archdeaconry rather than with the Cathedral.[8] Already Wilberforce was breaking lances with Lord Brougham on the hotly debated matter of education.[9] On the other hand, his learning was such that he was elected to preach the Latin sermon at the opening of Convocation in 1841 where the ceremony continued of opening a parliament of the Church which really did not exist, and Wilberforce voices that complaint.[10] Later, when Bishop of Oxford, he was more able to bring pressure to bear to cause the resumption of the meetings of Convocation.

Returning to the Winchester letters there is possibly only one reference which may have a link with the Cathedral. This is a letter to A. Way who edited a manuscript of the Cathedral *Promptorium Parvulorum*[11] (the first Latin-English Dictionary) for the Camden Society. Possibly for this, Way had approached Wilberforce to secure the support of the Prince Regent in his project. But the link is not explicit. In any case, Wilberforce felt unable to approach the Prince for a work that was not completed. He must see the finished work and then he felt he might be able to use his good offices.

Already Wilberforce had written a good deal. His Clapham connections like those of his colleague Dealtry, are clearly visible in the interest which he had in the Church Missionary Society and also (somewhat suprisingly for those days) in the Society for the Propagation of the Gospel. For most men such missionary support was *either/or* and rarely *both/and*. He edited the *Journals and Letters of Henry Martyn*, a heroic figure who, after unspeakable hardships, translated the Bible and Prayer Book in Hindustani and Persian before dying at the age of thirty one.[12] By way of contrast Wilberforce wrote a book of devotions, *Eucharistica*,[13] a devotional anthology based on the Caroline divines. He also helped publish a five volume work on the life of his Father, the celebrated William Wilberforce.[14] Arising out of his parochial experience he wrote a book of stories for young children to be read in true Victorian style on Sundays. The book was called *Agathos*[15] (Good) and went through many editions and was translated into French and German. All this the young canon had achieved before he left Winchester to be Dean of Westminster for a few months in 1845, before going on to Oxford where between 1845 and 1869 he remodelled the episcopate. The Cathedral seemed to offer no sphere commensurate with the abilities of this restless and very able man. The last work he wrote while at Winchester was a *History of the Protestant Episcopal Church of America,* in 1844.

David Williams, 1833-1860

Another gifted canon who served the Cathedral but found his scope elsewhere was David Williams.[16] Williams was one of those who found complete fulfilment within the foundations of William of Wykeham. A scholar of Winchester College, Fellow of New College, he returned to Winchester to become tutor, under-master and finally Headmaster. Thereafter, he proceeded to twenty years as Warden of New College. At the same time he was from 1833 to 1860 one of the canons. A memorial to him in the south transept states that "his powerful and melodious voice was singularly impressive, whether raised in solemn accents of prayer and praise, or when enforcing the holy doctrine of God his Saviour." As in the case of Wilberforce the Cathedral was a base for activities outside the cathedral and 'residence' was a quiet, almost holiday-like, interruption of his main activities. No wonder there were those who wondered what the role of a cathedral should be.

Samuel Sebastian Wesley.

Samuel Wilberforce.

The Role of a Cathedral

This question was raised both officially and individually on many occasions during Queen Victoria's reign. The first official enquiry was clearly that of the Ecclesiastical Commission.

In 1852 further Commissioners were appointed to inquire into *The state and condition of the Cathedral and Collegiate Churches in England and Wales.* Questions were sent to Winchester. As a result it appeared that at this stage the foundation was reduced from 12 canons to eight and from six minor canons to four. The Report, published in 1854, is most famous, so far as Winchester is concerned, because of the lengthy reply of its organist, Samuel Sebastian Wesley in which he championed in his typically doughty way the cause of Cathedral music. Already the Dean and Chapter were paying to the Commissioners in one year £4,794. In a shrinking revenue it is hard to see how an expanding and improved musical foundation could be established.

The London Gazette (in three issues of April 16th, 1861, August 23rd, 1867., and March 24th., 1889) revealed the further reforms that took place, thus bringing to an end a system of financing the Cathedral which had lasted for over a thousand years. By this time the Cathedral was deprived of all property and received a sum of money from the Commissioners.

Besides these official actions, there were individual writers who entered the lists with their contributions. One was Mackenzie E. C. Walcott (already known as a writer on Winchester), who wrote a work entitled *Cathedralia, A Constitutional History of Cathedrals of the Western Church,* 1865. In it he examines the rôle played by the different office holders in a cathedral not only in England but in Western Europe. He took, almost as a text for his work, some words of Richard Hooker: "Most certain truth it is, that churches cathedral and the bishops of them, wherein the face and very countenance of apostolic antiquity remaineth even as yet to be seen, not withstanding the alterations which tract of time and the course of the world hath brought." Cathedrals are, he maintains, temples to the whole diocese. His book gives, in detail, the establishments and procedures of a large number of cathedrals, from Salisbury to Salamanca.

In 1870 E. M. Goulbourn gave eight sermons on *The Principles of the Cathedral System vindicated and enforced upon members of Cathedral Foundations.* He was concerned with the daily office and saw the cathedral with three other main functions: retreats for contemplation; schools of music; and homes for theological study. He quotes Westcott as writing that "the most conspicuous schemes of Cathedral Reform which have lately gained currency appear to agree in one thing: they are all alike formed without any attempt to understand, still less to realize, the essential ideas which were first contemplated in Cathedral Foundations."

Edward White Benson, himself destined for the highest office in the Church, wrote on *The Cathedral; Its Necessary Place in the Life and Work of the Church* (1878). He saw cathedrals as closely linked with their bishop serving him as a Council. He had some experience of this at Truro, a recent foundation which, whilst excellently suited for new ideas, was not typical of long established foundations with their own traditions. He pointed out that while at the Reformation monastic establishments were swept away, the nine old cathedral foundations remained untouched and eight new ones (of which Winchester was one) were added. Thus, he claims, the Cathedral is an institution approved throughout Europe for many centuries "by Governments, by potentates, by landowners and by the Christian masses". Writing at this late date when the work of the Commissioners was more or less complete, he asserted that Cathedral loss had not proved Church gain. Little had been done to abolish the 'languor' of cathedrals. They must seek out new spheres of activity and service. He looked to clergy training, diocesan missioners, music, library and archives. Schools and hospitals were other possible spheres of activity. It has to be admitted the answer was not yet.

Samuel Sebastian Wesley, 1849-1865

Amidst this uncertainty, the Chapter appointed the most famous organist that the Cathedral has ever known. And whatever problems Wesley may have felt that he had to endure, he was gracious enough to dedicate his *Anthems* to Dean Garnier though he was possibly not fully aware that a diminishing income is not the best recipe for expanding activity. Nor did he always seem to realise that the Chapter suffered from the diminishing income every bit as much as he and his fellow musicians.

Charles Knyvett, with his peculiar sense of humour, supported Wesley's application:

'I have written *this post* to the Bishop and Dean of Winchester . . . having taken every possible shape in *abusing* your detestable talent and your unaccountable presumption in offering yourself as candidate. I now wish you, my dear friend, all success, but I much fear the result proving as I could wish, for there is a person nam'd *Long,* not only so nam'd, but measuring 6 ft. without his night-cap who has serv'd as Dr. Chard's Deputy for many years, and therefore may stand in your way . . . [Dr. Chard] altho' possessing a very nice feeling for music . . . was much more attach'd to fly-fishing and hunting, for frequently, when on his journies to scholars . . . if perchance he heard the hounds, "Tally ho 'tis the merry ton'd hour" says he. "Have at ye go it my Pippins, over hill and dale into the adjoining County" and with or without the brush of the Fox wd. brush into the first Public house handy for brandy, pipes and backie, till sometimes breakfast was next morning waiting his return, besides the many pupils that had been hard practising (during his absence) the *Battle of Prague* . . . . [17]

In due course, Wesley made his application in these words:

Leeds, July 17th. 1849

Reverend Sirs,

I beg leave to submit myself to your notice as a Candidate for the office of Organist in your Cathedral, and to lay before you several Testimonials in my favor from the Clergy connected with the Church at which I have served and from eminent musicians.

I trust these testimonials may obtain your consideration and attention, as well as go far to remove the but too favorable impression under which my pretensions have hitherto laboured.

Should you deem it due to me to confer on me the appointment I do earnestly solicit, I beg to offer my assurances that every possible opportunity shall be taken by me to do justice to its duties, to merit the high honor of your esteem, and to secure for the Musical offices of your Cathedral the approbation of all competent judges.

I beg to subscribe myself,
  Reverend Sirs,
    your obedient humble Servant
      Samuel Sebastian Wesley. [18]

The Dean and Chapter were courageous, if not reckless, in appointing a man who had set out quite plainly his ideals for cathedrals in a volume published just before he left Leeds in 1849 — *A Few Words on Cathedral Music and the Musical System of the Church with a Plan of Reform.*[19] In it he makes it quite clear that he wanted a raising of the professional status of cathedral organists and a raising of musical standards. For sixteen years at Winchester, he strove to do this and despite contemporary difficulties, it can now be said that Wesley's ideals have been generally achieved. So far as Winchester was concerned he achieved three main purposes:

1. The purchase of a better organ. This was the one used at The Great Exhibition in 1851 and which came to be installed in the Cathedral in 1854 In order to secure access to the instrument he caused a spiral staircase to be constructed which went through the roof of the Holy Sepulchre Chapel. His action illustrated perfectly one of the constant dilemmas of any Cathedral. To-day the outcry against such vandalism would have been so strong that such an erection would have been totally out of the question. Mural paintings are an art treasure of highest import.

2. In 1852, he submitted a weighty memorandum to the Report entitled: *State and Condition of the Cathedral and Collegiate Churches in England and Wales.* It is significant that Wesley's return was the longest of those submitted including those by the Bishop and the Dean and Chapter. This was published in 1854.[21] In the main, his plea was that "religious musician should no longer rank as a Lazarus" and should be given the means and resources to offer music of the highest order.

3. In 1853 he published his anthems by Samuel Sebastian Wesley, Vol.1.

To the professional musician Wesley appeals primarily because of his anthems and his organ music. His centenary celebrations in 1976 did much to reveal the wide range of Wesley's ability.[21] For the general churchgoer these achievements are little known and what influences him is a simple matter such as a hymn tune. Here too Wesley had great influence and three tunes alone assure him of continual service to the Church: *Harewood* to which the hymn *Christ is our Corner Stone* is often sung; *Aurelia,* to which is sung *The Church's One Foundation;* and *Hereford* to which is sung *O Thou who camest from above.* There are others but these three alone suggest that the less musical churchmen are also indebted to Wesley for his genius. It is doubtful if ever a Sunday passes without a hymn or an anthem of his being sung somewhere in the Anglican Communion.

"What Chopin did for the piano," wrote Henry Ley, "Wesley did for the English Cathedral Service."

The Fabric

Victorian churchmen at Winchester could not complain that their immediate predecessors had neglected the fabric of their Cathedral According to the *Record of Winchester Cathedral and Close*[22], £40,000 were spent on the Cathedral during the years 1817-1827. For several years choral services were suspended and services took place in the Lady Chapel.

In 1860-1, extensive repairs were carried out on the West Front, as a result of Ewan Christian's survey of 1860. These cost £2,862.[23] A new figure was placed on the gable of the west end and the old figure, variously thought to be Swithun, Edington or Wykeham was taken down and put into the Feretory, later to be removed to the Crypt.

Less important but proving a stage towards the modern heating and lighting of the Cathedral was the installation of gas standards in the Quire in 1867 and heating stoves in the Cathedral generally two years later. This was the first attempt to heat the building as a whole since it was built nearly eight centuries earlier.

Rufus' Tomb

The most famous archaeological work within the Cathedral during Dean Garnier's time was the opening and removal of Rufus' Tomb, in 1868.

Two reports on the opening were published. The first by F. W. Richards,[24] published in 1868, and the second by J. G. Joyce in 1870.[25]

It was opened on August 27th., 1868. The bones discovered in it had been disturbed at some stage, possibly at the time of the Cromwell. Besides the skeleton, a number of objects were found in the tomb:-

1. fragments of a lead coffin
2. cloth of gold
3. red cloth
4. seven gold braids of Norman pattern
5. three kinds of muslin
6. remains of cloth lining to the lead coffin
7. other fabrics resembling serges
8. a turquoise
9. an ivory griffin's head
10. fragments of small wands
11. some flat pieces of cork
12. some broken nutshells, small twigs, and pieces of bark
13. remains of a weapon

Richards considers at some length the truth or otherwise of the tradition that Rufus was buried in this tomb. After examining the evidence of one of the mortuary chests, the evidence of the Cathedral Register, Gale, and other sources he writes:

"We conclude, therefore, that if absolute certainty cannot be arrived at, there is a strong probability in favour of the old and general belief that the remains we have recently seen are in truth those of William Rufus . . . "

Joyce's communication to the Society of Antiquaries two years later concludes after a parellel examination of sources: "There is, I would submit. reason to conjecture that its present occupant filled it from the first, though rudely disturbed at the Rebellion. If it be so, he was probably an older inhabitant than Rufus, and may have had a place in the Cathedral that preceded Walkelyn's."

After the opening of the tomb and its examination the tomb was moved from just in front of the sanctuary steps to a site between the chantries of Beaufort and Waynflete where it remained until 1886 when Dean Kitchin, convinced that the remains were not those of Rufus but of an eminent ecclesiastic, removed the tomb to the quire between the quire stalls.

The Glass of the East Window of the Quire

The other main change in the fabric of the Cathedral during the time of Dean Garnier was the restoration of the window over the east end of the Quire in 1852 by Edward Baillie, of Wardour Street. Hitherto in the centre light had been a broken figure of St. Bartholomew. The view was taken that such a figure was in an inappropriate position and was replaced by a figure of our Lord seated on a rainbow. The fragments were sent to the South Kensington Museum for preservation. The Winchester architect had already published this *Ancient Painted Glass of Winchester Cathedral* in 1845[26] in which he illustrated the windows built in Fox's time above the Great Screen.

The Close

The slimming down of the number of canons left the Chapter with a practical problem. As only five canons existed in 1865, the houses of the canons were no longer needed by their intended occupants. Some, of course, could be let but it is clear that (possibly due to the Dean) thought was given to the general improvement of the appearance of The Close. The House at one time occupied by Thomas Ken fell vacant in 1854. It was a historic house. At the same time it lay in the middle of the Dean's garden. The opportunity was taken to re-draw the lines of the boundaries of No.1. and of the Deanery and to make some subsequent improvements. Thomas Ken's house was pulled down and the Dean's garden extended to the river.

What had hitherto been part of the Dean's garden covering the old Chapter House was tidied and made into a lawn in front of No.1. In addition, a wall on the west side of the arches leading into the old Chapter House was removed, leaving the arches free standing. The whole plan added to the amenities of the Deanery, No.1 and The Close in general. A further improvement in this area which has benefitted the general visitor was the making of a through way past No.1 to the Water Gate. On the other side of The Close what was then No.11, just north of No.10, was partly demolished and partly added to No.10.

Cathedral Services

The influence of Wesley may be further detected in 1857 when what had been the muniment room on the west side of the south transept was given to the choir as a practice room. Previously they had practised in the Exhibition Room belonging to the Library. The *Attendance Registers* indicate that services were continued regularly in accordance with statutes. Occasionally because of some event within the Royal Family or because of some national event, whether in peace or war, special services were authorised to be used. From the 19th century onwards the archives contain many such examples. Sometimes they are services of mourning or repentance, sometimes of celebration or rejoicing.[27] To sum up, during Dean Garnier's time though there was general retrenchment so far as people and money were concerned, the Cathedral was trying to find a new role particularly in the encouragement of a higher standard of music within the parishes of the Diocese.

Dean Bramston, 1872-1883

John Bramston was unique among the deans of Winchester. He came to Winchester after forty two years as incumbent of parishes in Essex, successively of Great Baddow and Witham between the years 1830 and 1872. In five years prior to 1830, he had been a Fellow of Exeter College, Oxford. No sooner was he installed than Bishop Wilberforce was killed in a riding accident and succeeded by E.H. Browne. He decided to revive a right which had long lapsed, that of 'visiting' the Cathedral. This he did in 1874. Evidence of the first visitation can no longer be traced. In 1878, he circulated a questionnaire of fifty-one questions to the Dean, canons, honorary canons, minor canons, organist and lay clerks. The Dean answered the questions as fully as possible. Most of the other recipients of the questionnaire referred to the Dean's answers. He reveals that there were

The Deanery.

only four canons (not the statutory five) and four minor canons, nine lay vicars, 16 choristers, two virgers and two sub-sacrists, three clerks or bellringers, one porter, a chapter clerk, and 12 bedesmen. Coming to the fabric, he is of the opinion that the sum of c£650 which is available each year for fabric maintenance and repairs to the roads is altogether insufficient. The Cathedral services are at 8.30 am, 11 am and 3.30 pm on Sundays and at 10 am and 4 pm on week days. The Muniment Room is reported as for many years disused; the Library had some books for loan to the clergy; sermons were preached regularly on Sundays.

Bramston himself has left us a small volume of his own sermons, *A Few Addresses from the pulpit in Winchester Cathedral* (1887), covering the years 1872 to 1883. The first one to be printed is of especial interest as it was delivered shortly after assuming his duties as Dean and indicate the humility of the man: "When I think, therefore, of myself installed as chief Minister of this great and glorious Cathedral I am filled with dismay at the thought of inefficiency and unworthiness, the very magnificence of this Cathedral seems to tell us that the kingdom of God is acknowledged here, the ample provision for the service and worship of God in the harmony of musical sounds, and the union of many voices uttering the praises of the Almighty ought to impress us all every day ...every Lay Clerk and Chorister, every Clergyman connected with the Cathedral and above all the Dean, ought to be by his heart worship to be raised to a higher tone.... I can conceive no sadder thing than....to sink into a mere formal iteration of beautiful words without heart or meaning."

There is one paper of interest which indicates that like one of his successors he had to secure at least the degree of B.D. in order to be appointed Dean. Among his addresses is an exercise for the degree which he took in 1872, on the subject of Christian Baptism. It is, in fact, a short essay and can only have been a formality rather than a serious academic examination.[28]

For the first time in the Cathedral's history and indeed the history of the Diocese, it is possible in Dean Bramston's time actually to see the clergy and some of the other members of the Cathedral staff e.g. the virgers. Mrs Bramston collected in a large album the sepia photographs of the Bishop, the Dean, the Canons Residentiary, the Honorary Canons and the clergy of the diocese. It is a gallery of Victorian Churchmen. The photographs are all of characteristic gravity and cover the years 1873 to 1883.

Cheyney Court in the 19th century and to-day.

Bishop Browne's Charge, 1878[29]

The Bishop Browne (1873-1890) was acutely sensitive of the fact that his exercising of his undoubted right, which his predecessors had neglected, possibly for centuries, might be mis-construed as questioning the faithfulness or efficiency of the Dean and Chapter. This was far from the case. He surveyed what he took to be the origin of the work of the bishops and their cathedrals in the very early days of the history of the Church. He thought that their first use prompted ideas as to their use in the nineteenth century. They should be, as once they were, centres from which priests went out to evangelize the Bishop's *parochia* or diocese. It is true that in time it was felt that a resident rather than visiting priest was more satisfactory. Then the clergy of the cathedral acted as a council to the Bishop. They should do so again. Though he had to admit a certain confusion in the emergence of councils and committees in the diocese and in the central organs of the Church which were undertaking this very work. One further work which the Cathedral might undertake was the immediate training of men for the ministry, though again he had no wish to take men away from Oxford or Cambridge. The Bishop had courageously addressed himself to the problem of the Cathedral's role but he too had not yet found the answer.

The Ecclesiastical Commissioners, 1879

Mid-way through his time as Dean, Bramston and the Chapter were asked by the Commissioners twenty questions about the current financial position of the Cathedral, now that its numbers were reduced and its resources reduced. The considered answer of the Dean and Chapter was forwarded in 1879 though not published until 1884. The report indicates that the resolution to take away all the lands from the Cathedral had been modified and that some had been returned. Despite this help the Commissioners themselves admitted (in 1884) "that since 1879...the income of the Cathedral has fallen so seriously that at one time it seemed very doubtful whether the Dean and Chapter would be able to perform the duties entrusted to them, or to maintain the fabric of the Church, and the musical services and charities proper to it." They undertook that the stipends of Dean and Canons should not fall below the figure set in 1861. If they did the question of residence would be re-considered. The position, therefore, of the Cathedral was not altogether assured.

Cathedral Music

During Bramston's time G.B. Arnold established himself as Organist and Choir Master. A former pupil of Wesley, he had inevitably been overshadowed by his teacher. Whether or not Wesley first had the notion of a Diocesan Choral Festival it is impossible to say. What does emerge is the fact that the first of such festivals took place in 1866 and continued at intervals during Bramston's occupation of the Deanery. These were great occasions indeed from the point of view both of numbers and organisation as the detailed plans of the Cathedral drawn up for the Festivals clearly indicate. Train loads of choristers converged from every part of the diocese. For the first time Cathedral music was actively reaching out beyond the Cathedral walls and helping to encourage organists and choristers within the parishes.

Arnold was no mean musician. He was the youngest person ever to receive the Doctorate of Music from Oxford, being only twenty years of age. He was both organist and pianist and had learned singing under one of the best Italian teachers of the day. On the eve of his appointment to Winchester his oratorio *Ahab* was performed by the National Choral Society at Exeter Hall, London and was favourably received. It received its first performance in Winchester at St. John's Rooms in 1867. A reporter observed: "numerous and distinguished guests praised the work." Some of Arnold's songs, however, were less favourably received and readers were warned: "Poverty of melody is so often concealed by being nicely harmonised in four parts and sung without accompaniment. "Arnold himself never set out to be a popular composer. Locally he was generally well received, as for example when he performed his oratorio *Sennacherib* in 1883. Local critics spoke "most flattering words of approbation". Critics further afield were divided. In London the music was dismissed as "common place". Yet in Berlin a critic wrote "I perceive that I have to do with the work of a first class composer." [30]

Dean Kitchin, 1883-1895

In 1883, Gladstone nominated George Kitchin to succeed Bramston. Kitchin had a brilliant career at Oxford and was already well known as a writer on historical subjects ranging from a three volume *History of France* to learned monographs. Winchester was not new to him for as a young man he had been Headmaster of Twyford School before returning to Oxford. One obvious aspect of the Cathedral which he exploited, really for the first time, was its historical muniments. He did much to edit and publish a number of volumes: *The Obedientiary Rolls of the Cathedral, 1308-1573* which lists the income and expenditure of the various officers who worked for the monastery; *A Consuetudinary of the Fourteenth Century for the*

Refectory; A Charter of Edward III; Cathedral Documents from 1541-1547
giving in great detail the documents relevant during the crucial years of the
Reformation, so far as Winchester Cathedral is concerned; and the Manorial
Rolls of *Manydown,* one of the manors of the Monastery. Kitchin also
produced a popular history of *Winchester,* [31] He also did a great deal of
lecturing and in recent years many of his papers have found their way into
the Cathedral Archives. Here are some of the subjects on which he lectured
in and around Winchester: *Dante, Man and his Tools, Gregory, English
Church History, The Great Rebellion.* Having married an English lady
brought up in Denmark, he was interested in Danish History and translated
Danish works into English. We owe a great deal to him for making available
so many of the archives of the Cathedral.

The Churchyard[32]

Kitchin also was the first to undertake the work of excavating the area
north of the Cathedral. This too appealed to his historic sense. He dug
trenches in the outer churchyard as he realised that earlier buildings lay
under the grass. One result of this was a great campaign, not long after his
arrival, to tidy up the Churchyard. A Committee was formed in 1885 and
quickly decided to move some grave stones "without enquiry as to objection
by any person who might be interested." These graves are all numbered and
correspond to a plan of the burials which is still available. Shortly afterwards
a notice was published which was more conciliatory:

> It is purposed to **REMOVE** some of the **GRAVESTONES** now standing
> in the Churchyard. Relatives having an interest in any stones and who
> may object to such removal, are requested to communicate at once with
> the Very Rev. the Dean.
>
> Deanery, Dec. 21. 1885

Communications were sent in, some reasonable and accepted: others
simply objections for the sake of objection. Amongst the correspondents was
one who pleaded for the preservation of the stones of Matthew and Mary
David who had lived in College Street and owned the house when Jane
Austen lived her last two months. While this campaign was being conducted
there were those who were sending donations "for improvement of
Winchester Cathedral Churchyard."

The ground level outside the west wall of the north transept was lowered
by four feet, so revealing the original level of the entrance in that wall. A
striking discovery was a majestic piece of sculpture representing some priestly
or royal person.

CITIZENS OF WINCHESTER
PROTEST

THAT you *will not* see the Graves of the Poorer Citizens of Winchester in the Cathedral Church Yard violated to serve the ends of certain Aristocrats who desire a better approach to their homes in the Close.

The Stones are numbered and will soon be no more if you do not move in the matter.

Are we poorer ones in this OUR CITY going to see a repetition of what has occurred here before and also in London through the avarice and greed of the Aristocracy?

Fellow Citizens, this Appeal is to you! What will you do?

The Aristocrats were the ones who robbed the Charities and fleeced the poor and now they are going to rob the dead of their right to rest in peace.

Don't be moved but stand firm.

Who will take the first step and inaugurate a Public Meeting at the Russian Gun?

Issued by one of the

" GREAT UNWASHED."

GOD SAVE THE QUEEN.

The Close

The Close too received attention. The plaster which had covered Cheyney Court, certainly since early in the nineteenth century, was removed in 1886 and its beams revealed. In 1896 the Dean and Chapter sold No.4, The Close for the use of H.M. Judges at a cost of just under £4,000 in a 999 year lease and a rent of £10 per annum. It is now maintained by the Department of the Environment.

The Crypt

From Churchyard and Close to Crypt was a logical development of archaeological and historical interest. Sometime in the 18th century its floor had been covered with nearly five feet of earth in order to absorb the flooding of the Crypt. The proportions of the structure were, therefore, seriously affected. When the original level was recovered no harm seemed to ensue. There was, however, an interesting discovery under the east wall of the Lady Chapel.

Bishop Courtenay's tomb

Bishop Courtenay died on September 2nd, 1492. The location of his burial place had been lost. However, when work was undertaken at the very east end of the Crypt under the groined vault of the Lady Chapel, there was found in it a leaden coffin, built up with stone and brick. The coffin was over six feet long and on it was a plain Latin cross and at the foot of the cross the shield of the Bishop's family arms. This pointed strongly to the conclusion that the body inside the tomb was that of Bishop Courtenay. Inspection of the tomb supported the inference. There were remains of the funeral pastoral staff. It may also be noted that the burial is above the water level. The question then arose as to whether the tomb should be left where it was, or be given a more prominent burial. In the end the fragment containing the cross and the Courtenay arms was placed in a new ledger stone, the coffin carefully removed, and a new monument placed in the south east corner of the Quire near the altar rails.

Rufus Tomb

We have already referred to the removal of the Rufus Tomb in 1868 to a place in the retrochoir. Kitchin was strongly of the view that such a place was inappropriate and decided that it should be returned to the Quire, not indeed to its former situation near the altar steps, but beneath the Norman tower where tradition says Rufus was originally buried. This was carried out in 1886. At the same time Kitchin raised again the identity of the person buried in the tomb and agreed with Joyce that it was almost certainly not Rufus (for his bones are mingled with those of Canute in one of the mortuary chests), but of some eminent but unknown ecclesiastic.

The Duke of Beorn

The Dean continued his researches and revealed for the first time, certainly since the Fox screen was built, the tomb of Rufus' younger brother who was also killed while out hunting. A careful drawing of the discovery was made by the eminent local historian Francis Baigent. Passers by in the south presbytery aisle can see where the burial took place for it is marked with a Latin inscription: *Intus est corpus Richardi Wilhelmi Conquestoris filii et Beorniae Ducis* (Within is the body of Richard, son of William the Conqueror and Duke of Beornia.)

Nicholas de Ely

Adjacent to the young prince is another discovery made by Kitchin in 1887. All that is visible now is the Latin inscription: *Intus est cor Nicolai olim Winton Episcopi Cuius corpus est apud Waverlie* ("Within this wall is the heart of Nicholas, late Bishop of Winchester, whose body lies at Waverley".) Again Baigent comes to our rescue with his clear drawings of what was found in 1887.

Over the casket containing the heart is a lead plate which bears a Latin inscription:

> Hic humatus *est* cor Nicholay de Hely
> Wintoniensis Epi qui abiit anno gra
> cie Mil.CCLXXIX die lune ante festu
> Sci Valentyni

> Here is buried the heart of Nicholas of Ely
> Bishop of Winchester who departed in the year
> Of Grace 1279 on the Monday before the Feast of
> Saint Valentine

The date represented February 12th., 1279/80.

Mary Sumner, Charlotte Yonge and Josephine Butler

An impression could easily arise that Kitchin's tenure of office was solely concerned with history and archaeology. It would not be unkind or untrue to say that these were his predominant interests. He found it difficult, after discharging the routine of the services, to see the spiritual ministry of the Cathedral. One of his colleagues Canon Durst found him unaware of strongly held views by churchmen as churchmen. There was an occasion

Mary Sumner's one-time home

when a Canon, on first entering into 'residence' conducted the Holy Communion after his wont, in accordance with the more tractarian views that he held. This caused some pain to others and some surprise. The Canon immediately offered to resign rather than cause any disturbance. To the credit of all concerned it was agreed that each should conduct the service in accordance with his own scruples.

There were, however, in The Close at the time of Kitchin's work, two very remarkable women: Mary Sumner and Josephine Butler. Mary Sumner was wife of Bishop Sumner, himself the son of the Bishop Charles Sumner, who was at that time Bishop of Guildford, a suffragan of Winchester. To the year 1885 a later generation ascribed the origin of the Mothers' Union. On one of the buttresses added to the Cathedral in the years 1905-1912 is affixed

Mary Sumner.

Josephine Butler.

Charlotte Yonge.

the following inscription:

> To the Glory of God and in gratitude
> to Mary Elizabeth Sumner, Founder of
> the Mothers' Union, A.D. 1885, this
> buttress is given by members of the
> Empire in recognition of her work for
> the sanctity of home life. A.D. 1912.

This inscription summarisies a whole chapter of the history of the Anglican Communion. Before coming to live in The Close, the Sumners had been at Old Alresford and there as Rector's wife, Mary Sumner began to take great interest and concern in the women of the parish. When she moved to Winchester she was asked to speak on the subject to a Church Congress at Portsmouth in 1885. She was extremely nervous and hesitant about doing so but finally overcame her reluctance. From then onwards the Mothers' Union grew in strength and influence. It withstood the break up of the British Empire and has spread its influence wherever the Anglican Communion is represented. To say that it has had problems is to say no more than that it has had to undergo the trials that beset any living organisation as it lives from generation to generation.[33]

Charlotte Yonge

One of the women Mrs. Sumner invited to help with the literary work involved in disseminating the news and views of the Mothers' Union, was Charlotte Yonge who lived at Otterbourne, near Winchester. She was also an ardent worker in her parish and much influenced by John Keble. It is not surprising that when Charlotte Yonge died in 1901 Bishop George Sumner, in his capacity as a member of Chapter, proposed a memorial to Charlotte Yonge in the Cathedral in the form of a reredos in the Lady Chapel. Somewhat unenthusiastically the motion was accepted — provided the Dean and the Chapter incurred no expense.

Josephine Butler

About the time Kitchin was appointed to Winchester, George Butler, Headmaster of Liverpool College, was offered, also by Gladstone, a canonry at Winchester. His wife was the more famous of the two. For while her husband was running a modest public school in Liverpool, Josephine Butler became aware of the intolerable conditions under which many women and girls lived in a great sea port. With quiet courage she went out to tackle the problems of prostitution and the White Slave Trade. The slums of Liverpool were very different from The Close at Winchester but she did not forget her crusade and pressed forward until she secured legislation for the repeal of the Contagious Diseases Act (1886). Her influence was so great that foreign governments sought her help and guidance in dealing with similar problems in their own countries. Mary Sumner began a great work in the Church. On the other hand Josephine Butler began a great work in the world. The initiatives of both women are still very much alive. The Cathedral can be proud of such pioneers.[34]

The Great Screen[35]

Dean Kitchin's greatest work was the restoration of the Great Screen. Somewhat wistfully Dean Bramston had previously regretted that his age prevented his undertaking it, much as he saw the desirability for the work. In 1878 he had written: "It would indeed be desirable to complete the entire restoration of the Screen, and to provide suitable figures for all the niches, but the present Dean shrinks from so great an undertaking. A commencement however might be made, which would lead at some future time to an entire restoration".

He then made certain suggestions, some of which were followed and some of which, in the event, were not followed. He suggested a beginning might be made with the figures of St. John and of the Blessed Virgin under the Cross, the figures of St. Peter and St. Paul. In the same year the eminent architect, Sir Gilbert Scott, who had recently completed the west side of the Quire Screen, was approached. He replied that he would have to make careful measurements before any ideas could be proposed.

Dean Bramston died and the architect Street came into the picture in 1880. He was sympathetic towards the general idea of restoration and proposed that a fund be set up to carry out the work. The only decorative feature of the Great Screen was Benjamin West's picture above the altar.

In 1884, one of the Cathedral's most loved clergymen, Archdeacon Jacob, died. Cathedral and City held him in the highest esteem and a deputation, headed by the Mayor, waited on Dean Kitchin, to suggest that a worthy memorial ought to be erected in memory of the Archdeacon. In the end, and by an unanimous vote, it was agreed that the memorial should take the form of the Restoration of the Great Screen.

The Society for the Protection of Ancient Buildings

News of the Dean and Chapter's intention to appeal for funds reached the knowledge of the Society for the Protection of Ancient Buildings. They were quick to lodge a formal protest:-

23rd February, 1885

To the Very Rev. The Dean and Chapter.
Gentlemen
......"These alterations whether they be in themselves things of beauty or as the Committee think merely disfigurements, can only be carried out at the cost of irreparable damage to the original work. The modernizing of the Screen and its consequent discord with its surroundings is probably not desired, but similar restorations have conclusively proved that such a result is inevitable. Nor will this be atoned for by any intrinsic merit in the new work. Those who engage in the trade of supplying the demand created by the wish to restore old monuments are neither original nor trained artists, but merely copiers....."

The Committee, therefore, strongly urged the Dean and Chapter to withdraw their consent to the proposed alterations.

The Dean and Chapter were not convinced by the objection and decided to continue the project. They received sufficient funds to set the work in hand. On March 25th, 1885 the following resolution passed at a meeting of the Committee for the Restoration of the Great Screen of the Cathedral as a Memorial to the late Archdeacon Jacob was read:- "That the money collected for the purpose of the Restoration of the Great Screen as a Memorial to the late Archdeacon Jacob be expanded on the Stonework and Canopies throughout, and of the Statues in the Central Compartment, and in the erection of a Cross without a figure thereon.

"That the names of Mr. Bodley and Mr. J.D. Sedding be forwarded to the Dean and Chapter with a recommendation that one or other be selected as architect".

Mr. Sedding was selected and the sum of £2,109 was made available for the initial work.

On September 25th of the same year Mr. Sedding was instructed to prepare a general design of the Screen, reproducing as far as possible the stonework as originally constructed, and shewing the character of the statues and the mode of treatment of each. The statues to be treated in accordance with the style and date of the Screen. No statue was to be carried out until the cast of it has been placed in its niche and approved by the Cathedral Committee and the Dean and Chapter. After about two and a half years the Dean and Chapter were so dis-satisfied with the work that they terminated Mr. Sedding's appointment and chose Mr. G.H. Kitchin instead.

Lord Montagu of Beaulieu

In November, 1886, Lord Montagu of Beaulieu addressed a protest to the Dean and Chapter:

> "I was quite horrified the other day, just before I left home, to hear that there is a proposal on foot to put a statue of Izaac Walton into one of the niches of the Great Screen. I hope you utterly refuse to give your sanction to any such thing".

The noble Lord was horrified that a layman should be portrayed on a Screen on which the central Figure was to be our Lord surrounded by the saints.

The Dean replied: "It was always intended to have a number of small figures of those distinguished in the history of Winchester..." It seemed to him that the Screen would then connect together the different ages during which Englishmen had worshipped God together in the Cathedral; and so become a real representation of the English Church.

The Work Resumed

By 1888 work on the actual figures could begin. The artists to be employed were Miss M.L. Gaunt, Mr. Geflowski and Mr. R. Boulton who worked under the supervision of Mr. G. Buckle, "Surrey Extraordinary" of the College of Heralds. Within three years all the figures on the screen were completed, the Central Figure alone excepted, in time for the enthronement of Bishop Thorold on 3rd March, 1891. During the course of the project, a further artist, Mr. Nichols was invited to undertake some of the work.

The Crucifix

The most important part still remained to be completed: the Central Figure and what was to be done with the space still occupied by Benjamin West's picture.

Religious views of the time were such that much feeling was caused between those who considered that a plain simple cross was appropriate and those who thought that a Crucifix was appropriate. Then a further idea was mooted following an ancient idea that Christ reigned triumphantly from the Cross and that he should be represented crowned. Incidentally this took up the fact that for centuries the crown of Canute had been given to the Cathedral.

On Easter Day, March 25th, 1894, it was decided to display a model of the Christ Crowned and reigning from the Cross. The Figure was to wear royal robes in the attitude and act of benediction. The Diocesan Chronicle for May 1894 simply records the chilly paragraph: "The Dean and Chapter have decided not to take any further steps for the present with reference to the filling up the central space of the Great Screen." Clearly public opinion was too strong and the idea was dropped.

Dean Stephens, 1895-1903

In 1895 Dean Kitchin was appointed Dean of Durham, a post which carried with it that of Warden of the Durham Colleges. The double appointment was eminently suited to his particular gifts and combined ecclesiastical and academic interests in a way that suited his many and varied abilities. He was succeeded by William Richard Wood Stephens, a voluminous writer, son-in-law of the celebrated Dean Hook, Dean of Chichester and author of his biography. He also wrote a biography of the distinguished historian E.A. Freeman. While at Winchester, as joint editor of a series of volumes on *The History of the English Church,* he wrote the volume covering the period between the Norman Conquest and the end of the thirteenth century. This was published in 1901.

More Work on the Great Screen

On arrival he was faced with the incomplete work on the Great Screen but seems happily to have carried on with the work begun by Kitchin and indeed co-operated with him in writing the definitive work about it. This appeared in 1899, the year in which the work was completed. It was left to the new Dean to sell Benjamin West's picture, The Raising of Lazarus, to Pierpont Morgan. At that stage it was intended for the Cathedral in New York. The first intention did not materialise and finally the work rested alongside a portrait of West in the Wadsworth Athenaeum in Hartford, Connecticut.

Another area in which the new Dean was happy to complete the work of his predecessor was to join in the publication of the second volume of *Winchester Cathedral Documents, 1636-1683* for the Hampshire Record Society.

Reparation of the Nave Roof

Work on the Great Screen was interrupted yet again because more essential work had to be undertaken in connection with the repair of the roofs of the Cathedral in 1896. J.B. Colson, the Architectural Surveyor to the Dean and Chapter, reported at first on the problem at the western end of the Nave. Here the wooden beams were resting on the inside stone roof of William of Wykeham and threatening to destroy Wykeham's lierne vaulting. The problem was how to continue with the wooden beams which supported the outside roof and yet take the weight off the inside stone roof. This Colson did by re-designing the structure of the beams. The tie beams across the nave were able to be raised and thus abolish the downward thrust upon the stone roof. At the same time, the wooden beams were strong enough to support the outside lead roof. One problem was the impossibility at the time of securing oak beams of the length and size to do the work required and the timber had to be brought from Stettin. Attention was given to the damage done to the beams by woodworm *(sirex gigas)*. Traces of the fire of 1698 recorded in manuscript diary of William Emes, Fellow of Winchester College, in 1698, were also noted. Over fifty cartloads of rubbish were removed from the roof. Repairs were undertaken, once the scaffolding was in place, to the roofs of the Chancel, the North Transept and part of the South Presbytery Aisle. The Belfry floor was also repaired. The whole of this work lasted from 1896 to 1898. Colson gives some striking statistics of his work. He needed 9,678 cubic feet of new timber weighing 198¼ tons. He required 16,274 cubic feet of pitch pine weighing 326¾ tons. He used nearly 40 tons of iron and 197½ tons of lead. Altogether about 17 miles of battens were used.[36]

The Completion of the Great Screen

At long last the work of the Great Screen could be completed. It was finally decided to have a Crucifix as the centre of the screen, it being considered that this was the original design. Finally, below that and in the place of West's painting, it was decided with generous help from Mrs. Valpy, to sculpt a representation of the Holy Family and to carve six saints:St. Margaret, St. Catherine, St. Anne, (Mother of our Lord and holding a tabernacle, She is the patron saint of carvers) St. Agnes, St. Cecilia (patron saint of music) and St. Faith.

Thus the project put forward by Dean Bramston in 1878 was finally completed twenty one years later and two deans later in 1899.[37]

The Lady Chapel Windows

East Window

Between1897 and 1900 the three main windows of the Lady Chapel were filled with glass. This was very much a project dear to the heart of Dean Stephens. The East window or Jubilee window had as its main theme the central Christian doctrine of the Incarnation, the royal line of David culminating in Jesus Christ. Such a window is often called a Jesse window as it depicts the royal line from the father of David, Jesse, right down to the birth of Christ. Jesse's descendants are depicted. In addition, royal and ecclesiastical personages of England are also depicted doing homage to the Son of David. Among English royalty are Queen Elizabeth of York, wife of Henry VII, by whose liberality the Chapel was extended, and Queen Victoria whose Diamond Jubilee was celebrated in 1897. The window was the work of C.E. Kempe. He preserved such fragments as he could of earlier glass. A local feature is the depicting of the Mayor of Winchester of that time, Mr. H. Webb, in his robes of office and representing the citizens of Winchester, the donors of the window.

South Window

This window, installed in 1897 to recall the ministry of Bishop Thorold from 1891 to 1895, contains representations of scenes in the life of Our Lord in which the Virgin Mary appeared. Among the saints represented in the window are St. Birinus and St. Swithun and St. Alphege. St. Anthony is also represented as being appropriate in view of the Bishop's Christian name. Kynegils, Bishop Fox, Henry VII and Prince Arthur are also, appropriately, represented.

The North Window

The last window to be added was the north window. This was made possible by realising part of the funds produced by the sale of the Benjamin West's picture, The Raising of Lazarus. This window too is a work of C.E. Kempe

The Visitation of 1900

The year 1900 marked the end of a century and, as it turned out, the end of a reign and of an era. Even then a service to mark the end of the century indicates an awareness of this. It is not surprising, therefore, that Randall Davidson, the Bishop, should think it fit to "visit" his Cathedral.

This was more than a formal occasion with a long list of questions. It put three searching questions about the place of the Cathedral in the life of the local Church.

1. What methods, if any, can you suggest whereby the Cathedral could be brought into fuller practical connexion with Diocesan work?

2. In your opinion, could either (1) the Dean and Canons Residentiary, or (2) the Greater Chapter as a whole, advantageously act as a Council to the Bishop on Diocesan affairs? If so, what suggestions can you offer as to place, time, subjects, manner of consultation?

3. Can the corporate unity and life of the Cathedral be increased? If so, how?

The Dean's Reply

Although 71 out of 80 members of the Foundation attended, the questionnaire this time seems only to have been sent to the clergy. There are no existing replies from the laity, the musicians and other officers of the Dean and Chapter. The Dean seems to have been sent a supplementary list of 24 questions of a more detailed nature. By this time the Dean could report not only about special sermons but about a number of special services. The Army and Winchester also made regular use of the Cathedral for their services. It is noteworthy that only the Lady Chapel ever had a service of Holy Communion in it, apart from the Quire. Wykeham's Chantry had recently been furnished with an altar but had not so far been used. Residences and Chapter Meetings were regular and presented no problems. The Minor canons all had extra duties either in a parish or at the hospital. Canon Madge also looked after the Library. There are nine lay clerks, and choristers were educated under their own master in one of the Dean and Chapter houses. There were sixteen choristers but the Dean, out of his own purse, had provided two more. Dr. Arnold was well spoken of as still regular in all his duties. There were 12 bedesmen and the officers of the Dean and Chapter; Receiver, Chapter Clerk and Architectural Surveyor discharged their duties satisfactorily. The Receiver, it may be noted, lived at Oxford. As for the fabric it was 'in good substantial repair' Another £3,000 should meet all requirements. The Library was on good order. The stipends were approximately £1,200 for the Dean and £600 for the Canons.

The discussion arising out of the answers to the questions was not reported.

The Bishop's Charge

The Bishop's Charge was characteristic in that it was set in a detailed historic setting. He goes back to the time of the Reformation when the monastery was suppressed and reveals that Cranmer was not in favour of prebendaries. He favoured the encouragement of learning. Prebendaries were only good 'vianders' (providers of good viands). The Bishop reminded the Dean and Chapter of their own charter by which they were established in 1541, then of the statutes of Charles I and Archbishop Laud, and then finally of the legislation of 1840 which reduced the numbers and finances of the cathedrals. The reforms were necessary because of the abuses of the eighteenth century. He quotes Archbishop Benson's description about cathedrals being "enervated, paralysed, devitalized." He went on to show that the suppression of prebends had released sums of money which now served to vitalize life in the parishes of England. Moreover, the Commissioners were managing estates more efficiently so that in fact the estates of which cathedrals had been dispossessed were producing more both for cathedrals and for parishes than ever before. In all, the reform was necessary and had in fact proved beneficial, not least to the cathedrals. He believed that the services in the cathedrals in 1900 were far better conducted than ever they were in his boyhood. There had been a marked improvement.

By the end of the century the Cathedral was finding its new role and was conducting the *opus Dei* better than it had done for many years. Indeed the Cathedral had reached a turning point in its long history.

FURTHER READING

A.R. Mss. 6 vols. 1839-1909
C.A. 4 vols. 1824-1914. Each volume indexed by E.Foss.
D.N.B. Butler G. 1819-1890 Butler J. 1828-1906 Carter O.B. 1806-1859 Garnier T. 1776-1873 Hoare C.J. 1781-1865 Noel G.T. 1782-1851 Wilson W. 1783-1873
Davidson R.T. Visitation Mss. 1900. *Charge*, 1900.
L.B. Mss 5 Vols. 1841-1875. (the end of the Ledger Book)
London Gazette re Church Commissioners and Winchester Cathedral: 16 April, 1861. pp. 1582-1597 23 August, 1867 pp.4668-4678. 23 March, 1899 pp.1975-2014
Matthews B. *Samuel Sebastian Wesley*, 1976. Privately printed
R.S. First such volume begins in 1896
Records of the Cathedral and Close, 1739-1966
Report *State and Condition of the Cathedral and Collegiate Churches in England and Wales, 1854*
P.W Sergeant *The Cathedral Church of Winchester*
T B. Mss. 4 vols. 1838-1892 (last volume)
H.Wray. *Catalogues of books in the Library of Winchester Cathedral.* Mss.

NOTES

1. *Church Commission, Memorials and Communicators from the Cathedral and Collegiate Churches of England. London, 1838.* pp. 1-5. Hoare was canon of Winchester, 1831-1865.
2. *Ibid.* pp.59-63.
3. *Ibid.* p.63.f.
4. E. Venables. *Thomas Garnier* (1776-1873) *D.N B.* s.v. "The garden...at Bishopstoke was very celebrated, especially for rare shrubs".
5. *Conspectus of the Diocese of Winchester, 1854.* A further edition, brought up to date, was published in 1864.
6. Dean Kitchin Papers. MSS.
7. A.R. Ashwell. *The Life of...Samuel Wilberforce.* London, 1880. Vol.I.cc.v.vi.
8. R.K. Pugh. *The Letter Books of Samuel Wilberforce, 1843-1868.* Oxfordshire Record Society.1970
9. S. Wilberforce. *A Letter to the Rt. Hon. Henry, Lord Brougham on the Government Plan of Education.* London, 1840.
10. *Concio ad Clerum Provinciae Cantuariensis in Aede Paulina habita* London, 1841.
11. Winchester Cathedral MSS XV. 14th cent.
12. S. Wilberforce. *Journals and Letters of the Rev. Henry Martyn.* London, 1839.
13. S. Wilberforce. *Eucharistica.* London, 1839
14. R.I. Wilberforce and S. Wilberforce. *The Life of William Wilberforce* Five volumes. London, 1838
15. As late as 1896 the book was still being published S. Wilberforce *Agathos and Other Sunday Stories.* (In full prize calf)
16. T.F. Kirby. *Annals of Winchester College.* London, 1892. p.424.f.
17. B. Matthews. The Music of Winchester Cathedral. London, 1974. p.21.
18. Winchester Cathedral MS.
19. Leeds, 1849. (Reprinted, 1961)
20. S.S. Wesley. *Reply to the Inquiries of the Cathedral Commissioners.* London Separately printed. n.d.? 1854.
21. P. Chappell. Dr. S.S. Wesley. In 1976 there was published the first number of the *Gazette* of The Wesley Society of Great Britain.
22. Winchester Cathedral MS.
23. *W.C.C.* 1800-1865. p. 190 (MS.)
24. F.W. Richards. *William Rufus. His Tomb.* Winchester, 1868.
25. J.G. Joyce *On the Opening of a Tomb in Winchester Cathedral,* 1871.
26. O.B. Carter. *The Ancient Painted Glass of Winchester Cathedral,* 1845.
27. *Special Services, 1797-1937.*
28. John Bramston. *A Few Addresses from the Pulpit in Winchester Cathedral. Winchester, 1887*
29. Bishop Browne. *Visitation. 1878.* G.2.4.
30. See typed thesis of M.J.F. Smith *Winchester Cathedral. A Musical Backwater in the Second Half of the Nineteenth Century.* 1978.
31. For a detailed record of Kitchin's publications see *Crockford's Clerical Directory, 1902*
32. *Churchyard and Crypt, 1885-1886.* MS.
33. J.Coombs. *George and Mary Sumner.* London, 1965.
34. G.W. and Lucy A. Johnson. *Josephine Butler. An Autobiographical Memoir.* 3rd edn. London, 1928. See c. XIII. Winchester.
35 G.W. Kitchin. *The Great Screen of Winchester Cathedral,* 1899.
36. J.B. Coison. *The Reparation of the Nave Roof,* 1898.
37. F.Bussby *W.C.R.* 1978 and 1979. Illustrated.

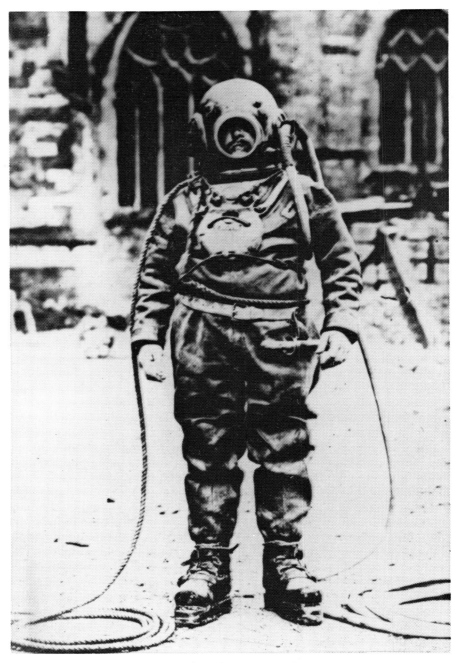

Weight of Dress 200 lbs.

William Walker the diver.

Chapter XII

The Edwardian Era

Preaching at the completion of the underpinning of the Cathedral which had taken nearly seven years to complete between 1905 and 1912, Archbishop Davidson said, on July 15th, 1912, St. Swithun's Day: "The names of Ryle and Furneaux, with the trio of redoubtable men, the great architect Thomas Graham Jackson, the resourceful engineer Francis Fox, and — for it must be added — William Robert Walker, will hold place for good in the annals of our century's beginning."

Dominant as these men were and still are, as we look back on those opening years, the remarkable fact is that an enterprise which might justly have claimed the total energies of the Dean and Canons and all their helpers, did not in fact exhaust their contribution to the life of the Cathedral, the City or indeed to the Church at large.

It is a platitude to say that the death of Queen Victoria marked the end of an era. The platitude, however, is a truth. R.C.K. Ensor who contributed the volume in the *Oxford History of England (p.268)* which covers the years 1870 to 1914 writes: "...the shock of her death struck the nation at a dark hour, when it had just discovered that the war (i.e. the South African War), presumed to have been won, was still not in sight of an ending. Men felt that a great epoch had closed..." What was true of the country as a whole was true of Winchester in particular. The Queen died at Osborne in the Isle of Wight, then in the Diocese of Winchester. It fell, therefore, to Randall Davidson, Bishop of Winchester, to offer his ministrations to the dying sovereign. The more so, because between 1883 and 1891 he had been Dean of St. George's, Windsor and in that capacity had enjoyed the special confidence of the Queen. The story is set out in great detail in G.K.A Bell's monumental biography of *Randall Davidson.*[1] The Cathedral shared the sorrow of the Diocese and its Bishop. Reflecting the mood of the time, the Dean in his address on the Sunday after the Queen's death could say: "Farewell, venerable, beloved Mother of the English Nation".[2] Such was the sentiment of the day.

The Cathedral Fabric

The episode best remembered within the annals of the twentieth century's beginning is the underpinning of the Cathedral which began in 1905 and ended in 1912. In 1905, J.B. Colson, the Cathedral Architect, assured the Dean and Chapter that they could congratulate themselves upon the good work done in the closing years of the previous century. Nevertheless, there was still work to be done, but a sum of about £3,000 would probably meet the cost. The estimate was wildly wrong. Instead of £3,000 the Dean and Chapter had to find £113,000. That monumental sum, for such it was, centres round the story of William Walker the Diver.

William Walker the Diver

His routine work as a diver is remembered only in official reports. But his work as a diver under the tottering foundations of the Cathedral struck the popular imagination then, and has continued to do so with increasing vigour right down to the present time. So much so that all the others who laboured faithfully and persistently are generally forgotten. Those who planned the work, who raised the necessary money, and who contributed so largely to its success, have to be content with a footnote in history. Today there is a statue to William Walker between the chantries of powerful prelates and within hailing distance of Joan of Arc. But architect, dean and engineer have to be content with short lives in the *Dictionary of National Biography,* and the myriad others have neither statue nor biography. The legend of 1906 to 1912, the actual years of Walker's own work, is now furthered by the modern Press, Radio and Television.

Walker was born in London in 1864. At the age of twenty-three he began working in Portsmouth Dockyard, as a diver's attendant. In due course he became a diver's signalman, and finally a fully qualified diver. In 1892 he joined the firm of Siebe Gorman and Company and became their chief diver in a staff of over two hundred divers who worked all over the world. For, even while working on the Cathedral Walker and his mate were called away to work in Italy. On other occasions he was called to work in South Wales or on the Thames. How then did he come to be working under Winchester Cathedral?

Sir Thomas Jackson Architect *Sir Francis Fox Engineer.*

Architect and Consultant Architect

In January 1905, Mr. J.B. Colson architect at that time, made his regular report on the state of the building. He pointed out that there still remained some work to be done at the West End, in the Crypt, beneath the Lady Chapel, and to the south wall of the Presbytery which was leaning outwards to a dangerous degree. The cause of these defects was the fact that the site of the Cathedral was flooded with water, which ebbed and flowed with the seasons, and which would make the work of restoration more difficult. He concluded his report by saying that he in no way wished to appear alarmist, but he felt it his duty to invite the serious consideration of the Dean and Chapter to these matters.

William Walker descending to work in 14 feet of water underneath the Cathedral.

The Dean and Chapter acted immediately upon their architect's report and called in the further advice of Mr. T.G. Jackson. Jackson dug an exploratory trench about ten feet deep outside the south wall of the retrochoir and found that the builders of the thirteenth century had rested their structure on a timber raft, whose purpose it was to fill the gap between the actual stone foundations of the retrochoir and the peat bed below, and to spread this great weight. Jackson worked with Messrs John Thompson of Peterborough and had his long-trusted clerk of works, Edwin Long. We are fortunate in that we still have the notebooks both of the architect and of the clerk of works so that the weekly progress of the under-pinning and reconstruction can be followed. Long asks frequently for the architect's guidance and both give pencil drawings indicating the various stages of the work. Long's notebooks end with the laconic entry: *"This completes the work of under-pinning the Cathedral after six years and seven months' labour. E. Long."* Already he was working on Eastrop Church and his next weekly report comes from Eastrop itself. No man ever supervised so important a work in so calm a manner and so free from heroics. But Jackson had not proceeded very far when he realised that he needed not only the skill of an architect but also that of a consultant engineer.

Consultant Engineer

The engineer he consulted was Francis Fox, a member of the Fox family which in earlier days provided a Richard Fox as Bishop of Winchester from 1501 to 1528. Fox made five recommendations setting them out in the order in which he considered they should be followed:

1.   The Building should be shored up on the outside.
2.   The arched vaulting of the retrochoir should be centred to avoid collapse.
3.   Steel tie-rods should be inserted where absolutely necessary.
4.   The walls should be grouted wherever necessary, beginning from the base.
5.   The walls should be under-pinned down to the hard gravel.

Fox realised that with so much water below the building, it would be necessary to employ the services of a diver.

On Fox's recommendation the diver began work in May, 1906. The diver was William Walker and his mate William West. Long's notebooks show how the work force steadily increased from one mason, two carpenters and five labourers in November 1905, when Long's notebook first begins, to a total of forty-three workmen in May, 1906 when the diver first appeared. At the period of peak working there were well over a hundred men on the site. But it was the diver who attracted the attention then, as now. In Edwardian journalese we read paragraphs like this: "To pass from the work of restoration into the nave of the Cathedral is to enter another world. The rolling glory of the *Te Deum* echoes through the vaulted space as it did in the days of William of Wykeham. The last *Amen* is sung, and the choir and clergy pass slowly and silently into the vestry. Outside the foreman blows his whistle. The great helmet of the diver with its staring goggle eyes, appears above the brink of the shaft, and the diver is helped out of his slimy, dripping shell. And soon choristers and workmen mingle beneath the shadow of the Cathedral." So wrote *The Standard* on September 24th, 1906.

From May onwards and for over five years Walker worked, with few breaks, in this way. It is estimated that he handled 25,800 bags of concrete

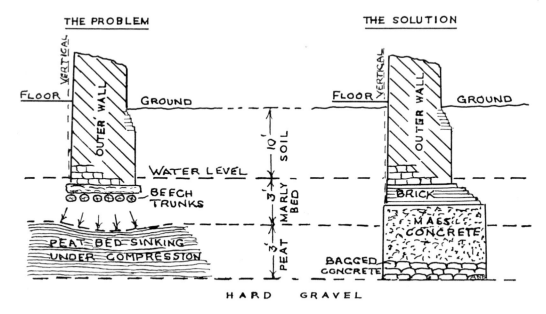

The underpinning of the foundations.

and 114,900 concrete blocks. In addition some 900,000 bricks were used. The diver's work was not able to be supervised constantly but Fox did from time to time inspect what Walker was doing and always pronounced the view that all was being done in the best and most conscientious manner.

Grouting and Tie-rods

But although the diver's work has almost completely monopolised the interests of contemporary and subsequent readers, it is only fair to remember that much other work was necessary and was carried out. For example, it is estimated that some five hundred tons of grouting were forced into the cracks and walls of the building further to strengthen it.

In addition, it is estimated that about sixteen and a half tons of tie-rods were employed to strengthen the building. The most obvious of these can be seen on the south side of the retrochoir not far from where Walker's statue now stands. Other tie-rods, less obvious, but no less important can be seen in the South Transept. The ends of these rods are visible on the outside of the South Transept wall.

Buttresses on South Side

Then, some time after the work of restoration was initiated, it was thought that the Cathedral would be further strengthened if buttresses were added to the south side of the Cathedral. It was felt that the removal of the monastic buildings in earlier generations which lay on the south side of the Cathedral removed support given to the main structure. And so ten buttresses were added. To the ordinary visitor they seem an original part of the Cathedral. One was given in memory of old Wykehamists; two were by members of the Mothers' Union; one was built in memory of Thomas Ken; another in memory of John Keble. Jackson hoped that there might be a cloister between the buttresses and a drawing of his proposal still survives.

Retrochoir

The walls of the Cathedral could not be dealt with by themselves. The whole of the inside of the retrochoir was particularly affected. The stately chantries were endangered. Fragments of the ceiling fell to the floor below. The pinnacles of the chantries were removed and the foundations of the chantries strengthed. Magdalen College Oxford generously undertook the restoration of the chantry of Bishop Waynflete who, as Bishop of Winchester from 1447-1486, was the founder of the College.

Crypt

As the crypt is below the retrochoir, repairs to the crypt were a consequence of the general restoration. For when the crypt was cleared it was found that the chantries in the retrochoir above were standing perilously on the edge of a bank of made-up ground. Under-pinning therefore was necessary and the whole of the crypt vaulting was made good. For this the grouting machine was of great service.

West Front

At the same time too the West Front of the Cathedral was put into a state of thorough repair. Under-pinning was not necessary here; but much refacing had to be done. For this special work the Goldsmiths' Company gave a donation of £5,500.

The Cost

The total cost, orginally estimated by Mr. Colson to be in the realm of £3,000, proved to be £113,000, an enormous sum by the standards of 1905 1912.

The Celebrations

The completion of this vast undertaking merited appropriate celebration. There was organised a whole week of services of thanksgiving between July 14th and July 21st, 1912. The main service was on St. Swithun's Day itself. The special service booklet had on its cover a design based on the *Benedictional of S. Aethelwold,* a design which is more than a century older than the oldest part of the present Cathedral. Within the framework of this design were the words:

WINCHESTER CATHEDRAL

BUILT

TO THE GLORY OF GOD

1079-1093

PRESERVED FROM DANGER

BY THE GOODNESS OF GOD

1905-1912

CONSECRATION

S.SWITHUN'S DAY 1093

THANKSGIVING SERVICE

S.SWITHUN'S DAY 1912

The day was a day of glorious sunshine and a day of high festival for Winchester, not only in the Cathedral but throughout the whole city. The King and Queen attended in state; the Archbishop of Canterbury, Dr. Randall Davidson, who himself had earlier been Bishop of Winchester, preached the sermon. He took as his text the words of *Psalm 90 verse 17:* Prosper thou the work of our hands upon us, O prosper thou our handiwork.

After the service the King expressed a wish personally to meet the diver who had done so much to preserve the Cathedral. A contemporary Press account says: The King shook him (Walker) by the hand. In reply to His Majesty's question Walker stated that he had been at work on the Cathedral six years, working six hours a day. "Really" said the King, "I congratulate you on your feat in saving the Cathedral." Walker had also been mentioned by the Archbishop in his sermon: "In days to come, when men are talking of Walkelin, and De Lucy, of Wykeham and Fox, there will be more to add. The names of Ryle and Furneaux, with the trio of redoubtable men, the great architect Thomas Graham Jackson, the resourceful engineer Francis Fox and — for it must be added — William Robert Walker will hold place for good in the annals of our century's beginning." Walker later confessed that he felt uncomfortable as he heard the words of the Archbishop, but supposed that few of the congregation would be able to recognise him. The more so for he was no longer in a diver's suit but in the unfamiliar frock coat.

Recognition

This "trio of redoubtable men" received due recognition. Fox was knighted in 1912; Jackson received a baronetcy the same year; and Walker was summoned to Buckingham Palace to receive the Royal Victorian Order, an honour which is in the exclusive control of the Sovereign. Writing to his employers on December 12th, 1912, Walker said:

> Dear Sir,
> I have received a letter commanding me to be at Buckingham Palace on the 19th to receive the Royal Victorian Order at the request of His Majesty. I would be thankful if you would inform me how to go on and anything I could do for the firm, and I must thank you with all my heart for all you have done for me in the past.

Earlier, on July 31st the Dean and Chapter made a presentation to Walker in the Deanery. The Dean and all the Canons with the Chapter Clerk were present. Their gift was a silver rose bowl. On it was the inscription:

> Presented to Mr. W.R. Walker, diver
> By the Dean and Chapter of Winchester
> In grateful recognition of his
> Valuable service in the work of underpinning
> The Walls of the Cathedral, 1906-1911.

In his reply Walker said he valued the gift more than anything else. He had honestly tried to do his best and was confident that his work would stand the test of time.

A few years later, despite the war of 1914 to 1918, it was resolved to place a tablet on the west wall of the Cathedral as a memorial of what was done. As it sums up admirably the whole work, its wording is here given in full. It was placed in position in 1916.

MEMORIAL TABLET

William Walker
1905-1912

During these years
£113,000 was spent upon the Fabric
The safety of which had been gravely imperilled
By the subsidence of the walls.
It was necessary to construct new foundations
And to carry them through the underlying peat, and
Considerable depth of water, to a bed of hard gravel.
The diver employed was W.R. Walker.
The reparation of the West Front
Was carried out by J.B. Colson, Architect
At the cost of £5,500 the munificent gift of
The Worshipful Company of Goldsmiths.
The walls throughout the greater part of the building
Were underpinned, grouted and bonded:
And when necessary tied with rods.
New buttresses were built on the South Side
Of the Nave and of the South Transept.
The Beaufort and Waynflete chantries
Were underpinned and their pinnacles restored.
The greater part of the vaulting
Was either re-set or reconstructed.
The timber roofs were largely repaired.
Much of the lead covering renewed
And the flying buttresses restored
T.G. Jackson, Architect.
Francis Fox M.Inst.C.E., Consulting Engineer.
John Thomson of Peterborough, Contractor.

Their Majesties King George and Queen Mary
Were present at the Service of thanksgiving
On the completion of the Work.

S. Swithun's Day 1912
Laus Deo[3]

*Opposite: The front page of the supplement to the "Hampshire Chronicle"
to commemorate the Royal occasion.*

King Alfred's Millenary, 1901[4]

Although the early part of 1901 was dominated by the death of the Queen, the City had already planned to mark in 1901 the millenary of the death of Alfred the Great. An ambitious programme was planned covering the many sides of Alfred's achievements. In the preface to the printed programme, Alfred Bowker, a name honoured for several generations in the history of the Cathedral, wrote as Mayor of Winchester for the millenary year: "The guiding principles of such lives as those lived by King Alfred and our revered Queen Victoria should be ever present".

Very properly the Cathedral played a part in the unveiling of the statue of King Alfred now dominating the Broadway, Winchester. An appropriate *Chorus of Praise* had been composed by the Cathedral Organist, Dr. G.B. Arnold;

> Hail to the mighty one
> Your voices raise,
> Sing loud the praise
> Of England's greatest name.

Lord Rosebery unveiled the statue. In addition, there were learned addresses and countless speeches. Every side of Alfred's achievements was covered. Over 4,000 people attended a special service. This time the music was Wesley's *Ascribe unto the Lord* and with it the began the practice which has led to the Southern Cathedrals' Festival. The choir of Salisbury and Winchester Cathedrals joined with the Cathedral choir and the choir of the Chapel Royal. The service was attended by the Lord Mayors of London and Liverpool along with about forty provincial mayors. The celebrations came at a much needed time and helped re-assure people of the long tradition of England's greatness.

The deaths of Organist and Dean, 1902

Soon after the Millenary celebrations, the Cathedral Organist died. Dr. Arnold had been associated with the Cathedral since 1849 when he started as a pupil of S.S. Wesley. In due course he succeeded him and continued to hold office until 1902. His monument is in the North Transept of the Cathedral, the Cathedral's musicians' corner. It consists of a portrait of him in profile on carrara marble surrounded by alabaster. The inscription briefly sums up his life:

> In memory of George Benjamin Arnold
> Mus. Doc. Oxon. 37 years organist in
> this Cathedral. Born December 31st., 1832
> died Jan. 31st., 1902.

Perhaps popular opinion of him is summed up in the music at the foot of the tablet, the notes of what was then felt to be Arnold's best composition, *The Lord is my shepherd.*

Later that year the Cathedral suffered another serious loss in the death of Dean Stephens. He began what has not been achieved since, a multivolume History of the English Church. The work was finally completed by his fellow editor, W. Hunt. Stephens contributed the volume covering the years 1066 to the end of the thirteenth century.[5]

And, as though to shake the Cathedral completely, the Bishop of the Diocese, Randall Davidson, was shortly afterwards preferred to Canterbury. It was a year of new beginnings. This loss of Dean and Bishop provided ecclesiastical lawyers with a legal problem, in fact with two legal problems.

Dean Furneaux, 1903-1919

Canon Furneaux, Headmaster of Repton, was already living in Winchester and undertaking a Canon's duties at the Cathedral. His appointment as Dean was impossible by statute because he had not qualified with the degree of B.D. or D.D. This first failure was soon remedied by the Archbishop exercising his prerogative of conferring a Lambeth D.D. This overcame the first legal impediment. And so on March 24th, 1903 at 10 a.m. in the morning Canon Furneaux, with his new doctorate, became Dean Furneaux. This left the legal way open for the Dean and Chapter to elect their new Bishop, Herbert Edward Ryle. Some idea of the haste of the proceedings can be gleaned from the fact that the election took place on that same day, March 24th., at 4 p.m.

Thus within a day Cathedral and Diocese had a new Dean and a new Bishop.[6] Furneaux's new life was early blighted by the death of his wife in the following year. Within a year of that tragedy he had to shoulder what rapidly emerged as the vast problem of the underpinning of the Cathedral. This he did with persistence and resolution, writing over three thousand letters with his own hand begging for funds and acknowledging donations. Side by side with this monotonous task he somehow found time to write and in the very year that saw the completion of the work on the building, to publish his commentary on the *Acts of the Apostles*[7]. Scarcely were these two achievements accomplished before the country was overtaken by the Great War. Altogether his tenure of office was arduous and the brief inscription by the iron gates leading into the south transept from the south aisle of the nave probably hints at his own assessment of his work at Winchester: the restoration of the Cathedral itself. The brief summary of his life is followed by the terse comment:

> During whose tenure of office
> The Foundations were made secure.

It was a dour and heroic achievement.

Cathedral Music: The Precentor

Another department of Cathedral life which saw a new beginning was the sphere of Cathedral music. A new Organist and a new Precentor were appointed within a short time of one another. The germ of what later became the Southern Cathedrals' Festival was sown; there was the financial problem of maintaining full time lay clerks; and choristers needed to be educated. A new edition of *Hymns Ancient and Modern* brought forth the considered comments of Dean and Precentor.

In 1902, the new Precentor who was appointed, was the Rev. W. Slater. He soon revealed himself a man of ideas. At the end of his first full Church year, Advent 1902 to 1903, he produced an analysis of the services and anthems sung during the year. The most memorable service was the one held to mark the deferred Coronation of Edward VII held on August 9th., 1903. A service of this kind he considered to be unrepresentative and, therefore, not within the scope of a proper appraisal of the place of music in cathedral worship. His conclusions give a clear idea of the convictions of the time. He writes: "In my opinion every kind of Church music which is of sufficient merit should be represented in Cathedral worship..." and in this, he goes on to say, that the Organist is fully in agreement. He instances Palestrina, Gibbons, Purcell, Boyce, Wesley, Stanford and Brahms, together with selections from the oratorios of Handel, Mendelssohn, Spohr and Gounod. Plain-song he felt was sufficiently represented in the Litany, the Responses and the Liturgical Chant at the Holy Communion. He commended the use of Psalm Tones when services were sung by men only. There was, however, one kind of music which he felt was totally barred "that of the great masters set to Latin or other foreign words, and arranged by English editors to words having no connection with those for which the music was originally written." Music must always be appropriate to the season of the year. He was proud that "a large quantity of modern music" had been introduced during his first full year. He pleaded for custodians of Choir Libraries to look to the future and so avoid the desolate inheritances which so many cathedrals have in the first years of the 20th century.

The Southern Cathedrals' Festival

Although it is to anticipate a later description, it was during this first decade of the century that the germ was sown for what finally became the Southern Cathedrals' Festival. The idea arose as a result of the King Alfred's Millenary celebrations when the choirs of Winchester, Salisbury, Chichester and the Chapel Royal were brought together.[8] In 1904 the choirs of Winchester and Salisbury visited Chichester to join in the opening service for the new organ there. From this arose the suggestion that such a service might be held, in rotation, at each of the cathedrals. It was emphasised that there was "no intention of establishing anything beyond a Festival Service." Such a service was held in Salisbury in 1905. The centenary of the birth of Samuel Sebastian Wesley in 1910 gave the notion a new impetus. This year the festival was held at Winchester. The music was wholly that of Wesley, and Dr. Prendergast received high praise for his performance throughout. An anonymous correspondent in the *Winchester Diocesan Chronicle* at the time. (1910 p.152) observed:

> The usefulness of these annual gatherings from a religious, social, and artistic point of view is becoming increasingly manifest, and it is to be hoped that the original idea of the Festival may be kept steadily in view, namely, that on one day in each year, instead of three choirs singing their Evensong separately, they should combine to render their *ordinary* worship, so that with the exception that more than one anthem is sung, there is no variation whatever from the regular course of the daily cathedral service."

Not inappropriately, in view of the commanding influence of Wesley upon the music of Winchester a tablet was placed to mark the centenary of his birth earlier that year in the north transept.

Hymns Ancient and Modern

The new Precentor was ready not only to make known his views on Cathedral music but also on the new edition of *Hymns Ancient and Modern* which appeared in 1905. He concentrated on the music of the book, the Dean made known his views about the words. So far as he could judge 167 of the old tunes had been dropped and about 200 new ones added. While regretting the omission of some of the tunes of Dykes and Stainer, he was pleased to note a distinct improvement in the use of plain-song melodies. He congratulated the editors in writing the tunes (where used more than once) in different keys. Such provision would be welcomed, he said, by any used to taking services in a mission room, particularly where an amateur might not be able to transpose a tune. His best hope was that the book might in the end prove a stepping stone to something better.[9]

The Dean too had shown interest in the book. He began by observing that the earlier edition appeared at a fortunate moment in time but it had been over-rated. The publication of a new edition offered an opportunity to improve the book. He was disappointed. In the old book he saw four main failings:-

1. One third of all the hymns were translations.
2. Many poor English hymns.
3. Unaccountable omission of fine hymns.
4. Words frequently and badly edited.

In the new edition he was bound to say:

1. There is still a disproportionate number of translations.
2. Being a head-master he had marked the English hymns alpha, beta, gamma or delta. He noted that in the new edition over a 100 which he had marked gamma or delta had disappeared; seven marked beta had disappeared. All his alphas had remained.
3. There is still an inexplicable omission of fine hymns. e.g. *Come thou long-expected Jesus* (Wesley); *O Little Town of Bethlehem; According to Thy gracious Word* (Montgomery).
4. There is an improvement in editing but the original words could and ought more often to have been used.

In conclusion, the Dean said that though there was improvement, the ordinary congregation would not be justified in incurring the expense of new copies. And finally, he asked, why and by what right are the editors a self constituted body with regard to whose capacity, taste, and knowledge the public has no security. [10]

Dr. Prendagast, 1902-1933

To succeed Dr. Arnold, William Prendergast was appointed. Born in Yorkshire he was, for a time, articled to Dr. Arnold, before taking up appointments at Berwick-on-Tweed and later in Edinburgh. This meant that there was an unbroken tradition from Wesley to Prendergast which covered the years 1849 to 1933, in all eighty-four years. In 1904 Prendergast received his Doctor of Music from Oxford. One of his first tasks was to make better arrangements for the training of the choristers. "Accordingly in 1905 the Dean and Chapter decided that it was wisest to make the Choir School exclusively a Boarding School without any admixture of Day Boys. They agreed to pay the Headmaster £256 per annum i.e. £28 for each of 2 solo boys and £12.10 for each of the sixteen choristers. They agreed to try and provide four probationers but could not guarantee such a provision. Instruction in playing the piano was to be given, where desired. So far as costs were concerned the Dean and Chapter would pay the £15 usually paid by parents but would discontinue the £9 (£5 for clothes and £4 foundation money) hitherto paid to parents.[11]

There were problems about the lay clerks. These came to the surface in 1912 immediately after the exhausting labours of providing the finances for the underpinning of the Cathedral. The main problem of the lay clerks was that as they were expected to sing daily at 10 and 4 they were unable to undertake any other employment, save at night. They suggested a return to the £100 per annum formerly paid to them. At present they received 28/- per week and were expected to give primacy to their musical duties and not allow their business commitments, where they existed, to interfere in any way. Once appointed a lay clerk had a freehold so that moneys were paid to men who could no longer sing which made it difficult to pay adequately the younger men who actually did the singing. If this practice were stopped then those who actually did the singing could receive the more adequate stipend which they suggested, 'with practically two voices for most of the parts'.

In the end it was possible for the Dean and Chapter to go a good way to meet the request and the stipend was increased to £85 per annum.[12] The organist's main task in his early years was therefore the establishment of the proper conditions for securing an adequate provision for men and boys just at a time when Cathedral finances were strained to the utmost.

Charlotte Yonge

The Cathedral had found it hard in the nineteenth century to be sympathetic to the Tractarians. John Keble had certainly not received that recognition which later generations accord him. When therefore one of his great supporters died, Charlotte Yonge, it was natural that as she had worked so closely with him both practically at the parish level and also through the pervasive influence of her books and other writings, that she should be buried near him. However Bishop George Sumner, who was also a Canon of the Cathedral and husband of Mary Sumner, proposed in Chapter[13] that a memorial be erected to her in the Cathedral and should take the form of a reredos in the Lady Chapel. The suggestion was coolly received by the Chapter and while not preventing it would not accept any financial responsibility. We may suspect that Mary Sumner had put the notion into her husband's mind. Writing from The Close on the occasion of Charlotte Yonge's death she wrote to Charlotte's first biographer, Mary Coleridge.[14] She told how she had approached Charlotte to publish for her in 1890 the journal which she had for the members of her Mother's Union; *Mothers in Council*.

Thereafter their friendship became very close and her admiration became ever greater. She concluded, on the morrow of Charlotte's death: "Miss Yonge was a great personality in the Winchester diocese...and from a national point of view she has left us an invaluable inheritance. She has bequeathed to the English nation a wealth of good and wholesome literature, which has touched and influenced many of our greatest thinkers". So despite the reluctance to act in the matter the Reredos to her memory was built. It was as though as time passed the Cathedral was being forced into absorbing a tradition which is part of the Church of England. A great cathedral should try to be as comprehensive as that Church. Charlotte Yonge is now remembered and, as in a symbol, the Cathedral is now buttressed by John Keble, after his death even though during his life time he was rejected.

Since the early days of the century Charlotte Yonge has fallen into neglect if not contempt. As so often happens, fashions change and there has recently been a quickening interest in her life and works. This was sparked off by Georgina Battiscombe's *Charlotte Mary Yonge*[15] which went through four editions in the year 1943. About thirty years later a Charlotte Yonge Society came into existence of whom the first historian is Marghanita Laski. The Society has published its own *Chaplet for Charlotte Yonge.*[16] Denigration is steadily giving way to appreciation.

The South African War, 1899-1902

The South African War, first thought of as a petty irritation to a great Empire, shook the confidence of Empire, and has left its mark upon the Cathedral in the form of two major memorials to men of the Hampshire Regiment and men of King's Royal Rifles. The first memorial to be put in place was on March 14th, 1904, the Hampshire War Memorial Window. This is just east of the south door entering the Cathedral. Its theme is based on the text in *Ephesians VI*. Put on the whole armour of God... the girdle of truth...the breast-plate of righteousness... the sandals of peace... the shield of faith... the helmet of salvation... the sword of the Spirit. Above the whole armour of God are two angels and above them the figure of Christ. At the actual ceremony an acknowledgement on behalf of all the relatives was made by the Rev. A. Harland Vicar of Harefield near Uxbridge who had lost one of his sons just before the relief of Mafeking.

On April 5th, 1910 in the south wall of the south aisle of the Quire the Riflemen's window was dedicated in the presence of the Prince of Wales. The theme of the window was suggested by Princess Christian whose husband H.R.H. Prince Christian Victor, was among the fallen from the

Opposite: The Lady Chapel with the Reredos in memory of Charlotte Yonge. In the corner can also be seen the Chairs used by King George V and Queen Mary on 15th July, 1912.

Regiment. This time it is St. George who is depicted with events from his life. In the lower part of the window Patience and Fortitude are commemorated and in the bottom right hand corner is a rifleman wearing the topee then worn in tropical and semi-tropical countries by serving members of the Army. Below the figures runs the inscription: "We pray you to remember all those soldiers of the Kings Royal Rifles who laid down their lives for their Sovereign and Country in South Africa, 1899-1902. On the ledge below the window is a Book of Remembrance recording the names of all who fell not only between 1899 and 1902 but also in the earlier wars in South Africa from 1886 onwards.

In the following year Sir Redvers Buller who had seen forty years active service from 1860 to 1900 was commemorated by a memorial cenotaph in the north transept.

The Epiphany Chapel and the Chapter Room: 1908-1910

The West side of the North transept after adaptation was dedicated in 1908 as the Chapel of the Epiphany. The furnishings of the chapel were the gift of Canon Valpy. Two sides have been filled with oak screens: that on the south side with four stalls. The floor of the sanctuary was paved with marble. In 1910 his widow added the four windows in her husband's memory: the Annunciation, the Salutation, the Nativity, and the Adoration. The windows were produced by Messrs Morris and Co. Members of Chapter in their turn wished to commemorate him, and refurbished the corresponding area of the South Transept making it into a Chapter Room for the Residentiary Chapter. Commenting on this modern work Simon Jervis of the Victoria and Albert Museum informs us that the architect was G.H. Kitchin and the craftsman Thomas Laverty, a name well known in Winchester for solid craftsmanship. Again it had not been possible at such a time to appeal for non-essentials. At the same time the additions are among the most used parts of the building and it is remarkable that both were added between 1908 and 1910 when the disorganisation of the daily running of the Cathedral was at its maximum.

The National Pageant, 1908[17]

As in 1901 so in 1908 the Cathedral still had energy to spare to share in events within the life of the City. Indeed for a whole week beginning June 25th. 1908 special services were held in the Cathedral. An added attraction was the number of visiting bishops (fifty in number) who were in England for the Pan-Anglican Congress being held that year. Visiting preachers were the Bishop of Massachusetts and the Bishop of Niagara. The pageant consisted of a string of historic episodes in the life of the city for which special music was composed. The wedding of Philip and Mary was the event most closely linked with the Cathedral. On the personal side Canon Valpy assisted on the planning committee and the Cathedral Architect found time to advise on all matters of heraldry.

The link between the Pageant and the Pan-Anglican Congress was emphasised in a series of four articles contributed to the *Winchester Diocesan Chronicle* (1908 pp. 15.ff; 30.ff; 47.ff; and 66.ff.) by Canon Storr[18] All four articles were preparatory to the Congress. As might be expected by one who was at work on English theological thought he considered the most important theme before the Congress to be "The Church and Human Thought". It was, he claimed, essential before all things that we give valid reasons for the hope which is in us. He also drew attention to the need for a consideration of the relation between Faith and Science. This last theme was really the burden of his three final contributions. Men were still grappling with the impact of evolution upon Christian faith. His closing words reflect this pre-occupation: "If we are to understand the world, ourselves, our religion, the growth of our institutions in Church or State, our Bibles, our God, we must learn the meaning of development, and how to apply the conception".

The Cathedral Library

Presiding over the Library at the beginning of the century was Francis T. Madge. His faithful and scholarly work for the Library is still of great value. He had enlisted the help of Sir George Warner to describe the manuscripts in the possession of the Library. That report is the basis of all our information about our Cathedral manuscripts and is in frequent use. Madge also anticipated the *Short Title Catalogue* of all books printed before 1640 by producing such a list of the English books in the Cathedral Library printed before that date. Turning to the books printed elsewhere in Europe he listed all the publications up to the year 1600. His work is basic to any cataloguing of cathedral books. In this field Madge had enlisted the help of Charles Sayle of Cambridge. Sayle drew attention to the losses sustained by the Library among its printed books since publication of Beriah Botfield's *Notes on the Cathedral Libraries of England*, 1840. Sayle noted that in the sixty years intervening eight valuable books had been lost, perhaps the most valuable being *Coverdale Bible of* 1535.

Other missing volumes include a Cranmer's Bible, another incunable *Decreta Gratiani* of Nuremburg, 1494; and a volume from the press of W.de Worde. In his will Bishop Lyttleton, Bishop of Southampton, left his Library to the Dean and Chapter for the benefit of the Diocesan clergy. For some reason this request was not fulfilled.

The most memorable discovery in the Library during these years arose out of the restoration work undertaken between the years 1905 and 1912. The decision had to be made to examine thoroughly and carefully the wall behind the books on the north side of the Library. This led to the temporary paralysing of the Library as a working instrument but it did reveal some wall paintings. When books and bookcases were moved, two arched recesses were uncovered which had been originally Norman windows. Surrounding them were wall paintings. A first examination by the architect Mr. Nisbett and by such authorities as Francis Baigent and C.E. Keyser found that there were in fact two layers of painting. Along the wall there is a band of red and yellow forming a kind of "dado" line at the level of the springing of the arches, some four feet above the floor. Below the line there are remains of a conventional pattern of squares placed diagonally. At the east end of the Library wall is a representation of the west doors of a church (? the cathedral) with iron hinges. There is also a tiled roof, coloured a reddish tint. The tiles are diamond shaped. There is also a representation of an altar draped with a cloth of light green and upon it a chalice. Above the chalice is a pendant lamp. Upon the altar appears to be a reliquary or casket. Besides the Church is the figure of a Benedictine monk, outlined in dark red but filled in with black.[19] Arrangements are made from time to time to remove a row of books and a panel in the woodwork so that the painting of the church and altar are visible.

Books from a Cathedral

We have already referred to the publications of Dean Stephens and Dean Furneaux. Dean Furneaux was carrying on the tradition of his early predecessor, Prior Godfrey, who amidst the noise and confusion of great building work was able to detach himself to produce a work of scholarship. And not only the deans but also the canons produced works of lasting value.

Canon Storr in 1913 produced what he hoped would be the first of two volumes covering the whole story of English Theology during the nineteenth century. It was entitled: *The Development of English Theology in the Nineteenth Century. (1800-1860).*[20] It is still the best book on the subject and had to wait until L.E. Elliott-Binns concluded the history up to 1900 in a work entitled *English Thought*, 1860-1900. London, 1936.

The other work of reference produced by a member of Chapter, Canon Braithwaite was published in 1909, *The Church Plate of Hampshire*. This describes the Communion Plate of the Cathedral and of all the parishes in the county. It is a work that has increased in usefulness over the years due to the erection of a Cathedral Treasury where Church Plate from the Diocese is

(Albert W Kerr)

Buttresses added on the south side of the Cathedral during Edwardian period

shown every summer. Again we can only wonder that these books were written at a time of immense activity and concern with the raising of great sums of money to preserve the fabric of the Cathedral.

Arising out of the restoration of the Cathedral, architect and engineer, Sir Thomas Jackson[21] and Sir Francis Fox had opportunities to present to more specialised readers the principles on which they undertook their work of restoration in a series of learned monographs for fellow architects or engineers. Jackson has left his manuscript books and also a small work published in 1910 *An Account of the building and Repairs now in Progress.* Fox (in 1910) published a work on the use of the grouting machine used to fill the cracks of the building which had threatened its collapse.[22]

Canon A.G. Robinson is most remembered for his pre-eminent part as Treasurer in connection with the raising of funds for the under-pinning. His administrative ability found further scope when he was made Archdeacon of Winchester. In 1913 the annual Church Congress, a feature of the life of the Church in those days and attended by large numbers of laymen and clergymen, met in Southampton. The Congress fell therefore very much under the notice of Winchester Churchmen. Canon Robinson shewed that he was not simply a man concerned with money and administration. He wrote on *The Christ of Experience*[23] as dealt with by contributors to the Congress. He noted that much had been done to discover the historic facts concerned with our Lord's earthly life. But however accurate our historical appreciation, we come up against a baffling mystery. The writers of the Gospels were not historians, they were men who worshipped a Christ who had risen from the dead and ascended into heaven. What they wrote was "that we might believe" and that we "might have life through His name". That life, the Canon continued, was found in the Society in which His spirit dwells.

These words were written on the eve of the Great War and after a decade of intense activity of a very down to earth nature which the Cathedral body had been compelled to undertake. Through it all the main purpose of the Cathedral was not lost. Its life could easily have degenerated into a struggle simply to maintain an ancient monument. So far as Dean and Canons were concerned they were looking after more than a monument and their thoughtful and scholarly contributions indicate very plainly that they were fully aware of the Cathedral's highest purpose and in this they were aided by the musical foundation which did not allow the immense difficulties to overwhelm them.

Detail from Izaak Walton Window.

The Izaak Walton Window, 1914

The last work of adornment of the Cathedral before the outbreak of the First Great War was the contribution by the fishermen of England and America of the Izaak Walton window in the Silkstede Chapel in the south west corner of the south transept. Izaac Walton, the angler is remembered in two of the bottom corners of the window. In the one, he is represented in Dovedale; in the other on the Itchen with St. Catherine's Hill in the background. Below is a favourite text of his from 1 Thessalonians iv.II: Study to be Quiet. Other references to fishing may be seen in the window. There are the apostolic fishermen, Peter and Andrew. And above all, in the central light of the window, the Lord sitteth upon the water flood. There is also St. Anthony, friend of St. Francis. Full details can be read in c.40 of the Little Flowers of St. Francis of the miracle which God wrought, when St. Anthony, being at Rimini, preached to the fishes of the sea. Having failed in his mission to the people of Rimini, "Anthony sat himself one day by Divine inspiration on the bank of the river...and began to speak to the fishes... "Hear the word of God, ye fishes of the sea and of the river, since the infidel heretics refuse to hear it." The story goes on to tell how the fish "held their heads out of the water, and all gazed attentively on the face of St. Anthony." This story is portrayed within the window. The window also commemorates the Short Lives written by Walton of the eminent churchmen of his day: Donne, Hooker, Herbert, Sanderson and Sir Henry Wotton. The window was dedicated on June 8th, 1914, the address given by Sir Herbert Maxwell and one of Thomas Ken's hymns sung ending with his famous doxology:

Praise God, from whom all blessings flow[24]

Walton's exhortation to study to be quiet was to be shattered irrevocably within a few weeks on August 4th., 1914.

NOTES

1. G.K.A. Bell. *Randall Davidson* 2 Vols. O.U.P., 1935. c.IV. *The Queen and her Chaplain.* c. XII. *The Bishop of Winchester.*
2. *W.D.C.*, 1901. p.17.
3. F. Bussby. *William Walker, The Diver.* Winchester, 1970
4. A. Bowker. *King Alfred Millenary*, 1901. London, 1902.
5. W.R.W. Stephens. *A History of the English Church.* Vol. II. From 1066 to the close of the thirteenth century. London, 1902.
6. *W.D.C.* March 24th, 1903.
7. W.M. Furneaux. *The Acts of the Apostles.* Oxford, 1912.
8. A. Bowker. *op.cit.* p. 129.
9. *W.D.C.* 1905 pp. 77-80.
10. *ibid.* 48 -51.
11 *C.A.* April 25th., 1905.
12. *C.A.* September 24th., 1912.
13. *C.A.* 1896-1914 p.163
14. C. Coleridge. *Charlotte Mary Yonge.* London, 1903. pp. 288-291.
15. G. Battiscombe. *Charlotte Mary Yonge.* London, 1943.
16. G. Battiscombe and Marghanita Laski. *A Chaplet for Charlotte Yonge.* London, 1965.
17. *Winchester National Pageant.* Winchester, 1908
18. *W.D.C.* 1908 pp.15ff., 30ff., 47ff., and 66ff.
19. *W.D.C.* 1909. p.121.f. Illustrated.
20. V.Storr. *The Development of English Theology in the Nineteenth Century (1800-1860).* London, 1913.
21. T.G. Jackson. *An Account of Building and Repairs now in Progress.* London, 1910.
22. F.Fox. *Foundations: The Use of Divers and Grouting Machines.* Journal of R.I.B.A. 1910. pp. 247-291.
23. *W.D.C.* 1914. pp. 38-41.
24. F. Bussby. *Isaac Walton in Winchester.* 1970.

FURTHER READING

A.R. Mss. 2 vols. 1898-1921.
C.A. 1896-1914. Index by E.Foss.
D.N.B. F.Fox, W.M. Furneaux, T.G. Jackson.
G.H. Harris. *Vernon Faithful Storr.* London, 1943.
B. Jackson. Life of Sir T.G. Jackson.
Jackson Collection Mss.
Mayhew A.K. *Promptorium Parvulorum.* Early English Text Society, 1908. (One of the Cathedral Mss.)
R.S. 3 vols. 1896-1925
Records of the Cathedral and Close, 1739-1966 Ms.
J. Vaughan *Winchester Cathedral Close.* London, 1914.
Walker Collection Mss.
Sir G.Warner and H.A. Wilson *The Benedictional of St. Aethelwold.* Roxburghe Club, 1910.
Winchester Cathedral Library. Early Printed Books, 1479-1640 (1902).
Winchester Diocesan Chronicle Vols. IX-XXII (1901-1914) has many references to the Cathedral.

U.K. & U.S.A. Troops in the Cathedral, 1918.

Chapter XIII

Between Two Wars

The Cathedral, like the rest of the country, was shocked and unprepared for the outbreak of war in 1914. On the first Sunday after the commencement of hostilities, a letter was read in the Cathedral written by Bishop Talbot which included these words: "An unspeakably solemn and momentous time is upon us." His own family was to share fully in the ordeal and tragedy of war for it is due to one of his sons that the movement which came to be known as Toc H was founded.

The task of the Cathedral was to strive to re-inforce the spiritual resources of the people. Intercession services were held regularly and the troops paraded Sunday by Sunday. Collections were given to good causes; those already well established like the Red Cross, and new ones which emerged due to the requirements of the time: The Destitute and Starving in Belgium. Later, echoes of the Middle East campaign appear in collections to help the Jerusalem Mission and Khartoum Cathedral. On one occasion Welsh troops were welcomed at the Cathedral with a special service paper prepared in the Welsh language on September 19th, 1915. Memorial services came to be a sadly regular feature. Often they were private services: occasionally they were of a more general nature. Among those remembered were Lord Kitchener and all who perished with him on the H.M.S. *Hampshire.* The large stone cross at the west end of the Cathedral still recalls that tragedy. Among individuals there was a service for Lt. Colonel Baring, M.P. for the City of Winchester, and many others who made an equal sacrifice and were equally remembered. A notable service was one to mark the entrance of the United States into the War on the side of the Allies in 1918 when the Stars and Stripes hung in the Cathedral.[1]

The staggering losses of human life in the conflict which raged for more than four years and cost millions of lives left their mark on the Cathedral in the form of numerous memorials. Books of remembrance recording the lives laid down by men of the 60th Rifles and the Hampshire Regiments bear poignant witness to the supreme sacrifice made by many thousands of young men. In the 1970s these men continue to be remembered not only on Remembrance Sunday but also each month in a brief but moving ceremony held by a contingent of the Royal Green Jackets who recall the dead of their three regiments.

In addition to books of remembrance, there are many names upon the walls of the Cathedral, and statuettes on the south side of Fox's Chantry in memory of individuals who gave their lives during the same war.[2]

Dean Hutton, 1919-1930

When William Hutton succeeded Dean Furneaux in 1919[3], he came to Winchester with a formidable academic record[4] and with a new ecclesiastical outlook. He was in line with the Caroline divines of the seventeenth century and with the more catholic tradition within the Church of England. He had given his Bampton lectures at Oxford on *The English Saints* and at Winchester his observance of the Martyrdom of Charles I revealed where his sympathies lay. He also introduced Eucharistic vestments, and encouraged Reservation of the Sacrament, steps which caused great concern within the Diocese at that time and led to protest. His remains are buried in the south presbytery aisle and in the most factual way the inscription over him sums up his career:

Pray for the soul of
WILLIAM HOLDEN HUTTON
D.D., D.C.L.
Dean of this Cathedral
Chaplain to the Order
of St John of Jerusalem
Who was formerly
Fellow of St. John's College, Oxford
Archdeacon of Northampton
Canon of Peterborough
Reader in Indian History in the University of Oxford
Born May 24 1860
Died October 24 1930

Hutton's first book was written in 1881 and was entitled: *The Political Disturbances of the Early Period of the Reformation.* His range of interests can be judged by the fact that, *Highways and Byways in Shakespeare's Country,* was published in 1913.

Amongst other works he edited *New Readings in Indian History* in 1916 and, during his stay at Winchester, he joined with Canon Goodman in editing in 1925 an edition of *Winchester Cathedral Statutes,* originally issued by Charles I.

The Times in its obituary of 25th October, 1930 outlines his career and then turns to his period at Winchester: "The chief drawback to his happiness, and, in some degree to his usefulness, during his eleven years at Winchester was the state of his health and in the corresponding depression of his spirits... Yet there was no diminution of his own charming hospitality. He loved to have guests at the Deanery, and beyond all, young people." It goes on to comment on the fact that due to the immense work completed during the time of his predecessor he was free "from the pressing anxieties about the fabric which nowadays are apt to beset the head of a cathedral establishment."[5]

Church Assembly and Convocation, 1925

In view of Hutton's great learning, it is not surprising to find that he was chairman of a committee of the Lower House of Convocation of Canterbury appointed in 1925 to enquire into *Cathedral Chapters regarded as centres of Learning.* This same subject had come up earlier in the Church Assembly. It was a subject with which the Dean was well able to deal. It was as part preparation for this work that he produced the scholarly edition of Winchester's own *Statutes.* The Commission came up with two main recommendations so far as Winchester was concerned. A more precise definition of the relation between the Bishop and the Dean and Chapter was required. It says: "There is a strong tradition (how ancient or modern we could not rightly discover) that jurisdiction ordinary rests with the Dean, though the statutes refer things to 'the Dean and Chapter' and oaths are taken to obey the Dean and Chapter. The Dean expressed the hope that his power of veto might remain. The only purely academic recommendation which it made and which might be thought germane to the terms of reference of the Committee, was the fusion of the Morley and the Thorold and Lyttleton Libraries. Such a fusion of Cathedral and Diocesan Libraries it added, "would place the studious clergy and laity of the diocese in an enviable position."

Joan of Arc, 1923

There being no major work on the fabric in view of the immense labours of Dean Furneaux, the Cathedral could turn its attention to more decorative features within the structure. In 1920, Joan of Arc had been canonised by Pope Benedict XV. In the Diocese of Winchester it was felt that as the Diocese, in the person of its Bishop, Cardinal Beaufort, had been present at her trial and condemnation (1431), so it should make some act of reparation, so far as that was humanly possible. The lead was taken by Rev. A.H.Fletcher, the Rector of Merrow in Surrey, a parish then in the Diocese. He gathered a group of sympathisers, British and American, and it was finally agreed that a statue should be erected facing Cardinal Beaufort so that their tragic confrontation in life might be replaced by a symbolic reconciliation.

The artistic supervision of the work was entrusted to Ninian Comper, a well known artist of those days. The actual carving was the work of W.D. Gough while the decoration was by H.A. Bernard-Smith. The statue is just under four feet high and stands on a pedestal about five feet high, hexagonal in shape and containing in its base a tiny fragment of the stone of the dungeon in Rouen where she spent her last days. Statue and pedestal are richly decorated, the fleur-de-lys of France being particularly prominent. Around the base of the statue are the words: *Sancta Joanna de Arc.* Surmounting pedestal and statue is a tall canopy raising the height of the whole work to some seventeen feet.

The work was ready for dedication on May 30th., 1923. Sir Herbert Warren composed for the occasion a special ode which was set to music by Dr. Prendergast, the Cathedral organist. The ode begins:

> Sainted Champion of thy King and Land
> Old and New World, children of thy foemen,
> Here is holy honour bid thee stand.

The service of dedication was attended by the Dean and Chapter, the Lord Lieutenant of Hampshire and the French Ambassador. A hymn and an anthem were sung, prayers were said and an address given. The Ambassador said: "No place and no occasion could be richer in noble lessons than this cathedral and this ceremony....To-day at the foot of this statue...I find...a school of politics and high morality: two things which ought to be identical if politics are to be identical with what Joan of Arc understood them to be; devotion to the people and not a self-seeking profession which benefits only its votaries. Nothing but humble imitation of her virtues...can dispel the misery which is overwhelming the world. She is entitled to be a patroness of Franco-British brotherhood..." The crusade before England and France, he

(Arthur W. Kerr)

Statue of Joan of Arc, 1923.

concluded, was "to deliver a yet captive heavenly Jerusalem, if by that word we mean the promised land of peace among men of good will".

After the work was completed some money remained which was used to create a small copy of the original statue for presentation to the Church at Domrémy where it still stands with its inscription recording the fact that it had been given by British and American friends of France.[6]

The Shipping Festival, 1928

The shared sacrifices of England and France between 1914 and 1918 stirred the sentiment which led to the erection of the statue of Joan of Arc. It had also brought home to the people of Britain their immense debt to the men of the Merchant Navy.

It was fitting, therefore, that in 1928 Bishop Woods should give a lead through the inauguration of the annual Shipping Festival in the Cathedral. One of the first visits he made after his enthronement in 1927 was to the Dockland in Southampton. For him, Southampton was "the hub of the Winchester Universe". Very quickly his interest won the respect of the exclusive Master Mariners, among whom he was received as a "Stowaway", a rare honour conferred, outside the Merchant Navy, only on such men as Admiral of the Fleet Earl Jellicoe, Sir Roger Keyes and Major-General the Right Honorable J.E.B. Seely, Lord Lieutenant of Hampshire. The men of the Merchant Navy responded and have done so ever since at their annual service in the Cathedral. A link with the merchant fleet of Britain is the ensign of the *Queen Elizabeth I* which is laid up in the Cathedral and drapes the altar at each festival service.[7] The toll inflicted on the Merchant Navy is movingly, if simply, told by the thousands of names of sailors who died during the war of 1939-1945. Many of them sailed from Southampton. Their names are preserved in three volumes kept in the Merchant Navy memorial at the south west corner of the Cathedral. Another link with the Merchant Navy was a model of the *Mauretania* for many years kept in the north transept but finally sold in the 1960s to help raise urgently needed funds for the repair of the fabric of the Cathedral. The same great ship is embroidered on one of the cushions in the Quire.

Canon Vaughan

Just after the end of the Great War, Canon Vaughan published his *Winchester Cathedral* (1919). Sixty years later it is still the most useful book on the monuments and memorials of the Cathedral. He felt that Professor Willis' classical exposition of the architecture of the Cathedral was still the supreme work on that subject, and could not be repeated. Round these monuments and memorials much historical information is given, though no continuous history of the Cathedral was attempted. A year later in the style in which he excelled, Canon Vaughan collected a series of essays: *The Music of Wild Flowers.* In that volume he devotes c.18 to *Where Izaak Walton Died.* This is an account of No.7 The Close where Prebendary Hawkins lived and where Izaak Walton died. Much of the information given by Vaughan derives from the so called *Wainscott Book,* then only recently discovered by the Librarian in an oak settle in the South Transept. The book tells of the expenses incurred by each house in the Close between 1662 and 1812. On the fourth Sunday after Trinity in 1922, he was in residence, and after preaching at Morning Prayer he celebrated the Holy Communion. As he spoke the words of the collect for that day..."that we may so pass through things temporal that we finally lose not the things eternal..." his speech failed, he never regained consciousness and died shortly afterwards. Few priests could wish other than that they should complete their life and ministry at the altar they were ordained to serve. His memorial is redolent of an age before the world of war:

> Let us thank God
> For the Gentleness Honesty & Learning of
> JOHN VAUGHAN
> Who loved the poor and the rich
> and won their hearts
> He loved this House of God
> and wrote its story
> He loved the birds of the Air
> and the Flowers of the Field
> And taught others to do likewise.

The tablet may be seen on the south wall of the Nave almost at the point where it joins the South Transept. A reprint of his work on *Winchester Cathedral* is a great need, perhaps with an extra chapter to cover the years 1919-1979. All the Cathedral monuments could then be described.

The Cathedral Library

Vaughan had been a lover of the Library and as early as 1914 included chapters in his *Winchester Cathedral Close* on St. Swithun's Scriptorium, Bishop Morley's Library, and then a more general chapter entitled, In the Library. He was not actually the Librarian. That office was held by Minor Canon F.T. Madge and was a duty he discharged conscientiously and assiduously from 1879 to 1925. During his term of office he helped make public more of the Cathedral archives. In 1925, he was joined by Canon Goodman as Co-Librarian who succeeded him in 1933 on the death of Canon Madge, though for the previous eight years he had in fact undertaken most of the work of the Library. He too produced a series of works of great learning. His successors can testify to his never failing accuracy. Noteworthy events during his tenure of office was the examination of the chained books of the Library by B.H. Streeter. The result of the visit is recorded in Streeter's authoritative work on *The Chained Library* (London, 1931) p.345.f.

In 1936, Mrs Lefroy presented to the Library a manuscript poem of Jane Austen written in Jane's own hand and which is noteworthy because it includes two verses not hitherto recorded in which she compares Mrs Lefroy of Ashe in Hampshire in 1808 with Dr. Johnson.

To the Memory of Mrs. Lefroy
who died Dec. 16 — my birthday — written 1808.

At "Johnson's Death, by Hamilton t'was said,
"Seek we a substitute — ah! vain the plan,
No second best remains to Johnson dead —
None can remind us even of the Man."

So we of thee — unequall'd in thy race,
Unequall'd thou, as he the first of Men.
Vainly we search around thy vacant place,
We ne'er may look upon thy like again.

In the following year the Library was presented with a gold ring connected with Bishop Lancelot Andrewes, Prelate of the Order of the Garter from 1619-1626. On the blue enamel on the outside of the ring are the words, *Honi soit qui mal y pense*. On the inside is a skull, the initials L.A. (Lancelot Andrewes) and the words *Novissima Memorare* — remember your last end.

In the early days of the Second Great War Mrs Goodman, who had been an invaluable colleague to him in the Library, died. Canon Goodman continued at his post until the war ended, producing what is probably the greatest of all his works for the Canterbury and York Society in 1940 and 1941, the two volume edition of Bishop Henry Woodlock's Registers. Woodlock, after being Prior of the monastery of St. Swithun, was Bishop of Winchester from 1305-1316.

Cathedral Music, 1914-1933

The organist in control of the destiny of Cathedral music between 1914 and 1933 was Dr. Prendergast who succeeded Dr. Arnold in 1902. The extensive repairs of 1905 to 1912 made many difficulties but despite these he maintained unbroken the tradition of Cathedral music. Then followed the years of war when men available to sing became fewer. The chances, therefore, of attaining any very high standard of music were hindered. The education of the boys was also less favourably pursued than was the case in later years. This led the Dean and Chapter to move the Choir School in 1925, from 34, Colebrook Street to 9, The Close, rather against the wishes of Dr. Prendergast. Extra classrooms were added in the garden of 9, The Close, where the organist lived. He felt so strongly about the change that he appealed to the Visitor but the Visitor (i.e. the Bishop) upheld the Dean and Chapter though he added a reprimand that they might have taken Dr. Prendergast into their confidence about the change of plans rather earlier.

There are one-time choristers who remember him still and who would respond to Canon Madge's limerick about him:

> A New Organorum Pulsator
> Of tones a tremendous Pulsator
> Gas may fail his bellows
> He'll fail not his fellows
> But will 'gas' like a wild agitator.

There is one contribution which Prendergast has made to the music of the Cathedral which still continues. He composed the music of many of the antiphons sung before Matins or Evensong, in the South Transept, which are a particular feature of Winchester. For a musician to live on so regularly in his music is reward indeed.

Glass and Wall Paintings

Shortly after Dean Hutton's arrival at Winchester, J. de Le Couteur brought out his book on *Ancient Glass in Winchester* (1920). The author became a close friend of the Dean who assisted him with his enormous library. He remained in close touch with the Cathedral and the College until he died on August 13th, 1925. Speaking at his funeral in the Cathedral, the Dean said: "To know was to admire and love him...he had three qualities which...always make for a happy life: intellectual curiosity, a sense of fun, and a sense of duty". After his death his *magnum opus* appeared: *English Mediaeval Painted Glass* (London 1926), a valuable work of reference for those wanting a general background.

Wall paintings too attracted attention in the Guardian Angels Chapel and in the Holy Sepulchre Chapel. W.G. Constable wrote on *The Paintings in the Guardian Angels Chapel* in 1929. The leading expert in these years was Professor E.W. Tristram, who was employed by the Dean and Chapter in any matter referring to wall paintings in the Lady Chapel and the Holy Sepulchre Chapel.

Dean Selwyn

The appointment of Selwyn to succeed Hutton as Dean of Winchester in 1931[8] began a new and important chapter in the history of the Cathedral. Before coming to Winchester he had followed a brilliant academic career at Eton and Cambridge. On leaving Cambridge he had experience as Headmaster of Radley and Vicar of the important parish of Redhill, in Surrey. He thus came to Winchester with wide experience and great gifts.

Immediately he made his mark and his initiatives are still felt. Perhaps the one which he found specially congenial was the creation of a new school for the training of Choir Boys.

The Pilgrims' School

On 28th September, 1931 the Bishop of Winchester dedicated The Pilgrims' School, "to the Glory of God and the service of His Church".[9] The school received its name as Dean Selwyn and Mr. H.J. Salwey, the headmaster, were discussing the project in The Close. As they looked at the Pilgrims' Hall, the idea emerged that the school should have the name the Pilgrims' School. Choir boys had been educated in Winchester for the best part of a thousand years. The Pilgrims' School, therefore, was the latest in a long line of schools. Its basic pre-supposition, however, was different from its predecessors. This was to serve both as a Choir School and a Preparatory School which might look particularly to Winchester College. Under the wise guidance of Humphrey Salwey, and with the devoted support of his wife, the school steadily prospered, enriching both the music of the Cathedral and producing a succession of pupils and scholars for the Public Schools.

The Friends, 1931

On July 15th, 1931 the Association of the Friends of Winchester Cathedral was founded. Their first patron was H.R.H. The Duke of Connaught and their first chairman, Sir William Portal. Their policy was formulated under four heads:

1. To undertake schemes of repair which the Dean and Chapter consider *necessary.*
2. To collaborate with the Dean and Chapter on schemes considered to be *desirable* and which commend themselves to The Friends.
3. To support the Dean and Chapter in cases of *special emergency.*
4. To set up a *Reserve Fund* to meet unforeseen emergencies. Friends promised to pay a certain sum each year.

Within a year The Friends reported repairs in The Close, classification of mediaeval sculptures and the provision of kneelers by the Cathedral Broderers.

Membership of the Friends has gradually risen but finds the 3,000 barrier difficult to surmount. Nevertheless, so large a membership is an immense personal, as well as financial, asset to the Cathedral. From time to time great corporate enterprises have been undertaken: a *Son et Lumière,* a Festival of Flowers, a massive sale. Less conspicious, but possibly even more valuable, is the day by day help of Friends with the many chores that need doing if a Cathedral is to be alive and welcoming: guides and holy dusters, cleaners, helpers on the door and at the bookstall, in Library or Treasury. Another area in which the Friends have done a great work is in their publications: Christmas cards, booklets on a number of subjects, transparencies and last but not least their annual *Winchester Cathedral Record.* This has provided necessary information about membership and financial statements and reports of annual meetings. In addition, it has provided a wealth of written contributions on every facet of cathedral life and history. Some of these contributions have reached a level of scholarship which would do credit to a national publication. Such contributors have included Dom David Knowles, Roger Quirk and Martin Biddle. Each year there is a Festival on or near St. Swithun's Day. This festival, begun in Dean Hutton's time, is characterised by an impressive roll call of men and women who have served the Church in Winchester for thirteen hundred years. It includes names illustrious in English History and serves to remind all present of the overwhelming continuity of the Cathedral as a great centre of Christian worship.

The Broderers

There is yet one more initiative taken by Dean Selwyn which is celebrated not only in Winchester but throughout the world. When Theodore Woods became Bishop of Winchester he broke the long succession of bishops who had hitherto lived in Farnham Castle. In 1927, the huge diocese of Winchester was divided into three dioceses: Winchester, Guildford and Portsmouth. Farnham Castle, so long associated with the bishops of Winchester, was now in the new diocese of Guildford. The Bishop of Winchester therefore, had to find a new home. This he found at Wolvesey in Winchester. For the first time in centuries the bishops of Winchester began to live in Winchester regularly and not in London or Farnham which had so long been the custom right down to the nineteenth century. The Bishop wished to refurnish the chapel at Wolvesey. Earlier in his career he had been Vicar of Bradford where he came to know Louisa Pesel who had won a great reputation as an embroiderer.

She was invited to design and execute the necessary kneelers and cushions for the restored chapel at Wolvesey. This achievement so attracted the Dean that he wished the Cathedral to be similarly furnished, and so invited Miss Pesel to undertake this larger task. Her reply was as follows:

April 24, 1931

Dear Mr. Dean,

      I shall be very pleased to undertake the work you propose & feel honoured that you are willing to trust it to me. Miss Blunt will be a very able assistant as you know......I think we should be able together to produce some good work. Anyhow we are prepared to attempt to do so.

      £25 will go a good long way in wools & canvas....

Yours sincerely,

Louisa F. Pesel.

Miss Pesel invited Miss Sybil Blunt to be her lieutenant. Together they trained women to help with the work, made the designs, and supervised the whole enterprise over a number of years. In the first year two hundred volunteers came forward and they produced 117 kneelers, 1 stall cushion, 10 alms bags, and a mass of borders for the edges of future bench cushions. In addition, some 200 pieces of work were nearing completion. Each year there was a short service of dedication. This practice continued for several years.

Opposite: Winchester Cathedral cushion embroidered with Queen Mary's Coat of Arms.

The contribution for 1934 was memorable for the visit of Queen Mary, herself a famous needlewoman. She added her name to the scroll of helpers who were listed each year with the work they had done:

MARY R
Her Majesty the Queen
Honoured the Broderers by
Inspecting their work
On April 11th
1934

This vellum scroll grew to be thirteen feet long and is most handsomely written and illuminated by Beatrice Forder and is itself a piece of modern calligraphy of the greatest beauty. As part of a memorial to Beatrice Forder, a means has been devised whereby some eighteen inches of the scroll can be shown at any time within a glass case and with the help of rollers any part of the scroll is readily visible without the danger of constant handling.

The work was finally completed in 1936 and the concluding tally of work done reads as follows:

360 kneelers for chairs
96 Alms bags
36 long cushions with 56 medallions
1 Lectern carpet
1 Litany Desk kneeler
3 seat cushions and 1 book cushion for the Bishop's throne
6 long seats for lay clerks
2 bench cushions for choristers
18 yards border for five communion-rail kneelers
25 borders for chapter kneelers

The value of this contribution to the Cathedral over the years has been immense. Its influence has spread throughout the country, across the Atlantic and as far as Australia. A recent authority in such work, Joan Edwards begins her book with the invasion of William the Conqueror in the Bayeux Tapestry and ends it with the medallion on one of the Winchester cushions showing a ship of William I. The implication is that the work is in the tradition of the Bayeux Tapestry. Certainly, the embroideries have stood up to heavy wear during nearly half a century, in which they have been under ever increasing wear. Careful cleaning is necessary from time to time and new backing has been required, especially for kneelers in constant contact with the stone floor. But the embroideries themselves are remarkably resistant to heavy wear. Groups of women frequently come to examine the work and return to their parishes at home and overseas inspired to undertake a similar work for their own church. What Miss Edwards calls *St. Swithun's Day Enterprise* has proved a continuing inspiration.

Louisa Pesel and Sybil Blunt also wanted their work to reflect the current life of the Cathedral. One reflection is the picture of John Elkins virger for fifty years. He stands for many servants of the Cathedral who give a life time of service. Born at Hursley, he was a parishoner of John Keble and used to walk into Winchester with the Vicar's letters and bring his mail. A few years later he was present at the enthronement of Samuel Wilberforce. He lived to be present when George V and George VI visited the Cathedral. *The Hampshire Observer* described "the prowess of Mr Elkins as a knight of the road". As a child he walked from Hursley to Winchester and back. As virger he took a walk over Magdalen Hill before opening the Cathedral at 7 a.m. It is said that he thought little of walking to Portsmouth.[10]

Selwyn, Scholar and Preacher[11]

So far we have written about the more obvious achievements of Dean Selwyn. He exercised his ministry in wider fields because of his scholarship and preaching. Before coming to Winchester he was widely known as editor of *Theology,* a monthly magazine with wide influence among the clergy. He relinquished the editorial task in 1933. He had already published *The Approach to Christianity* and had edited a compilation called *Essays Catholic and Critical* (1925) which was in the tradition of earlier compilations like *Essays and Reviews,* (1860) and *Lux Mundi,* (1889) and had marked epochs in the history of the Church. Selwyn's publication was to prove that the more catholic clergy could also be as critical and scientific in their approach to Theology and Biblical Study as any other scholar in any other discipline. The book had great influence on a whole generation of students.

Besides these major works, he wrote and preached a great deal. Of unusual interest is the fact that in 1932 he was chosen to preach the Latin sermon at the opening of the Canterbury Convocation in St. Paul's Cathedral. Thereafter he preached numerous University sermons at Oxford, Cambridge, Nottingham and St. Andrew's. He also had the ear of the editors of such journals as the *Quarterly Review* in which he was able to expand on themes which he considered important: *The Oxford Movement; The Church and the Outlook* (1941); *The Church and the Public Schools.* He was also one of the first to exploit the new medium of the radio. Two popular publications were: *Thoughts on Worship and Prayer and The White Horseman.* In this last collection is included a hymn of his which is still requested —

A Hymn of the Hampshire Countryside

Praise we the Lord, the great Author of Nature
Praise we the Maker of upland and plain
Praise we the Spirit through whom every creature
Gathers its life and renews it again...

See where his flock the young shepherd is guiding
Hard by the track on Old Winchester Hill:
See where 'mid Alton's shy slopes lie in hiding
Kilns where the hops their soft odours distil.

He also wrote a hymn for a special Scouts' and Guides' Service held in the Cathedral in 1935: *Hymn of the Hampshire Beacons.* Those who recall his preaching personally still speak with admiration of the polished preacher for whom the sermon was a very important part of his ministry.

The Dean and Mussolini, 1937

One sermon of his in particular achieved a fame he never anticipated. In March, 1937, he was invited to preach at a special service in London attended by the exiled Emporer Haile Selassie of Abyssinia whose country had been invaded by the Italians. This African war was a herald of the 1939-1945 conflict. During the course of his sermon the Dean expressed his regret that a country to which the world owed so much of its civilisation should be so mis-led by its Duce as to lead his country into war for which there was no possible justification unless territorial expansion was to be condoned.

The sermon was given wide press coverage in England and Italy and across the Atlantic. It is clear that some Italians at least thought that because the Dean was a leading figure in the Established Church he was representing the views of the British Government. Sensational reporting followed in which intemperate language was used by British, Canadians and Americans and the Italians.

The *New York Times* ran a headline: *British Dean Calls Mussolini Madman.* From Montreal came the headline *Dean in U.K. calls Duce Madman in New Anglo-Italian 'Incident'. The Times,* more soberly spoke of *Italian attack on British Dean. The Evening News* spoke of *Fiery Reply to "Anglican Hysteria" about Italy.* The source of the headlines was an academic reference in the Dean's sermon to the fact that in the second century B.C. Antiochus Epiphanes (Antiochus the brilliant) was nicknamed Antiochus Epimanes (Antiochus the madman).

Manorial History

A surprising and unexpected development took place between the wars in connection with monastic and episcopal estate papers. William Beveridge (later Lord Beveridge) and other economists as well as social historians realised that the manorial records contain the detailed history of ordinary people in ordinary every day life who dwelt on the farms and in the villages of earlier centuries.[12] These were not the chronicles of kings and queens or the registers of bishops. They were the evidence of the ordinary man. It needed highly gifted men to extract the evidence. The two-fold qualification to be able to read manorial rolls say from the 13th century onwards is given to few. Add to this the difficulties of British Latin and that few is reduced to a handful. The Cathedral was fortunate to have three scholars who could handle such material: they were Arthur Goodman,[13] his wife Florence,[14] and John S. Drew[15] gifted amateur historian with the precision of an expert and of a professional.

Arthur Goodman was in the line of meticulous scholars equipped both by temperament and learning to undertake works of scholarship of enduring value. His list of published works puts him in the highest category of scholars. Possibly only Francis Baigent and Dean Kitchen can vie with him in their contribution to our knowledge of the Diocese and Cathedral of Winchester. Mention has been made of Bishop Woodlock's Register (1305 to 1316) in two volumes. Canon Goodman's careful index of the three thousand manorial rolls of the monastery is of almost daily service to readers in the Cathedral Library. He also wrote several works on the Cathedral: *Winchester Chartulary, The Winchester Cathedral Statutes* as well as *The Manor of Goodbegot*. In his work he was partnered by his wife, a scholar in her own right with a gift for *haute vulgarisation*. She edited Dean Young's *Diary, Pretenders from the Pulpit* (eighteenth century sermons in the Library) and *Reverend Landlords and Their Tenants,* a readable account of the administration of Cathedral lands between 1660 and 1700.

During the years of the Second Great War, J.S. Drew, produced transliterations, translations, and notes on collections of manorial rolls relating to several manors: Chilbolton, Compton, Houghton, Silkstede, Michelmersh, and Thurmond. He also left two valuable card indexes on Compton and Silkstede. The value of his work has only begun to be explored.

The Cathedral Bells, 1937

Due to the generosity of The Friends of the Cathedral, bellringers themselves and the Barron Trust it was possible to re-cast all twelve bells of the Cathedral and for the first time the general public was able to see them all standing on the dais, in 1937. The work was undertaken by Messrs. John Taylor, of Loughborough. An opportunity was thus afforded to gather a brief history of the bells:-

Treble bell	Cast 1921 In memory of those who fell in the Great War.
2nd bell	Cast 1921. Gift of the Guild of Bellringers
3rd bell	Cast 1892. Gift of the citizens of Winchester
4th bell	Cast 1892. Gift of the Guild of Bellringers
5th bell	Cast 1772
6th bell	Cast 1742
7th bell	Cast 1734. Cracked and re-cast in 1797
8th bell	Cast 1804
9th bell	Cast 1734
10th bell	Cast 1814
11th bell	Cast 1737
Tenor bell	Cast 1891

The Tenor bell carries the inscription: I remember the hours as they pass; I mourn the departed; I summon the living to prayer; and I am commanded to sound out the Coronation of George VI and his name inscribed adorns the work. One peculiar circumstance of the re-casting and re-dedication, which took place on March 20th., 1937 is the fact that when the bell was originally re-cast, the King was expected to be Edward VIII and his name was originally on the bell. Due to the abdication in December, 1936 the name had to be altered to that of George VI. Since 1937 one extra bell has been added. To-day the bells play a vital part in the regular worship of the Cathedral on Sundays, the major festivals of the Church, the occasional wedding, the death of someone closely associated with the Cathedral and the passing of each old year. This last ceremony begins with the ringing of a muffled peal to mark the dying year. At a minute to mid-night prayers are said, the twelve strokes of mid-night follow and then a joyous peal rings out to mark the birth of a new year.

(A. W. Kerr)

Some of the Cathedral's 13 bells in the bell chamber.

Roger Lloyd

Like Gordon Selwyn his Dean, Canon Roger Lloyd, served the Cathedral for nearly thirty years. Lloyd came to Winchester in 1937, by which time Selwyn had taken his great initiatives and had settled the course of the Cathedral's ministry for nearly a generation. Roger Lloyd came from the Lancashire parish of Great Harwood. As Canon and Vice-dean he played his part. In this latter capacity he once acted as chairman at a meeting of Deans. He became a kind of elder statesman so far as cathedrals were concerned. His ministry of the word was widespread in the realms of theology, history, biblical scholarship and even fiction. As a hobby he had the characteristic of so many clergy: he was a train enthusiast. Indeed he was a brilliant writer on the subject, extremely knowledgeable and well known. His pen continued to be prolific all the time he was at Wincheser. In 1937, he published *The Beloved Community;* in 1938 *Revolutionary Religion;* and in 1939 *The Golden Middle Age.* His *Mastery of Evil* appeared in 1941 while in 1943 he published *The Inspiration of God.* This continued the theology which he worked out in his Society of Christ the King (S.C.K.), a series of groups of men and women who, in common worship and shared spiritual experience, found the inspiration of God. Many such groups arose and proved of great help to those who shared in them.

Mediaeval Figure Sculpture, 1935

In 1935, the Cathedral Architect, T.D. Atkinson, addressed the Society of Antiquaries on the fragments of mediaeval sculpture within the Cathedral. This was first attempt to offer a coherent description of the fragments that remain. He dated the fragments between the 13th and 16th centuries and estimated that at the time of the suppression of the monastery there were over two hundred statues within the Cathedral. Of these he estimated that sixty-one stood upon the Great Screen. The most famous statue and the most beautiful is the one variously described as The Synagogue or as Fortitude. This particular statue stood originally, not in the Cathedral, but in a niche on the south side of the Prior's House. There are many heads of great beauty and great strength. The most beautiful are the Virgin and Child, now generally known as the Winchester Madonna and the other possibly a Queen or Princess. One of the most powerful heads is that of The Almighty dating from the fifteenth or sixteenth century and which was found in 1886. There is a bishop's head wearing a mitre and other heads, one of which it has been suggested might be that of Richard II.[16]

Besides the figure sculpture there is also a collection of capitals. Two date from the twelfth century. On one is depicted the combat between the centaurs and the lapiths and on another there are figures of two tumblers. Both are strangely non-religious.

The Coronation Carpet, 1937

On May 6th., 1937, George VI was crowned King in Westminster Abbey. In July of the same year the Office of Works presented the Cathedral with part of the golden carpet used in the sanctuary of the Abbey on the occasion of the Coronation. Writing to the Dean on July 12th, the Controller of Supplies said:

"You will find in it some slight red marks; the two side by side represent the positions where stood the Chairs occupied by the King and Queen in front of the Royal Box. The third mark indicates the position of the Stool where the King knelt during the Communion Service. Most interesting of all, in the opposite corner, stood the Throne (i.e. King Edward's Chair, containing the stone of Scone) in which the King sat for his anointing, investiture and Coronation."

This carpet is now the sanctuary carpet of the Cathedral.

Royal Window of King George V. 1938

On July 12th, 1938 the American Ambassador unveiled a window over the South Door leading into the Nave. An inscription in the window sets out perfectly its purpose:

This window was given by Americans
as a tribute to the Life and Character
of King George V.
MCMXXXVIII

The window itself was the work of Hugh Easton, well known as an artist in stained glass. The window includes Edward the Confessor, William the Conqueror and a recognizable portrait of George V, kneeling and wearing the robes of the Garter. The vision in the light of the window comes from the Book of Revelation, chapter 19, verse 16: He hath on his vesture and on his thigh a name written KING OF KINGS AND LORD OF LORDS. Edward and William represent the Saxon and Norman royal lines which had their capital in Winchester.

The Second World War

The first War was sufficiently fresh in the memory of many to lead them to continue the practices of that earlier war so far as the Cathedral was concerned. There were the special services and the constant mindfulness of sacrifices made and lives lost. There was however one significant difference. The double threat of air attack and then of invasion meant that many children were evacuated from Southampton to Winchester. The Crypt was made into an air-raid shelter and fire watching parties manned the roof of the Cathedral to spring into immediate action in the event of an incendiary bomb being dropped upon it. It so happened that Winchester was spared any kind of 'Baedeker' raid such as had so seriously damaged Exeter or Coventry. Nevertheless losses were sustained, the Dean himself losing his wife and towards the end of the war a son, who was killed in action.

Field Marshall Wavell

Perhaps the noblest expression of the nation's spirit came from one of its greatest soldiers, a Wykehamist, Archibald Wavell, buried in Winchester College and remembered in the Cathedral. It was the author's privilege to meet him in Egypt and serve under him. Wavell won a legendary reputation as a great general. He became a distinguished Viceroy. But his own poem sums up the man: *Sonnet for the Madonna of the Cherries.* And it is the last couplet which is placed on his memorial in the Cathedral:

> For all that loveliness that warmth, that light,
> Blessed Madonna, I go back and fight.

He had kept his vision, enshrined in *Other Men's Flowers,* through

> Long Years of battle, bitterness and waste,
> Dry years of sun and dust and Eastern skies.

NOTES

1. *R.S.* 5 Vols. 1902-1947
2. R.F.K. Goldsmith. *The Military Memorials of Winchester Cathedral* Winchester, 1974.
3. *D.N.B.* 1920-1930. s.v. Furneaux W.M. (1848-1929)
4. *Crockford's Clerical Directory* 1930.s.v. *Hutton W.H.* gives a detailed list of Hutton's publications.
3. *D.N.B.* 1920-1930.s.v. *Furneaux W.M.* (1848-1928)
6. Winchester Cathedral Archives: *Joan of Arc.* For full details of relevant literature in French and English see V. Sackville West. *Saint Joan of Arc.* London, 1936.
7. E.S. Woods and F.B. Macnutt. *Theodore Bishop of Winchester* Pastor Prophet Pilgrim. A Memoir of Frank Theodore Woods, D.D. 1874-1932. London, pp.306-308.
8. From 1931 onwards constant use has been made of the annual publication the *Winchester Cathedral Record.* The Story of the Pilgrims' School is told in the annual issues of *The Pilgrims' School Magazine* (1932 onwards)
9. *School Magazine* 1932. p.1.
10. *The Hampshire Observer and County Advertiser.* 19 March, 1938.
11. The Cathedral archive contains most if not all of Dean Selwyn's published works. In addition it has many of his sermons and addresses, and a large number of press cuttings.
12. W. Beveridge. *Wages in the Winchester Manors.* Economic History Review VII. (1936), pp.22-43.
13. A.W. Goodman. *The Manor of Goodbegot.* Winchester. *Index of Manorial Records.* (Ms).
14. F.R. Goodman. *Barton Compotus Rolls,* 1248-1344.(Ms) Summary of Ledger Book 1.(Ms) She popularised her studies in *Winchester Valley and Downland* (i.e. the manor of Barton) Winchester, 1934. In addition she wrote an account of how the Dean and Chapter managed their estates in the seventeenth century: *Reverend, Landlords and their Tenants.* Winchester, 1930.
15. J.S. Drew *Manorial Accounts of St. Swithun's Priory.* English Historical Review 1XII (1947) pp.20-41. *Early Account Rolls of Portland, Wyke and Elwell* (estates of the Monastery of St. Swithun, Winchester). Dorset Nat. Hist. and Archaelogical Soc. Procs. pt. I (1944), pp.31-45; pt. 11 i.e.34-54 (1945) pp.34-54. 54
16. T.D. Atkinson. *Mediaeval Figure Sculpture* Oxford, 1936.

FURTHER READING

A.R. Mss. 3 vols. 1910-1946.

Atkinson T.D. *Winchester Cathedral Close* Ms; *Winchester Cathedral Memorials.* Typescript. Illustrated; *A Possible Foundation Stone.* H.F.C. xv. 263-268. *Mediaeval Figure Sculpture in Winchester Cathedral.* Oxford, 1936.

C.A. 4 vols. 1896-1939. Mss. Indexes to all volumes: E. Foss.

Church Assembly. *Constitution and Statutes of the Cathedral Church of the Holy Trinity,* Winchester. 1937.

Joan of Arc. Ms Collection.

Records of Cathedral and Close, 1739-1966.

E.G. Selwyn 1924 *Approach to Christianity;* 1925 *Essays Catholic and Critical;* 1936 *Thoughts on Worship;* 1937 *A Short History of Christian Thought;* 1940 *The Epistle of Christian Courage (1 Peter)* *Winchester Cathedral Chronicle,* 1914-1945 (Mss)
Winchester Cathedral Statutes, 1942.

The Bishop of Winchester, 1979

Chapter XIV

The Cathedral To-day

St. Swithun's Day, July 15th, 1945 fell between two major events: V.E. Day and V.J. Day. It fell between the days in May and August when victory was proclaimed against the Germans in Europe and the Japanese in the Far East. It was the eve of the atomic era. On July 15th there were very few indeed who knew that to be the case. For the Cathedral it was a day of rejoicing. Two months earlier war had ceased in Europe and the Far East was a long way off and likely to have little material impact upon Winchester. The Cathedral celebrated the anniversary of its patron saint with particular enthusiasm. There was something symbolic in the return of the Winchester Bible from its war time safe keeping to its original home. The lessons at evensong that day were read from it by Sir Frederick Kenyon, Dr. Oakeshott and the Vice-Dean.

The Winchester Bible.

In the following year Canon Goodman resigned from being Librarian after many years of distinguished and scholarly service to the Cathedral. The Dean and Chapter realised that it would not be easy to find in their number one so able as he for this particular kind of service. They, therefore, turned to Walter Oakeshott, the Headmaster of Winchester College to ask if he would serve as Honorary Librarian on the understanding that routine enquiries should be undertaken by the Precentor. This was agreed and linked the Cathedral with the world of scholarship. Already the Headmaster had produced his *Artists of the Winchester Bible* as a result of his studies, which went back to about 1933, when he started to visit the Library and to interest himself in the manuscript. On becoming librarian he proposed an Exhibition Room which would centre round the *Winchester Bible,* suitably displayed and rebound in four volumes. It had originally been bound in two volumes. In the days of Dean Rennell (1805-1840) it had been bound in three and now it was proposed to re-bind it in four. It also happened that Miss Beatrice Forder was able to undertake the actual work of re-binding and no more gifted craftswoman could have been found. Together scholar and craftswoman undertook the task, itself a great work of twentieth century art. It was completed in 1948 and as a brief account of the work is on one of the folios at the end of volume IV of the Bible and rarely seen, the wording is here given in full:

The Winchester Bible was rebound in the Cathedral Library in 1948. The section numbers show that the book was planned in mediaeval times as two volumes. In 1948 it was in three volumes in a binding which evidently dated from the beginning of the nineteenth century, probably from the time of Dean Rennell. It was presumably at the time of this binding that the edges were gilded. The fly leaves contained no evidence as to its state in the seventeenth and eighteenth centuries.

The book was sewn, in 1948, on seven double bands of linen parachute cord, the previous binding having had six bands only. It was bound in oak boards, the wood coming from Herriard Park, Basingstoke, with halfback and joints of unstained Niger goatskin. The old fly leaves and end papers were replaced by new. No paste-down paper was used. The book was bound in four volumes in order to bring the division between the original volumes I and II into place at the end of a volume. The book was lettered in Sangorski's Trajan style letter. The tooling of the bands was to a design based on the initial letter of the book Exodus.

During the course of the rebinding, the binder, Beatrice Forder of Winchester, sewed into place, with fine French linen thread, the initial to the book Obadiah, which had been bought for the Dean and Chapter by the National Art Collection Fund. This initial had been identified in a private collection in Yorkshire by the Cathedral Librarian of that time Dr. W.F. Oakeshott, who was put on the track of the initial by a remark made in a lecture by Dr. M.R. James on "The wanderings and homes of manuscripts." Dr. James had thought the initial came from the Lambeth Bible.

On the spine the title of each volume reads as follows:-

BIBLIA
SACRA
VVLGATA
LIBER
SANCTI
SWITHUNI
WINTON

Dean Selwyn

For a further twelve years the Dean wrestled with the problems of a post-war world which affected churches and cathedrals as well as other aspects of life. Funds were limited; building was hindered by various restrictions; and traditional beliefs and practices came under increasing pressure. Throughout the time he continued with rock-like steadiness, convinced that the Cathedral's role was constant and to bear witness to stately certainties at a time when everything was questioned, particularly when material progress began to increase and moral and religious convictions began to be abandoned. He struggled to maintain the weekday choral services of Matins and Evensong but had to admit defeat in 1954 when Choral Matins was replaced by said Matins on weekdays.

In 1946, Dean Selwyn produced the major scholastic work of his career, his edition, with commentary, on the Greek Text of *1 Peter* in the New Testament. This is a work of scholarship in the grand style in line with the great works of Lightfoot, Westcott and Hort of the nineteenth century. The work is marked by profound and detailed knowledge. Its main contention is that the 'Epistle' was designed for the newly baptised, setting out plainly for them the heart of Christian preaching and teaching as they faced a hostile world.

Royal Visit, 1946

However, in 1946 a royal visit set the seal on the continuation of ancient tradition. On May 17th, the King and Queen visited the Cathedral and spent forty minutes within its walls. They inspected the Winchester Bible, signed the Cathedral Book and were greeted by a cheering crowd of schoolchildren as they emerged from the south door of the Cathedral. This was the first opportunity which the King and Queen had of seeing the Coronation Window in the north aisle which had been unveiled just before the war on July 3rd, 1939.

Continuing Restorations, 1950

A particularly brilliant achievement, assisted by a generous grant from the Pilgrims' Trust, was the restoration of the wooden roof bosses in the Quire and the Tower. The last time the bosses had been seen at close quarters was in 1819, as a small scroll hidden behind one of the bosses revealed.

Roger Lloyd

Dean Selwyn wrote as scholar and preacher. Canon Lloyd on the other hand wrote perhaps in a more popular vein and on a wide range of interests. His special gift was that of popularisation of subjects which might otherwise have been confined to specialists. He was able to reach a wider public. His volumes on the *Church of England,* first published in 1946 and 1950 and then re-written in 1966, are among the few attempts to narrate the contemporary history of the Church. The style is always readable and though others with the benefit of hindsight will be able to point to defects of proportion, such writing is extremely valuable. He contrived too to make New Testament studies and studies in the Early Church readable in volumes of creative imagination: *Letters of Luke the Physician,* 1957 and *Letters from the Early Church,* 1959. He turned his hand to fiction in *The Troubling of the City,* 1962. The city is a cathedral city and readers can see Winchester in it. He also responded to the lively debate which arose out of John Robinson's book, *Honest to God* by writing *Ferment in the Church,* 1964. He had other books and articles to his credit. In fine he exercised a wide ministry with his pen in that difficult area between the works of academic scholars and the journalism which can so easily misrepresent a serious subject by over simplification and lack of comprehension.[1]

Railway Trains

Eccentricity is often thought to be a characteristic of the clergy. The canons of Winchester have included in their number those with unexpected interests. These interests have enriched the men themselves and often their contemporaries. In the case of Roger Lloyd he achieved considerable fame as a railway enthusiast. Some of his articles in *The Manchester Guardian* were journalism of a very high order as he described a run on the footplate of a steam locomotive out of King's Cross. In addition to his journalistic work, he wrote a number of books. Among them are *The Fascination of Railways* (London, 1951) and *Railwaymen's Gallery* (London, 1953). In the first of these he pays a warm tribute to the railwaymen who never abandoned their engines or signal boxes even in the heaviest bombing raids or in the most perilous situations during the years of war between 1939 and 1945.

Memorial to Bishop Haigh, 1942-1952

Bishop Haigh had been forced to retire in 1952 owing to ill health. He had served as senior chaplain to the Archbishop of Canterbury in his younger days, had been Bishop of Coventry at the time of the *blitz* in 1942 and shortly afterwards was preferred to the see of Winchester. As a memorial the low wall surrounding the Consistory Court (also used as a Minstrels' Gallery) was restored and had a suitable Latin inscription along the length of the south and east walls. It may be translated:

As evidence of their gratitude to Mervyn Haigh, on his leaving the Bishopric after ten years, the Dean and Chapter, with the help of the Friends of the Cathedral Church, saw to the renewal and restoration of the gallery, for many years appropriated to serve as a registry and consistory court.

On his retirement the Bishop went to live in North Wales until his death in 1962. He was brought to the Cathedral to be buried on May 26th. With his characteristic efficiency he had planned every detail of his funeral and of the service. The hymns included *Just as I am, without one plea*. It was the choice of a great man who knows that in the presence of his Maker he is wholly dependent on Another. The address was given by Bishop Williams, his successor.[2]

A very personal memorial to this great man is the gift of his pectoral cross which is kept in the Library. It is gold on wood and has the words *Fratres Fratri* which tell us that it is the gift of brothers to a brother. At the intersection of the cross are the arms of the See of Canterbury. It was, in fact, the gift of friends at Canterbury when he first became a bishop at Coventry in 1932. It was presented to the Dean and Chapter of Winchester by the Bishop's former secretary, Miss Jackson.

Monte Cassino, 1953

The Dean's good faith about his admiration for Italy was finally vindicated. During the invasion of Italy by the Allies in 1943, the monastery of Monte Cassino, the first house of the Benedictine Order, was regrettably destroyed for military reasons. It provided a strong point of German resistance which, if the invasion of Italy was to succeed, had to be removed. While the war was still in progress, the Dean and Chapter decided that as soon as opportunity offered they would approach all colleges and cathedrals which were indebted to the Benedictine Order during the course of their history and invite them to join together to replenish the Library of the Monastery by providing funds and or books. The suggestion was taken up and in 1953 it was possible to send books for this purpose. An inscription in Monte Cassino records the fact. Colleges at Oxford and Cambridge with Benedictine associations along with thirteen cathedrals joined with Winchester in the gesture. The bookplate placed in each book and specially designed for the occasion depicts a phoenix rising from its ashes.[3]

A Royal Visit, 1955

Queen Elizabeth II visited the Cathedral on July 25th, 1955. There were the customary presentations and once again the Pilgrims' School had its own real share in the visit. This particular visit took on rather more significance because the Queen gave an audience to Sir Anthony Eden, her Prime Minister, in the Deanery in what is now called The Queen's Room[4]. In due course the Prime Minister was created Earl of Avon. As Colonel of the King's Royal Rifle Corps his name was added to their memorial in the South Presbytery Aisle in 1977.

An Appreciation of Dean Selwyn

Harry Altham, summing up Dean Selwyn's work at Winchester on his retirement in 1958 writes much about his initiative in so many spheres of Cathedral life: Friends, Embroideries, Roof Bosses and the refitting of the Exhibition Room, and last, but not least, the Pilgrims' School. All these aspects of Cathedral life have been mentioned. He writes of him as a rare combination of the man of affairs with the scholar. In the wider councils of the Church he was a frequent speaker both in Convocation and the Church Assembly. He never hid his regrets over the division of the Diocese. In the world of scholarship he became President of the Society of New Testament Studies, a remarkable achievement, in a world where professors abound, for a busy churchman. He left memories of friendly converse with the choir boys, his beautiful reading of the lessons, and his distinction as a preacher. When he spoke he did so with authority, not only of mind but also of heart. He was one of the greater deans of Winchester. His retirement was brief for he died in the following year. On the very day of his death his last literary composition *Jane Austen's Clergymen* was received by the editor of *The Church Quarterly Review*. The article appeared in October-December, 1959 pp.424-435. The article shows that there was no failing in his literary powers.

Opposite: H.M. The Queen leaving the Cathedral on 25th July, 1955.

Central press photos.

Dean Sykes, 1958-1961

After the long tenure of office by Dean Selwyn, the Crown chose another scholar for the Deanery, Professor Norman Sykes, the Dixie Professor of Ecclesiastical History in the University of Cambridge. He came to Winchester as the foremost Church Historian in England. Scarcely a doctorate had been attempted for many years in Church History without reference to Norman Sykes. He himself had made the eighteeth century his particular field in three great works: *Edmund Gibson* (1926), *Church and State in England in the Eighteenth Century* (1934), and *William Wake, Archbishop of Canterbury, 1657-1737*, 2 vols. Cambridge, 1957. In these three works he proved beyond dispute that a facile dismissal of the eighteenth century Church as wholly lethargic and neglectful of its mission was far from the truth.

In 1958, Sykes came to Winchester not only with this formidable scholarship, but also with a great reputation as a speaker in the Church Assembly where oratory and learning blended in a unique way.[5] All seemed set for a distinguished career at Winchester. In his first year he published *From Sheldon to Secker: Aspects of English Church History, 1660-1768*. In the following year he published his lectures *Man as Churchman* and contributed valuable chapters to the *New Cambridge Modern History* (Vol.X.) and the *Cambridge History of the Bible: The West from the Reformation to the Present Day*.

Suddenly, so it seemed, he was taken ill and died within less than three years. During his time work continued on different parts of the Cathedral, the most outstanding being on the roof paintings in the Guardian Angels chapel under the direction of Professor and Mrs. Baker. The restoration of 1928 was held to be disastrous. An appeal for £20,000 had to be made to meet the routine repairs and the restoration.

Cathedrals in Modern Life

In 1958, the Church Assembly appointed a Commission "to prepare, in consultation with the Church Commissioners, a Measure to supersede the Cathedrals Measures and to make such other alterations in the Law relating to cathedrals as may seem desirable to meet the needs of cathedrals at the present time." The report, *Cathedrals in Modern Life* was published in 1961. It drew attention in particular to two points: the tourists who arrive in great numbers and who presented an evangelistic opportunity which "might be of considerable importance". In addition, this new mobility had created the possibility of diocesan services and of secular organizations seeking the privilege of regular or occasional services. Such organizations found the cathedral the "most natural *venue*". Never before, says the Report, have the cathedrals served "as living centres of worship for such a wide variety of ordinary church members."

Dean Selwyn

Dean Gibbs-Smith.

Dean Sykes

Twenty years after the commission was set up this two fold purpose was even more true but is only part of the ministry of the Cathedral. As Roger Lloyd pointed out in his last book written from Winchester *The Church of England, 1900-1965*, the commission did at any rate recognize the fact that cathedrals have a distinctive mission which only they can discharge and that it is not a place to provide a base for clergy to undertake other ministries. For long, cathedrals had been stultified because their canons had to give most of their time to other essential duties. Both are needed. In order to meet this recognised need the commission went on to say that henceforth each cathedral should have a minimal constitution of a Dean and two Canons whose ministry lay wholly within the Cathedral. They were not to be "suffagan bishops, Assistant Bishops or Archdeacons or to be appointed to substantial diocesan administration."[6]

Southern Cathedrals' Festival

In 1949, Alwyn Surplice succeeded Harold Rhodes as Master of the Music. Financial stringency and the continuing problem of securing men to sing two services a day on weekdays presented problems which were insurmountable. The regular worship was discharged as faithfully as possible but changes became inevitable. On weekdays Matins was now said each week day.

The number of lay clerks dropped to such an extent that the quality of Cathedral Music was deteriorating. It was still impossible to have the stimulus of a Southern Cathedral Festival. This was resumed when Dean Sykes came to Winchester, in 1961. That year the Festival was at Salisbury.[7] By the time Winchester's turn came round in 1963, Dean Gibbs-Smith was Dean. Already Salisbury and Chichester had extended the Festival from the old corporate Evensong to a two day Festival. The new Dean encouraged the Master of the Music to make the Winchester Festival a three day festival from Thursday to Saturday. The work of S.S. Wesley loomed large and musical concerts were added to the Evensongs sung each day. When the Festival returned in due course to Winchester in 1966 a Sung Eucharist had been established, first at Salisbury in 1964 and thereafter as a regular feature as the main act of worship within the festival. By 1969 the services and the music still continued but events of a 'fringe' nature were introduced and the Southern Cathedrals Festival was becoming one of the major festivals in the south of England with an atmosphere of its own given particularly by the spacious grounds surrounding the cathedrals of Salisbury and Winchester. In 1975, the Festival at Winchester was extended by a further day which began with a Choral Matins, a novel event given the liturgical atmosphere of the time. A little later patronage for a lecture or musical event was sought

Dr. Alwyn Surplice and the Cathedral Choir, 1971

and secured and first came to Winchester in 1978 when a well known publishing house sponsored a recital.

The hard struggle of Alwyn Surplice's early days had been finally rewarded by his having a choir sufficient for so great a cathedral and he was able to build up a choir of increasing reputation. It was a particular pleasure when it was announced, shortly before his retirement in 1971, that the Archbishop of Canterbury was to confer upon him the Lambeth Degree of Doctor of Music in recognition of his services to Church Music. The degree was conferred in the chapel at Lambeth Palace and the occasion attended by a representative of Chapter, members of his family and some of his friends. The whole company was later entertained by Archbishop and Mrs. Ramsey. It was a fitting conclusion to a career that had overcome many difficulties and which had so firmly laid the foundations of the Cathedral's music for the years to come.

Early in 1972, Martin Neary, organist of St. Margaret's, Westminster, took up duties as Master of the Music. he already had a good choir awaiting him and was able to build on the foundations laid by his predecessor. The choir continued to improve. The problem of men which had incapacitated the choir in earlier days was resolved because of the number of musical schoolmasters in the area who provided a supply of youthful voices. No longer were lay clerks life appointments who kept their places long after their voices had lost their musical qualities. Records and television appearances both extended the reputation of the choir. A first ever visit by an English Cathedral choir was paid to Notre Dame in Paris in 1978 and early in 1979 a tour of American and Canadian Cathedrals took place.[8]

The Cathedral Library

Dr. Oakeshott was succeeded by Canon Amand de Mendieta in 1962. His scholarship lay in an entirely different field. He concentrated his efforts mainly on the life and work of St. Basil of Caesarea (330-379), upon the Orthodox Church and especially upon Mount Athos. His pilgrimage from the Church of Rome to the Church of England is told in an autobiography called *Rome and Canterbury* while his hopes for the Church of England are set down in his work: *The Anglican Vision* (1971). On his death his many articles and reviews as well as his larger works were collected by his successor and are preserved in the Cathedral Library in fourteen volumes. His was a scholarship on the European scale of a highly specialised nature.

Miss Forder continued to serve the Library with self-effacing efficiency, setting the highest possible standards. The time came when she had to retire due to ill health though she continued, at home, to repair manuscripts. When she died it was widely felt that she should be appropriately remembered in the Library and the Archives. There is an inscription over the Winchester Bible which runs: *Remember Beatrice Forder who re-bound the Winchester Bible, 1948.*

A case was designed in which the 13 feet scroll that she wrote so perfectly to commemorate all the workers on the Embroideries is now preserved. And to link her with the Morley Library a disbound work of Bishop Morley was purchased and bound as near the 17th century style as is possible.

Canon Amand de Mendieta expressed a wish to give up his Library duties in view of his heavy commitments as a writer. He was succeeded by Canon Bussby. In recent years the main developments have been further furnishings to the Exhibition Room and Ante-room in memory of Bishop Alwyn Williams, an outstanding scholar, triple first, fellow of All Souls. Headmaster of Winchester College and Dean of Christ Church before becoming Bishop of Durham and finally Bishop of Winchester (1953-1961). His distinguished career is outlined on the cornice round the Exhibition Room.

The other main development has been the use of the east side of the South Triforium as a library and archive for the books and records of the Cathedral dating from 1700. This has relieved pressure in the Morley Library and Exhibition Room making them both more attractive and has helped visually to present the continuing life of the Cathedral from 1700 down to the present time. Much cataloguing has been done, especially in the older parts of the Library and also much indexing. Many helpers have furthered this work so that nearly all the Chapter Books are now indexed and the Cathedral is soon to have its own 'Wing' or catalogue of all its holdings between 1641 and 1700. Canon Madge had already catalogued all books printed before 1640 as long ago as 1902. Separate card indexes of Biblical, Hebrew, Patristic, Classical, Byzantine, German, French, Spanish and Italian works have also compiled. Manorial and topographical indexes are available as well as indexes of portraits. At least 30,000 entries have been made with the help of a team of workers.

Looking further afield, as in all departments of Cathedral life, there is a sharing with other cathedrals in the sphere of the upkeep and maintenance of books and archives. The Librarian promoted a Cathedral Librarians' Conference which first met at Lambeth Palace in 1976 and meets there annually. In 1978, there was held the first area conference of West of England Cathedral librarians at Wells. This mutual help and encouragement is much appreciated.

Dean Gibbs-Smith, 1961-1969

The death of Dean Sykes was followed within a few months by the resignation of Bishop Williams. A new chapter for diocese and cathedral was beginning. The new Dean Archdeacon Gibbs-Smith had been on the staff of St. Paul's Cathedral, London and Archdeacon of London. There his reputation stood high as administrator and organiser. He brought these gifts to Winchester, coupled with experience of parish life in the celebrated John Keble Church in North London. Winchester presented him with a superb opportunity to demonstrate the gifts which these experiences had brought him. He made a notable impact upon the services of the Cathedral and brought enhanced dignity to the Sunday Services and made available the musical support required for these services to be adequately rendered in so great a building. This meant more men and more boys.

The Appeal, 1966[9]

His bold and imaginative ideas could not be achieved within the straightened finances of the Cathedral. After much thought and careful preparation an appeal for £405,000 was launched. The response to the appeal was widespread and generous and the target was, in fact, surpassed. Its immediate consequences were new work upon strengthening the fabric of the Cathedral and the availability of resources in men and boys to bring the choir to the standard that the Dean envisaged and which it had long been the dream of the Organist to have at his command. Columns were strengthened, the organ case made secure, new tiles laid in the north presbytery aisle, and new pinnacles added to the north nave. The aim was to make the Cathedral as strong as it was when it was first built.

The Church Commissioners

The legislation promoted by the Report on Cathedrals in Modern Life was finally issued in new statutes and legislation in 1967. In that year the Dean and two canons were first paid by the Church Commissioners thus giving some easement to the strain on Cathedral finances. The Commissioners also make other small grants to assist provide funds for lay helpers in the Cathedral and look after investments on behalf of the Cathedral.

It became clear that both for cathedrals and for the Commissioners the individual dealings were a source of weakness to the cathedrals and increased work for the Commissioners. The issue crystalised over the strange relic of earlier days which still made Deans and Chapters responsible for part of the upkeep and insurance of chancels of certain parish churches. There are historical reasons why this was an equitable arrangement in earlier days. But in the 1970s any logic in such an arrangement had long vanished. Yet who wishes to take on new financial responsibilities? An approach by Canterbury, Winchester and Norwich on the matter elicited a helpful response from the Commissioners and already cathedrals who have responsibilities for chancels receive increased help. This was not the only problem and by 1978 as a result of initiative taken from Winchester, there is now an instrument representing all cathedrals which meets the Commissioners from time to time to discuss the increasingly complex practical problems of the cathedrals. In addition, the sharing of expertise between cathedrals is valuable.

Cathedral Statutes, 1967[10]

At the same time as the link with the Commissioners became closer, the Cathedral received its new statutes. The wording of Charles I is largely kept but new situations have arisen. For example, the position of the Pilgrims' School, of which the Dean and Chapter are *ex-officio* governors, had to be taken into account. In this particular matter a unique venture which linked the Quiristers of Winchester College with the Choristers of Winchester Cathedral had its effect upon the statutes. Appropriate room was left in the drafting of the statutes to include representatives from Winchester College upon the Governing Body should it be deemed appropriate. In 1978, two members of the College became full members of the Governing Body though for a number of years members of the College had acted and still act in an advisory capacity and contribute much skill to the running of this important school.

It will be news to most readers that such a body as a Cathedral Chapter with its Chapter Clerk (a legal officer) is the ultimate authority for the running of a cathedral. Each member of the Chapter, Dean and each of the four canons is bound by certain statutes. The statutes are given to the Cathedral by the Crown. The Dean is a Crown appointment: the canons are normally appointed by the Bishop though occasionally the Crown can (and did as recently as 1977) appoint a new canon. On the other hand, the Dean installs a new canon and the Vice-Dean installs a new Dean. A Cathedral has no parish for which it is responsible. There are 'parish Church cathedrals' but these are originally parish churches raised to cathedral status due to the increase in the number of dioceses in the last hundred years. The great historic cathedrals of Canterbury and York and Winchester have no such parochial duties. According to Law it is doubtful if a residentiary canon has a 'cure of souls.' The ministry of the cathedral and of its clergy is to look far beyond its local borders and among its many duties it should set standards of excellence as ideals for all. It is both traditional and experimental: its churchmanship is the churchmanship of the whole church and not just that of a particular section of it.

The Appeal, 1973

When Dean Stancliffe came to Winchester in 1969 he had been assured that the financial position of the Cathedral was secure. Even leading statesmen had not foreseen the raging inflation that struck the Country, and the Cathedral, in the 1970s. The appeal had not solved its financial problems. Although in 1973 the Cathedral was solvent it could only face retrenchment and a return to the stringency of earlier days. A further appeal was launched, this time for £175,000 with an emphasis on people: pensions for lay staff who served the Cathedral; bursaries for choristers; something for the archives of the Cathedral; and further provision for reparation of the fabric.

This second appeal on the completion of the first appeal lead to serious re-thinking of the Cathedral's finances. The main sources of revenue, the Commissioners and The Friends, were not able to increase their support at the rate that inflation demanded. Should another appeal be contemplated when the 1973 appeal (which ran for seven years) was completed? Salisbury Cathedral suggested that there was another way. That other way was to encourage visitors to support the Cathedral. Winchester pursued this idea. Visitors are invited to donate a modest sum to maintain one of the world's greatest fabrics. In this way what could be a crushing burden if faced locally is shared among the many hundreds of thousands from over sixty countries throughout the world who come to Britain to see cathedrals like Winchester because nowhere else has any nation succeeded to the same degree in keeping its tradition and at the same time maintaining a way of life within that tradition. Canon Wedderspoon has played a leading part in this development.

Archaeology, 1961-1971[11]

For a decade the churchyard of the Cathedral on the north side was annually opened up for the purpose of discovering as much as possible about the history of the first Church from the middle of the seventh century down to the time of Walkelin's present cathedral. The work was under the direction of Martin Biddle, and was part of the Winchester Excavations which were foremost in the country, with the backing of a local authority. Here we concentrate upon the work as it affects the early history of the Cathedral.

The work began in 1960, somewhat controversially, upon the Cathedral car park, a site which was let on a 99 year lease for the Wessex Hotel. Foundations of a late Saxon chapel were found. Thereafter excavations spread into the churchyard itself and continued for a decade. The main attraction of the site was that it had not been built on for many years and there was good hope that extensive remains of the Old Minster would be

Mediaeval graves being uncovered during Cathedral excavations.

found. In 1886, Dean Kitchin had undertaken a modest step towards excavating the site but new techniques were now available and an immense fund of enthusiasm for digging and excavating was provided by young people of many nationalities. Each winter the work excavated had to be filled in to prevent flooding. By 1963 not only was the Old Minster known but also Roman Winchester was revealed. In subsequent years further discoveries were made, revealing the various stages that the seventh century church underwent before it became the great Minster of St. Aethelwold in the tenth century. Some of the smaller finds were especially attractive: a ninth century piece of wall painting; the location of the original burial place of St. Swithun.

Each year detailed reports were presented in the *Winchester Cathedral Record* and for a wider world of scholarship in *The Antiquaries Journal.*[11] Inevitably the deductions reached at the end of a particular year were tentative but by degrees the complete picture emerged. The total work is now being written up in an impressive series of *Winchester Studies,* the first volume of which appeared early in 1977. This is of particular interest to the Cathedral and contains, quite literally, the foundation work on which the present story from 1079 to 1979 is constructed. When the full history of Winchester Cathedral is written from the seventh century onwards there will be available a wealth of material for these early years unknown to any of our predecessors.

For the general reader the plan of 1970 gives a visual impression of the nature of the buildings in the north churchyard. It is hoped in time that it will be possible to mark the outline of these discoveries in such a way that their gradual development from the seventh to the eleventh centuries will be understood. The first step was taken in 1971 when the site of St. Swithun's grave was marked. A second step was taken in 1978 when it was decided to outline on the ground the seventh century building. It is hoped that as time passes and funds become available that the whole complex will be suitably outlined and explained.

The Ecumenical Movement, 1962

It was Archbishop William Temple who in 1941 first introduced into the English Language the phrase, 'the ecumenical movement'.[12] Opportunities for the Cathedral to share in this movement have been numerous. Within its own area in Hampshire many Christians regard the Cathedral as their natural spiritual centre for a special occasion. Each year members of all Winchester Churches foregather in the Cathedral on such days as Good Friday. The Methodist Church requested (and was gladly granted) the use of the Cathedral to mark a special occasion. Roman

Catholics share in these ecumenical services. In 1975, appropriately on August 24th, St. Bartholomew's Day, Roman Catholics on pilgrimage celebrated Mass in the Cathedral. The Abbot of Quarr, (1971), and Archbishop of Rennes (1973) are among Roman Catholics who have. preached in the Cathedral.

In 1978, the Dean established a link with the Benedictine Monastery of St. Benoit-sur-Loire (or Fleury). It was from Fleury that Aethelwold brought Benedictine monks to Abingdon in the 10th century.[13] And it was from Abingdon that he brought the monks who introduced the Benedictine Order into Winchester. It is hoped that this association will be strengthened by annual visits.

Links have been forged with Orthodox Churches. In 1967, the Patriarch of Leningrad visited the Cathedral. From time to time the Orthodox Liturgy has been celebrated. In 1962, Bishop Allison appointed as Canon Residentiary Emmanuel Amand de Mendieta. A former Benedictine monk from Belgium he had made the spiritual pilgrimage from Rome to Canterbury. He had already established himself as a notable scholar with a long list of publications, articles and reviews dating back to 1945. He devoted much energy to this study of St. Basil along with Professor Stig Y Rudberg, of Uppsala. His studies led him farther to make a special study of the Orthodox Church in general and of Mount Athos in particular. His first work on Mount Athos, published in French, appeared in 1955. He was not satisfied with this work and published, this time in English, in Berlin a revised study, *Mount Athos,* in 1972. And now, posthumously, there has appeared from Thessalonica in 1977 his latest study *L'Art au Mont-Athos.* He illustrates his study with examples of monasteries, their mosaics and in particular their ikons.

This broad study led him to his *Anglican Vision* (1971) of a future Catholic and Ecumenical Church as a supra-national religious society. This vision nourished by his Catholicism, Orthodoxy and Anglicanism was one which he pioneered. His colleagues on the Chapter had their Anglicanism constantly challenged not by any word of his but by his wider catholicism. Thus the pragmatic approach to ecumenism of some Anglicans was reminded of expressions of the Christian faith of which they themselves had no personal knowledge. His writings should lead ecumenists in the years to come to greater mutual understanding and help to bring closer three great traditions.

The Cathedral and Scandinavia

Another aspect of ecumenism should be mentioned. The Cathedral's historic links with the Lutheran Church of Stavanger. In 1125 a Winchester monk, Reinald by name, crossed the North Sea to found the City and Cathedral of Stavanger and to make another cathedral of St. Swithun. Spiritual links between the two cathedrals certainly existed in the sixteenth century. The two cities are linked in a prayer in a breviary published in Paris in 1519:

Plebs Wintonie Gens Stavangrie[14]
The people of Winchester, the folk of Stavanger.

The links seem then to have been lost. They were resumed in 1962. When Winchester commemorated the eleventh centenary of the death of St. Swithun, the people of Stavanger presented a statue of the Saint to the Cathedral. Nine years later, in 1971, when Winchester celebrated the millenary of the translation of St. Swithun there was an exchange of gifts. The City of Stavanger presented to the Dean and Chapter a fine ledger stone to mark the grave where Swithun was orginally buried and which Martin Biddle, in his excavations, had been able positively to identify. The stone has on it but one word and that one words says all: SWITHUN. There was a special service to dedicate the stone on St. Swithun's Day, July 15th, 1971, exactly a thousand years to the day after Swithun's remains had been removed from their modest burial place outside the first cathedral and were translated into the massive Saxon Minster over three hundred feet long which is associated with St. Aethelwold. There are few places in the world where on the same spot at an interval of a thousand years the same office holders: bishop, dean/prior, monks/canons and a representative of the Crown assembled to do honour to the same person. In return, the Vice-Dean of the Cathedral took a gift from the Dean and Chapter to the Cathedral of Stavanger. It was a Saxon life of St. Swithun,[15] most handsomely bound in

Opposite: Dedication of the Stavanger Stone, 15 July, 1971

full leather and inscribed by the Dean of Winchester:-

In the year of our Lord
One thousand nine hundred and seventy one
and
in the thousandth year of the Translation
of
SAINT SWITHUN
Bishop of Winchester
This volume
was presented to
The Cathedral Church of Saint Swithun
STAVANGER
by
The Dean and Chapter
of
The Cathedral Church of Saint Swithun
WINCHESTER
as a token of their
unity in
the Lord Jesus Christ
and
the Communion of His Saints

Winchester   Michael S. Stancliffe
28 May, 1971   Dean

Friendly exchanges between the two cathedrals continue at regular intervals. The most important visit was in 1975 when the Bishop of Winchester and the Dean of Winchester visited Stavanger to mark the 850th. anniversary of the city of Stavanger and its Cathedral. It was a memorable civic occasion and was honoured by the presence of a member of the Norwegian Royal Family. The name of St. Swithun is as honoured among the people of Stavanger as it is among the people of Winchester.

From time to time a choir comes from Stavanger to sing in the Cathedral and as recently as 1977, in order to participate in a great festival, *Flowers in Pageantry,* the Dean of Stavanger sent an old print of the city. So historic links become contemporary links and Anglicans in Winchester are learning about Lutherans in Norway, and vice-versa.

Besides links with Norway, the Cathedral also has links with Sweden, or more accurately in the terms of the eleventh century with Denmark. In 1020, Canute the Dane was also King of England and his remains are in a mortuary chest on the South Presbytery Screen. In 1970, the City Fathers of Lund visited the Cathedral and presented to it a handsome leather bound facsimile of the *Missale Lundense* (1514) and inscribed it with these words:

TO
WINCHESTER CATHEDRAL
With greetings from the
CITY OF LUND
founded by King Canute
the Great in 1020.

Pilgrimages to the burial place of Canute are not infrequent and twice, in recent years, the Dean of Lund has been warmly welcomed in the Cathedral.

The movement of which William Temple spoke in 1941 has made itself felt in the Cathedral so that to-day three main traditions of Christendom, Roman, Orthodox and Reformed have all helped enrich our own Anglican inheritance.

The Treasury, 1969

The Consistory Court at the north-west of the Cathedral was originally used for the trying of ecclesiastical cases. When the legal use of the space was discontinued it became for many years an archive for diocesan records. After its restoration, the Goldsmiths' Company made a most generous grant towards its conversion into a Treasury where Church Plate from Hampshire might be appropriately displayed, suitably lighted, and housed in conditions of maximum security. It was opened in 1969 and each year for about twenty weeks in the spring and summer there is an exhibition of Church Plate from the churches, not always Anglican, in Hampshire. An average of something over 10,000 people visit the Treasury every year.

From time to time a special exhibition is arranged. For example, in 1972 and 1973 special exhibitions have been held of Saxon and Norman Art. These were smaller items found during the excavations in the Churchyard: wall painting, fragments of sculpture, a comb, a necklace, a bell mould, a strap end, and coins. Catalogues made in 1972 and 1973 give details of these finds, all of which relate to the early history of the Cathedral. The illustrations in the 1973 catalogue add particular value to it. In 1978 besides the Church Plate on exhibition, the County Council generously loaned the Titchborne Spoons so that they too could be seen by a wider public.

Dean Stancliffe, 1969

The giant step forward taken by Dean Gibbs-Smith proved costly to him personally. By 1967 it was clear that his health had been undermined. For two years he struggled on, never showing in public any sign of his illness, known only to those closest friends. By degrees he had to relinquish day by day connections with the Cathedral and leave more and more to members of the Chapter. The time came when he felt he must resign. This he made known early in 1969 and, to his great sorrow, his cathedral ministry ended at the Southern Cathedrals' Festival of 1969. It was a triumphant ending, the last music he heard in the Cathedral being Widor's *Toccata and Fugue*. Those who knew him realised the grief which it gave to him. Unhappily retirement did little to restore his health and he died in September, 1969, not unfittingly on the eve of the *obit* of William of Wykeham whose nave he had been the first to employ for the regular services of Matins and Eucharist, Sunday by Sunday.

He was succeeded by Canon Michael Stancliffe, Rector of St. Margaret's Westminster and Canon of Westminster Abbey. He came to Winchester with a reputation as a distinguished preacher. On the 29th November, 1969 he was installed in his new office.

His installation brings us down to the present day. The historian is too close to set in perspective the events of the last decade. It has certainly been a busy decade. It began with heavy financial commitments and continued during a time of raging inflation. Despite these problems, the essential *opus Dei* for which the building was raised nine hundred years ago has continued unbroken. There has been, somewhat surprisingly, given the intellectual climate of the day, increasing support for the services of the Cathedral. Here it may well be that factors which mitigate against the parish church assist the Cathedral. The mobility of the population means that a congregation may well assemble in the Cathedral not only from all parts of Britain but from many parts of the world. It is commonplace to speak to worshippers from U.S.A., Canada, Germany, Holland and many other countries. Then there is the factor of crowds. It is easier to join in worship with a large number. Here again the Cathedral has been greatly assisted by sound amplification. It is only in the last generation that it has become possible to use the whole Cathedral (556 feet long) for a service. Our forefathers just could not do this. New liturgical concepts, therefore, have arisen and been tested, some successfully, some less successfully. For the rest the many thousands who throng its vast spaces come with a mixture of interests from trivial curiosity and incomprehension and a few minutes to spare, to profound cultural appreciation of music, or illumination, of woodwork or embroidery, manorial research or some of the bye-ways of learning, perhaps painted glass

Dean Stancliffe

or mediaeval tiles. Children and young people come with their projects. Soldiers are given an orientation course and distinguished visitors are shown something of England's traditions. Thousands join in the worship of the Cathedral.

Those who have consulted the notes and the suggestions for further reading will have noticed that there has been no lack of recent literature on every aspect of Cathedral life. It would take a band of specialist scholars to ensure in the present work that there has been no omission. Morever, for one man to attempt to cover so many fields is to court academic disaster in each one. And yet a Cathedral, while indebted to specialised studies, is not a collection of specialisations. A cathedral is people living a life. There are many who are puzzled by it and are frankly disbelieving. Nevertheless it remains a way of life at the heart of which a small group of men, guided by Royal Statutes, who endeavour to continue in the twentieth century what their predecessors undertook nine hundred years ago: the daily worship of God. This is the vital clue to the living Cathedral of 1979. Take away that small group of men, the Dean and four canons, and Winchester would no longer have a Cathedral. It would have a large monument where men used to do certain things as in a thousand monuments throughout Europe.

People built in 1079 in order to worship Almighty God. They had no doubts about the fitness of such a project. People continue to maintain that building in 1979, in order still to worship Almighty God. It is the story of those people which we have tried to outline.

Opposite: The Cathedral to-day

(Dick Amey)

NOTES

The *Winchester Cathedral Record* and the *Hampshire Chroncle* covering the years 1945 to 1979 have detailed information about the life and activity of the Cathedral.

1. See also his *The Church and the Artisan*. London, 1952; An Adventure in Discipleship. London, 1953; and *The Borderland*. London, 1960. He died on September 15th., 1966 and his ashes repose in the Epiphany Chapel.

2. F.R. Barry. *Mervyn Haigh*. London, 1964. c.VI. Barry gives the text of the Bishop's sermon. An appreciation by Roger Lloyd is also added, p.220.f.

3. *Winchester Cathedral Library*. MS.f.198.

4. *The Memoirs of Sir Anthony Eden*. London, 1960. p.311.

5. Church Assembly. Autumn Session, 1958. pp. 419-421.

6. *op. cit.* c.28.

7. Southern Cathedrals Festival. Salisbury,1961., *An Introductory History*. Festival Programmes have continued since then to be issued annually in rotation by Salisbury, Chichester and Winchester and reveal the growth and extent of the Festival.

8. The Cathedral Music Lists, originally published separately, and now incorporated in the Monthly Bulletin, give a clear picture of Cathedral music sung and played day by day. Surviving music lists exist from 1964 down to the present time. Canon Boden's notebooks also give a meticulous account of the Cathedral's music, written in his capacity as Precentor from 1939 to 1964.

9. Two volumes of Press Cuttings have been made of all matters relating to the Appeal of 1966.

10. Winchester Cathedral Statutes were approved by the Queen in Council 28th June 1967.

11. Annual reports of this work may be found in the *W.C.R.* and in *The Archaeological Journal*, 1962. pp. 150-194. *The Antiquaries Journal,* 1964. pp. 202-211; 1965. pp.249-258; 1966. pp.319-326; 1967. pp. 266-272; 1968. pp. 268-280; 1969. pp. 321-323. The *magnum opus* is the *Winchester Studies* which will appear in a number of volumes. Vol. 1. *Winchester in the Early Middle Ages* has already appeared. C.P. 1976.

12. *A Supplement to the O.E.D.* Vol. 1. A-G: C.P. 1972. s.v. *ecumenical*.

13. *Chronicon Monasterii de Abingdon*. 2 Vols. R.S. 1858. Vol. 1. p. 129 and p. 344. Vol. 2. p. 259 and p. 278.

14. *Breviarium Nidrosiense*. Paris, 1519.

15. J. Earle. *Gloucester Fragments. Fascimile of Some Leaves in Saxon Handwriting on Saint Swithun*. London, 1861

FURTHER READING

The best way to continue reading about the Cathedral to-day is to read the *Monthly Bulletin* published by the Dean and Chapter and the annual *Winchester Cathedral Record* published by the Friends. Each year the Pilgrims' School publishes its own magazine. The Chapter still conduct their business which continues to be recorded by the Chapter Clerk and the Administrator. The historian of the future will not lack for source material.

Appendices

THE BISHOPS OF WINCHESTER
1079-1979

Walkelin was the 35th bishop of Winchester

1070 Walkelin
1100 William Giffard
1129 Henry of Blois
1173 Richard of Ilchester
    (also Tokelivus)
1189 Godfrey de Lucy
1205 M. Richard Poore.
    (election quashed).
1205 Peter des Roches
1238 Ralph de Neville (election quashed)
1239 William of Ralegh (much controversy over
    appointment)
1250 Aymer de Valence
    (alias Lusignan)
1261 Andrew of London
    William de Taunton
    (elections disputed)
1262 M. John of Exeter
    (alias Gervais)
1268 M. Nicholas of Ely
1280 Robert Burnell
    (election quashed)
1280 Richard de la More
    (quashed, 1282)
1282 M. John de Pontissara
1305 Henry Woodlock de Merewell
1316 John de Sandale
1319 Henry de Burghashe
    (election set aside)
1319 Adam de Wynton
    (election set aside)
1319 Rigaud de Asserio
1323 M. Robert de Baldock D.C.L.
    (election set aside)
1323 M. John de Stratford D.C.L.
1333 M. Adam de Orleton D.Cn.L.
1345 John Deveneshe or de Veneys
    (Royal mandate withdrawn)
1345 William of Edington
1366 William de Wykeham
1404 M. Thomas Neville
    (election set aside)
1404 M. Henry Beaufort Sch.Th.
1447 M. William Waynflete B.Th.

1487 M. Peter Courtenay D.Cn.L.
1493 M. Thomas Langton D.Th., D.Cn.L.
1501 M. Richard Fox D.Cn.L.
1529 M. Thomas Wolsey D.Th., Card. Pr. of S.
    Cecilia.
1531 M. Stephen Gardiner D.Cn. & C.L.
1551 John Poynet B.D.
1553 Stephen Gardiner restored
1556 John White D.D.
1560 John Pilkington D.D.
    (nominated to Durham)
1561 Robert Horne D.D.
1580 John Watson M.D.
1584 Thomas Cooper D.D.
1595 William Wickham B.D.
1596 William Day D.D.
1597 Thomas Bilson D.D.
1616 James Montagu D.D.
1619 Lancelot Andrewes D.D.
1628 Richard Neile D.D.
1632 Walter Curle D.D.
1660 Brian Duppa D.D.
1662 George Morley D.D.
1684 Peter Mews D.C.L.
1707 Sir Jonathan Trelawney Bart. D.D.
1721 Charles Trimnel D.D.
1723 Richard Willis D.D.
1734 Benjamin Hoadly D.D.
1761 John Thomas D.D.
1781 Hon. Brownlow North D.C.L.
1820 George Pretyman Tomline D.D.
    (established claim to baronetcy, 1823)
1827 Charles Richard Sumner D.D.
1869 Samuel Wilberforce
1873 Edward Harold Browne
1893 Randall Thomas Davidson
1903 Herbert Edward Ryle
1911 Edward Stuart Talbot
1924 Frank Theodore Woods
1932 Cyril Garbett
1942 Mervyn Haigh
1953 Alwyn Terrell Petre Williams
1962 Sherard Falkner Allison
1975 John Vernon Taylor

Sources

John Le Neve: *Fasti Ecclesiae Anglicanae*

1. 1066-1300 II. Monastic Cathedrals. Compiled by D.E. Greenway. London, 1971. pp. 85-87.
2. 1300-1541 IV. Monastic Cathedrals. Compiled by B.Jones. London, 1963. pp.44-47.
3. 1541-1857 III. Canterbury, Rochester and Winchester Dioceses. Compiled by J.M. Horn. London 1974. pp. 75-83.

Crockford's Clerical Directory
    1869 onwards.

PRIORS AND DEANS OF WINCHESTER
1079-1979

Simeon was the fifth prior of Winchester

1070 Simeon
1082 Godfrey of Cambrai
1107 Geoffrey I.
1111 Geofrey II.
1128 Ingulph
1130 Robert I.
1139 Geoffrey III
1165 William
1165 Robert II.
1175 Walter I.
1185 John
1187 M. Robert son of Henry
1201 Stephen (de Lucy)
1216 Walter II.
1239 Andrew
1243 John de Cauz
1244 Walter III.
1247 John of Cauz (again)
1250 William of Taunton
1255 Andrew of London
1262 Walter Rufus
1265 Ralph Russel
1265 Valentine
1276 John of Durevill
1279 Adam of Farnham
1283 William of Basingstoke
1295 Henry Woodlock de Merewell
1305 Nicholas de Tarente
1309 Robert de Enford
1328 Alexander Heriard
1349 John Merlawe
1361 William Thudden
1362 Hugh Basyng
1384 M. Robert Rodebourne D.Th.
1395 M. Thomas Neville D.Th.
1415 Thomas Shyrebourn
1435 William Aulton
1450 Richard Marlborough
1457 Richard Westgate
1470 Thomas Hunton

1498 Thomas Silkested
1524 Henry Brook
1536 M. William Basyng or Kingsmill D.Th.
1541 He became Dean when the
     office of Prior ceased.
1549 Roger Tonge D.D.
1549 Sir John Mason M.A.
1554 Edmund Steward LL.D.
1559 John Warner D.M.
1565 Francis Newton D.D.
1573 John Watson M.A.
1580 Lawrence Humphrey D.D.
1589 Martin Heton D.D.
1600 George Abbot D.D.
1609 Thomas Morton D.D.
1616 John Young D.D.
1660 Alexander Hyde D.C.L.
1666 William Clarke D.D.
1679 Richard Meggot D.D.
1692 John Wickart D.D.
1722 William Trimnell D.D.
1729 Charles Naylor LL.D.
1739 Zachary Pearce D.D.
1748 Thomas Cheyney D.D.
1760 Jonathan Shipley D.D.
1769 Newton Ogle D.D.
1804 Robert Holmes D.D.
1805 Thomas Rennell D.D.
1840 Thomas Garnier D.C.L.
1872 John Bramston B.D.
1883 George William Kitchin D.D.
1895 William R.W. Stephens D.D.
1903 William H. Furneaux D.D.
1919 William H. Hutton D.D.
1931 E. Gordon Selwyn D.D.
1958 Norman Sykes D.D. D.Litt.
1961 Oswyn H. Gibbs-Smith C.B.E., M.A.
1969 Michael S. Stancliffe M.A.

Sources

John Le Neve: *Fasti Ecclesiae Anglicanae*
  1. 1066-1300 II. Monastic Cathedrals. Compiled by D.E. Greenway. London, 1971. pp.88-91.
  2. 1300-1541 IV. Monastic Cathedrals. Compiled by B.Jones. London, 1963. pp.47-48.
  3.1541-1857 III. Canterbury, Rochester and Winchester Dioceses. Compiled by J.M.Horn.
  London, 1974. pp.83-86.

Crockford's Clerical Directory.
  1872 onwards

A. B. Emden *A Biographical Register of the University of Oxford, 1501-1540.* s.v. Basyng alias
Kingsmill W., Mason J., Warner, J., Watson, J.

PREBENDARIES AND CANONS OF WINCHESTER
1541-1979

SOURCE

Lists of prebendaries and canons who served the Cathedral from 1541 to 1857 are given in:-

J.Le Neve *Fasti Ecclesiae Anglicanae* ed. by J.M. Horn. Vol.III. London, 1974. pp.89-106. On p. 107 details are given of the reduction in the number of canons from 12 to 5.

In 1930 the number was reduced from 5 to 4.

Canons of Winchester
1857-1979

1st Prebend

1857 P.Jacob
1885 W.P. Warburton
1901 P.H.P. Braithwaite
1933 E.Moor
1950 C.P. Cowley
1955 F.R. Money
1961 W.D. Maundrell
1970 A.G. Wedderspoon

2nd Prebend

1857 G.T. Pretyman
1860 J.S. Utterton
1880 F.R. Atkinson
1888 J.H. Sapte
1906 F.E. Utterton
1908 A.G. Robinson 1st inst.
            see 4th prebend, 1922
1922 L.E. Blackburne
         Suppressed in 1930

4th Prebend

1857 W. Wilson
1874 F.T. McDougall
1894 A.S. Valpy
1909 J. Vaughan
1922 A.G. Robinson
    2nd inst.   2nd inst.
1934 L.H. Lang. 1st. inst.
1937 R.B. Lloyd
1967 F. Bussby

9th Prebend

1857 W. Carus
1885 G.H. Sumner
1906 A.E. Daldy
1925 C. Boutflower
1933 A.B.L. Karney
1943 H.R. Burrows
1947 L.H. Lang. 2nd inst.
1963 N.E. Cornwall
1973 C.C.W. James
1977 M. Manktelow

10th Prebend

1857 T. Woodroffe
1878 E.R. Wilberforce
1882 G.H. Butler
1890 H. Haig
1909 V.F. Storr
1916 C. Hepher

1931 L. Hodgson
1938 F.H. Brabant
1942 E.R. Morgan
1951 K.E.N. Lamplugh
1962 E. Amand de Mendieta
1976 A.D. Caesar.

Details of all the above mentioned canons can be found in the appropriate editions of *Crockford's Clerical Directory*.

WINCHESTER CATHEDRAL ORGANISTS
1402-1979

1402 John Dyes
1437 Richard Bygbroke
     John Langton
1530 Henry Perrat
1537 Matthew Fuller
1541 Richard Wynslade
1615 John Lante
1615 John Holmes
1621 George Bath
1631 Thomas Holmes
1638 Christopher Gibbons
1661 John Silver
1666 Randal Jewett
1675 John Reading
1681 Daniel Roseingrave
1692 Vaughan Richardson
1729 John Bishop
1737 James Kent
1774 Peter Fussell
1802 George W. Chard
1849 S.S. Wesley
1865 George Arnold
1902 William Prendergast
1933 Harold Rhodes
1949 Alwyn Surplice
1972 Martin Neary

SOURCES

P. Chappell.   *Dr. Samuel Sebastian Wesley.*

D.N.B.   G.B. Arnold; J. Bishop; G.W. Chard; J. Holmes; T. Holmes; R. Jewett; Jas. Kent; J. Reading; V. Richardson; D. Roseingrave; S.S. Wesley.

B. Matthews.   *The Music of Winchester Cathedral.* London, 1974. *The Organs and Organists of Winchester Cathedral.* 2nd Revised edition, Winchester, 1975.
Samuel Sebastian Wesley. Privately printed. 1976.
Typescript of more than 200 titles of works by Winchester organists.

W. Shaw.   Typescript of history of organists from Matthew Fuller to Alwyn Surplice. Archives

G. Willoughby.   Typescript. *The Organs of Winchester Cathedral.*

Plan of Statues on the Screen of Winchester Cathedral.

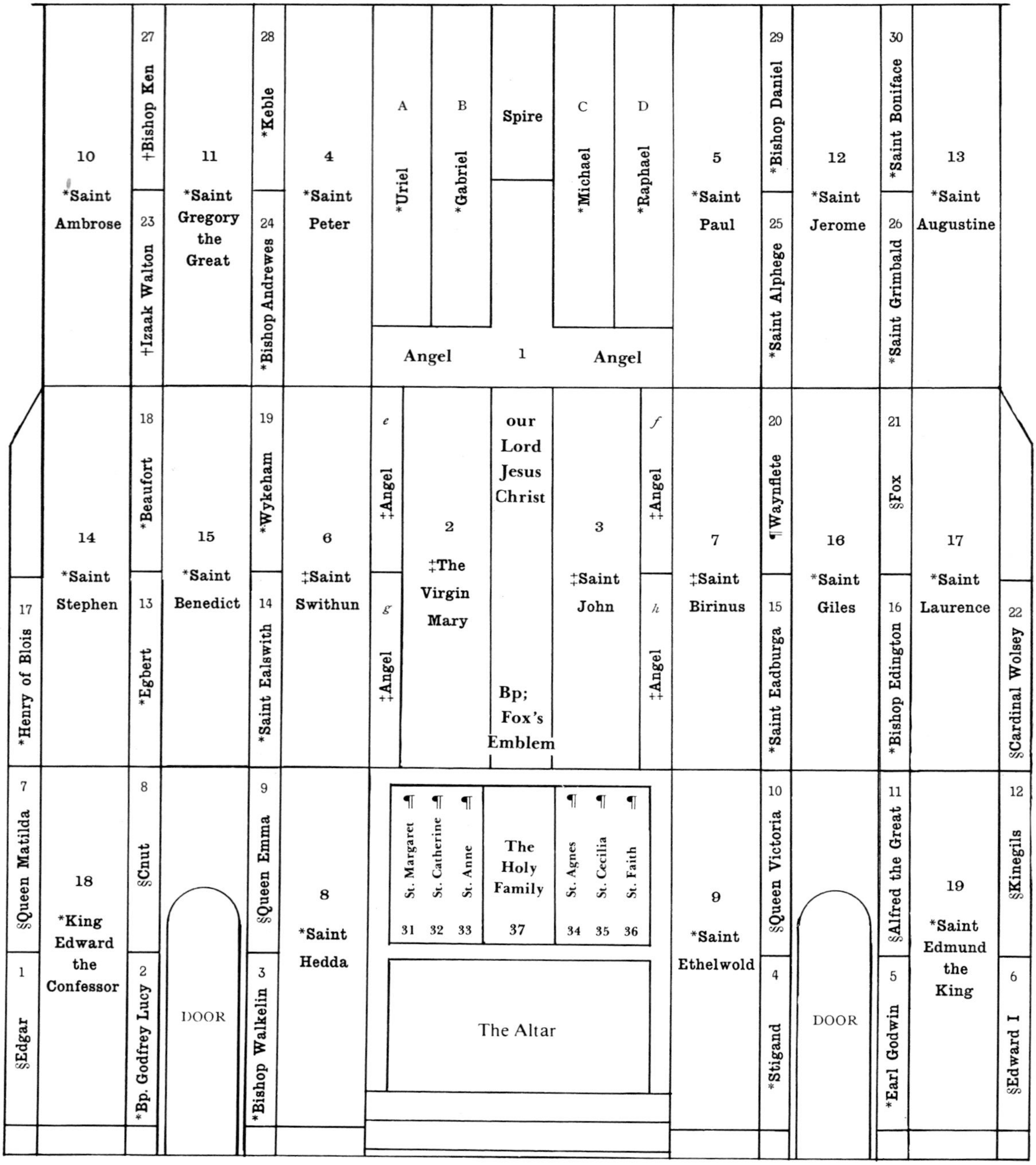

Top tier (left to right):

- 10 — *Saint Ambrose
- 27 — †Bishop Ken
- 11 — *Saint Gregory the Great
- 23 — †Izaak Walton
- 28 — *Keble
- 24 — *Bishop Andrewes
- 4 — *Saint Peter
- A — *Uriel
- B — *Gabriel
- Spire
- C — *Michael
- D — *Raphael
- 5 — *Saint Paul
- 29 — *Bishop Daniel
- 25 — *Saint Alphege
- 12 — *Saint Jerome
- 30 — *Saint Boniface
- 26 — *Saint Grimbald
- 13 — *Saint Augustine

Angel — 1 — Angel

Middle tier (left to right):

- 17 — *Henry of Blois
- 14 — *Saint Stephen
- 18 — *Beaufort
- 13 — *Egbert
- 15 — *Saint Benedict
- 19 — *Wykeham
- 14 — *Saint Ealswith
- 6 — ‡Saint Swithun
- e — †Angel
- g — †Angel
- 2 — †The Virgin Mary
- our Lord Jesus Christ
- Bp; Fox's Emblem
- 3 — ‡Saint John
- f — †Angel
- h — ‡Angel
- 7 — ‡Saint Birinus
- 20 — ¶Waynflete
- 15 — *Saint Eadburga
- 16 — *Saint Giles
- 21 — §Fox
- 16 — *Bishop Edington
- 17 — *Saint Laurence
- 22 — §Cardinal Wolsey

Lower tier (left to right):

- 1 — §Edgar
- 7 — §Queen Matilda
- 18 — *King Edward the Confessor
- 2 — *Bp. Godfrey Lucy
- 8 — §Cnut
- DOOR
- 3 — *Bishop Walkelin
- 9 — §Queen Emma
- 8 — *Saint Hedda
- ¶ St. Margaret 31 | ¶ St. Catherine 32 | ¶ St. Anne 33
- The Holy Family 37
- ¶ St. Agnes 34 | ¶ St. Cecilia 35 | ¶ St. Faith 36
- 9 — *Saint Ethelwold
- 10 — §Queen Victoria
- 4 — *Stigand
- DOOR
- 11 — §Alfred the Great
- 5 — *Earl Godwin
- 19 — *Saint Edmund the King
- 12 — §Kinegils
- 6 — §Edward I

The Altar

---

* Mr. Boulton, of Cheltenham.
¶ Messrs. Farmer and Brindley, London.
§ Mr. Geflowski, London.
† Miss Grant, London.
‡ Mr. Nicholls, London.

INDEX

ACKNOWLEDGEMENT

Every note and suggestion for further reading is also an expression of the author's indebtedness and gratitude to a vast number of writers upon the Cathedral. In particular he wishes to express his gratitude to the *Winchester Cathedral Record* now so much enhanced in convenient usefulness by the index recently compiled by General R.F.K. Goldsmith.